Encyclopaedia of SHIPS

Enzo Angelucci

Odhams Books

LONDON · NEW YORK · SYDNEY · TORONTO

THE ORIGINS OF NAVIGATION

The spirit of self-preservation must have urged primitive man, menaced by a flood, to cling on to a floating tree-trunk, and let himself be carried along with the current.

Man would probably have passed quickly from the tree-trunk to the raft, made from a number of trunks tied together with liana.

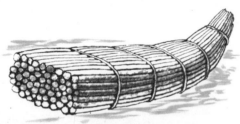

In places where there were no trees, man created his first boats by tying together bundles of rushes, balsa or papyrus. To propel them, a pole was used in shallow water.

THE origins of navigation are lost in the mist of ages. No one will ever know how, when and where a human being first ploughed across the water, so setting in motion a story which will only cease with the end of humanity itself. To attempt to pierce the haze of pre-history really means, that, for the most part, one is relying on supposition – giving imagination free rein on the difficult path back into the past but hoping that the discipline of common sense will lead to an approximation of the truth.

Man was in contact with water from his earliest days on Earth. Water constituted one of the principal difficulties of early man, as it was closely linked with the problems of shelter, provisions, and survival itself.

Did primitive man "wish" to accomplish his first navigational exploit – or was he "forced" into it because of some hazard of nature, such as flood? Who can say? It is, however, certain that in either case he had to sharpen his wits and seek a solution. The primordial idea of how to cope with water was certainly suggested to him by seeing something floating – probably a tree-trunk, rotten or struck by lightning, which had fallen into a river. To conquer water it was necessary to float and, since his own body did not float, he had to make use of something else that had this property. In the tranquil and clearly determined limits

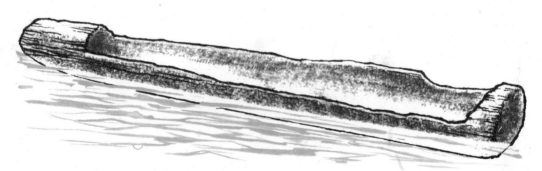

When man mastered the extraordinary power of fire he was able to make a cavity in a great tree-trunk, thus making a dug-out canoe. Boats such as these, which are still used by primitive peoples of Australia, South America and Africa, gave their passengers the protection of sides. With the canoe came the use of the paddle and the oar as means of propulsion.

of a river, he must have carried out his first experiments, clinging on to a tree-trunk and letting himself be taken along by the current. On that occasion he must have had two extraordinary experiences. The trunk, being unstable, was capable of being easily overturned, and so man had to find a way of giving stability to his craft. Secondly, the trunk, following the whim of the current, could not take him from one river bank to the other, and so he had to find a way of giving direction to his new-found craft. At this point he realised that he needed something that would float, that was sufficiently stable, and to which he could give movement and direction. More trunks tied together with plant fibres resolved the first two aspects of the problem, while a long branch which he could use as a lever on the river bottom resolved the other two. And so the raft was created.

If "to navigate" means to get about on water with a certain degree of safety and in the desired direction, it was probably with the creation of the raft that this great achievement was first made possible.

All this happened in parts of the world where there were large numbers of trees. But in zones where nature had not been so generous, man attained the same ends by utilising whatever lay to hand – rushes or papyrus plants, tied up in tight bundles, inflated skins of animals joined together, all things which had a good degree of buoyancy.

The raft, therefore, must have been the most important element in the origins of navigation. The dug-out tree-trunk, the canoe of tree bark, the canoe made of

Another type of primitive canoe was made of tree bark, either in one piece or of several pieces sewn together. Canoes like this have been found among the Yaghan people of Tierra del Fuego, who are so used to living on the sea that they are called "water nomads".

The lack of big trees forced the natives to build boats by joining two or three pieces of trunk together in rudimentary fashion. To prevent water seeping through, the joints were filled up with mud and clay.

Where wood and rushes did not exist, primitive man discovered that an inflated animal skin floated. At first he utilised it by balancing on it, but later he joined several inflated skins together with a wooden framework, thus creating a form of raft.

For use on the Nile the Egyptians developed papyrus boats to a remarkable degree, as engravings which date back to 3800 B.C. bear witness. These boats were capable of carrying up to ten people. One can see that the use of very large oars as rudders was already established. The bundles of papyrus were kept together by firm ties covered with sewn skins.

5

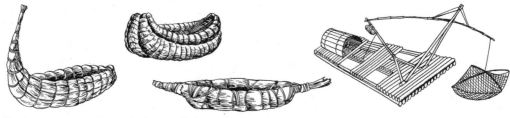

Papyrus canoe from Lake Tchad in Africa; a craft still in use by natives.

Balsa canoe from South America, and a Tasmanian canoe-raft made of rushes.

Bamboo raft from the Malay Archipelago, still used by the local fisherman.

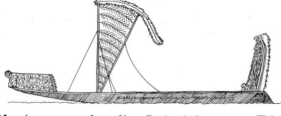

A Maori war canoe from New Zealand. Some are as long as 70 ft., and can carry 80 men. The sail is made of painted cloth.

This canoe from Tahiti has a single outrigger which prevents capsizing. It can be used with safety in the great Pacific rollers.

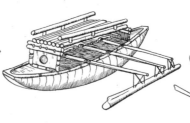

Double canoe from the Society Islands. Each hull paddled by up to two persons.

New Caledonian canoe. The hull is a tree-trunk, and has a wooden superstructure.

Indonesian canoe with outriggers and sail, from the Celebes Archipelago.

several parts of trunks joined together were subsequent inventions, of secondary importance compared with that of the raft.

When the oar was invented and by whom, when the sail was invented and by whom, when the first canoe was hollowed-out and by whom, we shall never know. It is certain, though, that these inventions followed upon one another, even though spaced out over centuries, and that each one contributed in its own complementary and decisive way to the development of navigation.

All that has been said so far about man's

first navigational experiments is not without foundation. To support it, we have the evidence of peoples who remained at a primitive stage even after civilisation had fully developed in other parts of the globe. The art of navigation reached such heights in the Mediterranean as to allow great voyages of discovery, and Europe came into contact with the inhabitants of America, Africa, the East Indies and Oceania. It was discovered that the people living in these places, without there having been any means of contact between them, had nevertheless each resolved the problem

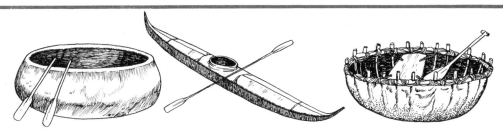

A "cufa" from rivers in Iraq. This consisted of wooden rib-work covered with skin.

Eskimo "kayak" from the Polar Arctic Circle. A light skiff, made entirely of skin.

Irish "coracle". A circular boat, covered in skin, similar to the Iraqi "cufa".

Ojibway Indian canoe. It has a wooden hull covered by skins sewn together.

A small craft from the Straits of Magellan, made of two inflated sea-pike skins.

A "kelek", raft made of inflated skins kept together by wooden boards.

Canoe with stabilising outrigger and strangely shaped sail from the Cameroons.

Canoe with large outrigger from Papua, which resembles that of the Cameroons.

Chinese Junk. These craft had a rudder aft, probably before European boats.

of navigation in more or less the same way, utilising just the same wood or rush rafts, dug-out canoes and floating skins, according to the raw materials available.

If these first observations were important, how much more important were the results of an ever increasing number of scientific expeditions which, even today, continue to be made. These expeditions are carried out in the name of a science which, although relatively young, is of extreme importance – ethnology, or the study of different peoples in their own environs and of their material, social and spiritual cultures. And it is precisely this science, which is the most appropriate ally for anyone who wishes to embark on a study of the dawn of navigation, for they will then have a good all-round knowledge of circumstances and background. One of the basic assertions of this science lays down that "primitive men, confronted with the same necessities and having the same means available, react in a similar manner." Thus is explained the fact that quite similar rush-built canoes have been found on Lake Tchad in the depths of Africa and on Lake Titicaca in the heart of

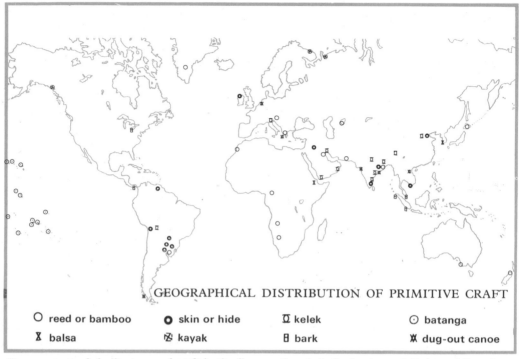

GEOGRAPHICAL DISTRIBUTION OF PRIMITIVE CRAFT

○ reed or bamboo	● skin or hide	◐ kelek	☉ batanga
✗ balsa	⊠ kayak	⊟ bark	✕ dug-out canoe

The presence of similar types of craft in the five continents is the best proof of the validity of one of ethnology's fundamental assertions which maintains that "primitive men, confronted by the same need and having the same means available, react in a similar way." Also there is a major concentration of primitive boats in areas near to the equatorial zones.

South America. According to the knowledge that we have today, no contact could ever have been made between the two indigenous peoples – yet they resolved the problem of tackling the waters of their lakes in identical ways.

Accepting this fact, it may be said that the raft was not invented just once but hundreds, or even thousands of times, in different places and at different times: this also applies to the oar, the sail and the rudder.

The first documents to have come into our hands which are of use in reconstructing the history of the ship and of navigation belong to the ancient Egyptian civilisation and go back to about 3500 B.C. – a period which, in relation to man's life on earth, can be considered "yesterday". All that goes before this period remains shrouded in uncertainty. From then, History has its beginning and the development of navigation follows the course of History.

No one can say if, in some corner of the world, navigation went beyond the phase of the raft and the canoe before it was known in the Mediterranean. It is possible that a type of craft more evolved than those on the Nile did, in fact, appear in the Far East, and particularly in the China Sea. But it is right to suppose that, if this were so, proof would have been found, just as has happened in the case of the ancient Mediterranean civilisations. In the predynastic period in Egypt, a primitive standard of navigation already existed. On the Nile trading was carried out by means of craft made of papyrus – in a way similar to those which were and still are used among the primitive peoples of Africa and America. Through the remains of Egyptian and Assyrian-Babylonian civilisations there can be traced the evolution of craft right up to the first Egyptian boat which deserved the title of ship. It is from this point that our journey in time starts, our panoramic survey of the development and evolution of the ship which could not have happened had not man, way back in pre-History, invented the raft, the oar and the sail.

SHIPS
YESTERDAY

From the boats of the Pharaohs of Egypt to the aircraft carriers of the Second World War.

IT would take thousands of pages to describe fully the process of development of the ship and of navigation from Egyptian and Phoenician times to the days of the Second World War. In fifty centuries so much has happened, from the fabulous Pharaonic undertaking in the Land of Punt to the air/naval battle of Midway Island. In this time the world has written its history, has travelled the road of civilisation. Ships can be regarded as milestones on this road, reflecting the technical standards achieved by the people who built them – as means of discovery, and instruments of power and wealth. To follow the course of the ship through the centuries up to the 15th century of our own era is not an easy task, since the more one delves back into time, the more difficult it is to find authentic material of any value. Nevertheless, from graffiti and sculptures, sketches and paintings, a sufficiently comprehensive picture can be built up, even though it is not necessarily entirely complete. Imagination has never been given an entirely free rein, even though it would have been useful to do so sometimes for the sake of completeness, and every illustration is reproduced from the most reliable source possible.

From the 15th century onward, the nearer we get to the present time the more prolific is the material available on ships of every type and country. It has been necessary, therefore, to be selective and only include ships which have been of technical, not merely historical significance, this in order to achieve a wide and objective view and provide international coverage of both merchant and naval shipping.

In this chapter the development of the ship is followed from the age of the oar, through the domination of sail to the establishment of steam. In these pages are reviewed the caravels of Columbus, the galleys of Lepanto, the galleons of the Great Armada and Nelson's men-of-war, Admiral Togo's battleships and Rizzo's motor torpedo-boats, the submarines of Doenitz and the Allied and Japanese aircraft-carriers of the War in the Pacific. And thus, by means of ships, the pages of the great book of History will be turned.

EGYPTIAN AND ROMAN SHIPS

THE meaning of the word "ship" is generally given in a dictionary as "any large sail or steam vessel" Certainly most dictionaries emphasise the fact that only a vessel of large dimensions may be called a ship.

Judging from its size, therefore the first ship of which there is any knowledge would have been the Ark, described in the Bible by Moses in the Book of Genesis. The Ark is said to have been 233 ft. long, 92 ft. wide and 56 ft. high, with four decks, and capable of giving shelter to all the men and animals which were destined to survive the Great Flood. But, strictly speaking, the Ark was not a ship – its movements could not be controlled or directed and it was therefore merely a great floating hulk.

So leaving Noah's Ark in the biblical legend let us examine the archaeological remains of the ancient Egyptian civilisation. The first wooden vessel – as distinct from one made of papyrus – was built by the Egyptians around 3300 B.C. Although it was still restricted, because of its structure, to use on the Nile, Pharaoh Sakure's ships of 2700 B.C. were, without doubt, capable of going to sea, in view of the tales of how they raided the coast of Syria.

About the 15th century B.C., Egypt was undoubtedly the greatest maritime power in the world. In 1500 B.C. Queen Hatshepsut was able to send an expeditionary force of ships, built at Suez, into the legendary

Egyptian ship – 3300 B.C. It is reckoned that the first wooden ships were built in Egypt between 3300 and 3000 B.C. They were constructed of planks of acacia or sycamore held together by wooden pegs. They had no keel or ribs. They numbered 26 oars of normal length and six larger ones which acted as rudders. The square sail was hoisted on a mast consisting of two poles.

Ship of Pharaoh Sakure – 2700 B.C. Passed down to posterity in a bas-relief are eight ships of this type – perhaps the first of which were capable of taking to the high seas and of emerging from the calm waters of the Nile. They raided the coast of Syria, returning home laden with booty and Phoenician prisoners. The craft had neither keel nor ribs. When the sail was not in use, the mast was taken down.

One of Queen Hatshepsut's ships – 1500 B.C. A bas-relief in a temple at Deir el Bahri portrays the ships which were sent to the Land of Punt in search of valuable merchandise. Built at Suez, of cedarwood from Lebanon, they were from 82 ft. to 90 ft. long. The sail was braced between two yards attached to the mast. Of special interest are the deck girders.

Land of Punt – perhaps the Somaliland of today – with the sole aim of replenishing her stocks of gold, myrrh and ivory – to add yet more lustre to her greatness.

The Egyptians, too, with their sea-faring mentality, were sharply conscious of the value of a waterway linking the Mediterranean and Red Seas. They anticipated by many centuries the cutting of the Suez Canal (effected in 1869 by Ferdinand de Lesseps), for in the early 20th century B.C., they had already dug a canal 44 miles long which joined one of the tributaries of the Nile to the Red Sea. In 617 B.C.

Pharaoh Necho employed 120,000 men on repairing this canal which was 150 ft. wide and 10-20 ft. deep. Only in A.D. 767 was this magnificent work obliterated, through the stupidity of the Second Caliph of Egypt who ordered the canal to be closed.

Before deterioration set in, the Egyptian navy owed its strength to Phoenician shipbuilders and sailors and, in 1200 B.C. it was one of the contenders in the first naval battle in history. At Pelusium, a district near the present-day Port Said, the Egyptian ships, under the orders of Pharaoh Rameses III, saved the country from in-

A ship of Pharaoh Ramses III – 1200 B.C. The first naval battle in history appears to have taken place in the waters around Pelusio, near to the spot where Port Said exists today. Ramses III's ships, built and manned by Phoenicians, defeated a combined force of Libyans, Syrians and Philistines. Especially interesting are the raised sides of the galley to protect the oarsmen.

Phoenician Merchant Ship – 1500 B.C. From a fresco in an Egyptian tomb. Although it has no keel or ribs, the ship appears sufficiently well equipped for voyages on the open sea.

Phoenician Merchant Ship – 100 B.C. From a sarcophagus at Sidon. It must have been in a vessel such as this that Saint Paul made his journey to Rome.

vasion, defeating the combined naval forces of the Libyans, Syrians and Philistines.

In effect, it was a victory for the Phoenician sailors who were to succeed the Egyptians in the domination of the Mediterranean. Not far behind the seafaring civilisation of Egypt were two others – the Cretan which dated back to 2000 B.C., and the Phoenician. Crete, which had reached a high level of civilisation by 1500 B.C., was destroyed by the Achaians in 1300 B.C. On the other hand, the Phoenician capital of Sidon continued to flourish for many centuries, thanks to her able seafarers.

The Phoenicians, who had their origins in Syria, were rich in long-trunked trees, the famous cedars of Lebanon. They were probably the first to build ships with keels and ribs and were certainly the first to construct one with two banks of oars, one above the other, thus producing the bireme. About 1000 B.C. they reigned supreme from one end of the Mediterranean to the other. They had bases on the African coast, in Malta and in Sardinia. They were the masters of the Red Sea. They made up King Solomon's Hebrew navy and the Egyptian navy. Their ability as sailors was great and, besides being good carpenters, they guarded the secret of their knowledge of astronomy for a very long time. They steered by means of the Pole Star and the Little Bear (Ursa Minor) and

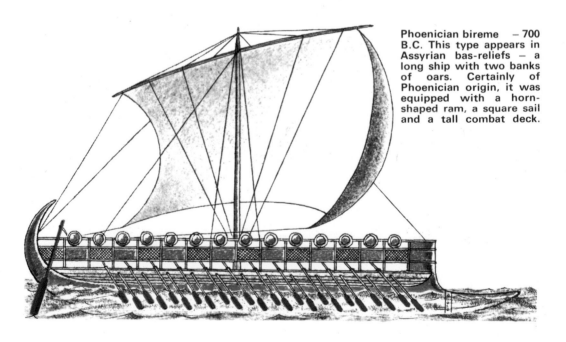

Phoenician bireme – 700 B.C. This type appears in Assyrian bas-reliefs – a long ship with two banks of oars. Certainly of Phoenician origin, it was equipped with a horn-shaped ram, a square sail and a tall combat deck.

even navigated at night, which was unheard of by the other navies of those days.

A good example of their superior seafaring qualities is the task carried out by the Phoenicians on the orders of the Egyptian Pharaoh Necho in 611 B.C., as narrated by Herodotus. Twenty centuries before Vasco de Gama they sailed round Africa. They left from the Gulf of Arabia and arrived back in Egypt through the Straits of Gibraltar. It took them four years to complete this incredible undertaking – but completed it certainly was; the details reported by Herodotus on the astronomical characteristics and on the different peoples seen and recorded – or actually met – by the navigators are exact and could not have been merely the fruit of a fertile imagination.

Meanwhile, in 1400 B.C. the Achaians who were of Greek stock had appeared in the Mediterranean. Later, they destroyed the Cretans' power and inherited their seafaring qualities. In 1180 B.C., as Homer tells, the Achaians opened up the way to the Dardanelles as a result of the Trojan War, and bases for Greek power in the Mediterranean started to spring up. The Greeks were the legendary Argonauts who, guided by Jason, went on their quest for the Golden Fleece. It was said that they did not even flee from the attacks of the Etruscan pirates who, coming from the town of Adria on the upper Adriatic were instilling fear and respect into all those

Greek Merchant Ship – 600 B.C. From the rare examples of pottery, it seems to have been used mainly under sail. The gangplank was placed directly above the cargo.

A Greek "Ceres" – 400 B.C. A light and fast ship used by almost all the Mediterranean navies of the time. It is likely that some of this type were used to carry grain.

A Greek bireme – 600 B.C. The first Greek biremes, according to designs found on vases, go back to the 7th century B.C. They were built with keels to which were fixed the sternpost, stempiece and ribs. 73 ft. to 100 ft. in length, one mast, 50 oars, a single rudder and a long beak.

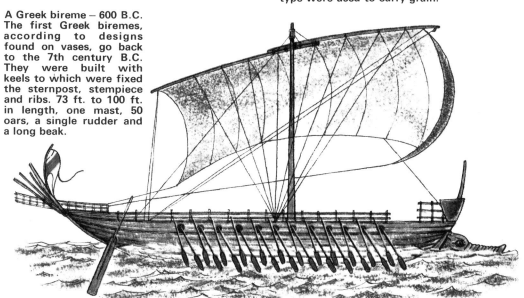

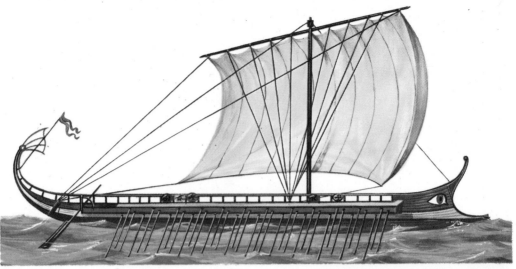

A Greek trireme – 480 B.C. The first triremes (long ships with three banks of oars) appear to date back to the 6th century B.C. At Salamis, in 480 B.C., the Greeks used only ships of this type. Faster than the biremes but less manageable, they were equipped with a single mast and a ram. Above the oarsmen was a deck for the armed warriors.

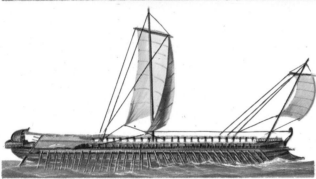

A trireme of Attica – 350 B.C. A long ship measuring approximately 115 ft. – 125 ft. by 20 ft. It had a main-mast and a secondary mast forward.

lands adjacent to the Ionian Sea, the Adriatic and the Aegean.

The ships of the Trojan War were of quite modest size, with only one bank of oars. Those that were to play such a great part in making the Greeks masters of the sea – the triremes (galleys with three banks of oars) did not appear until the 6th century B.C., some years after the biremes.

The triremes were to take part in the second great naval battle of history – the conflict which took place in the Straits of Salamis in September, 480 B.C., in which 310 Greek triremes took part against King Xerxes of Persia's incredible fleet of 1,207 ships. At the time when the Greeks were at the peak of their glory, with colonies all around the Mediterranean, they found themselves having to face up to a wave of invading Persians which could have swallowed up all the Mediterranean civilisations.

Although the great invading army, led by Darius, might have stopped at Marathon, it seemed to the Greeks that nothing could oppose King Xerxes' fleet, which consisted of 300 Phoenician ships, 200 Egyptian, 150 Cypriot, 100 Cilician, 100 Ionic and others, carrying at least 200,000 armed men. According to Aeschylus, however, only about 207 of these were triremes. Only Themistocles, at the head of the Greeks, never doubted that victory would be his. He drew the imposing enemy fleet into the narrow waters between Salamis and the peninsula and completely routed his adversaries. In the ratio of 4 to 1, the Greek triremes – which were tougher and faster than the enemy's vessels – got the better of the combined Persian forces. Mediterranean civilisation was safe.

Three centuries later, in 148 B.C., the descendants of those same Greeks were to fall under the domination of the Romans, who were then wearing the fulfilment of their plan to create the largest Empire in the world.

The Romans, too, in their need to expand their power beyond the limits of the peninsula, had to become sailors, above all

An Etruscan bireme – 600 B.C. The Tuscans and the Tyrrhenians, who were of Etruscan stock, were skilful sailors. On a vase found in the Etruscan necropolis (the town's cemetery) at Cerveteri was a painting of this bireme which must have been Etruscan. Some scholars, however, maintain that it was Greek. There is no doubt, however, that there were Etruscan ships of this type – fast and light biremes, equipped with a ram and a single mast with square sail.

to oppose Carthage, a city which had been founded in 810 B.C. by the Phoenicians and whose heirs were determined to maintain the traditions of their forebears.

It was not until 262 B.C. that Rome (founded in 753 B.C.), having by then succeeded in consolidating the unification of the peninsula, resolved to attack Carthage and to form her first fleet. Her ships were triremes and it is believed that they were modelled on the same lines as the Carthaginian triremes, one of which had foundered, almost intact, on the coast of Southern Italy.

In 260 B.C., the first encounter took place between Romans and Carthaginians off North East Sicily, at Milazzo. In Caius Duilius' fleet were 120 triremes all of them armed with "crows", a type of boarding gangplank fitted with a grappling hook which, when dropped on to the enemy ship, held it steady, so permitting the soldiers to attack. The Carthaginian fleet, under Hannibal's command, had an equal number of ships but the unexpectedness of the "crows" had the desired effect. The Romans sank 14 vessels with their ships' beaks, captured 31 (amongst them the flagship), and killed 7,000 Carthaginians. It is clear that the Romans were not completely unprepared as sailors, but it must be remembered that amongst their ranks were the direct descendants of those Etruscan corsairs who had once been the terror of the seas. Four years later a second naval encounter was to give the Romans temporary domination of the Mediterranean and allow them to land in Africa.

In 250 B.C. fortune turned her back on Rome when her fleet was destroyed by the Carthaginians, but in nine years she had completely rebuilt it and, in the battle of the Egades, she was able to attack the great Carthaginian fleet as it was taking supplies to Hamilcar Barca's army. The 200 Roman ships sank 50 Carthaginian ships and captured 70, taking 10,000 prisoners. Thus the First Punic War was concluded with a

A Roman trireme – 260 B.C. The first real Roman fleet was that which Caius Duilius led to victory against Hannibal's Carthaginian ships at Milazzo. The Roman triremes were distinguishable both by the turret and by the "crow" – a gangway used for boarding other vessels during battle. Underneath the "crow" was a metal hook which fastened itself into the deck of the enemy ship.

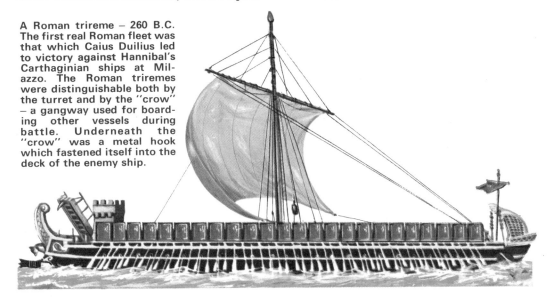

A Roman trireme – 150 B.C. In this reconstruction by the Archaeological Academy of Naples, the Roman trireme has only one mast, with a mainsail and a small triangular sail forward. The aft-deck and awning are clearly visible and here were accommodated the *praefectus navis* and the *magister navis,* the military commander and naval captain respectively.

request for peace by Hamilcar. In the Second Punic War, the most decisive moments actually took place on dry land, but the Roman fleet lent its indispensable weight to bring to a close the conquest of Macedonia and Greece.

The last great naval battle in which the Romans were involved was at Actium in which Anthony and Cleopatra and Octavian found themselves on opposing sides. It was a clash with 400 ships on each side, many of which were biremes, and it ended with Anthony's defeat – he lost 200 ships sunk or captured. This was in 31 B.C.

Actium saw proof of the decline of the trireme whose place was gradually being taken, during the period of the Roman Empire, by craft of a lighter build. Merchant ships, however, were being built ever larger and more spacious. They were indispensable to Rome for trading with her colonies. The belief that the main

part in naval history from the Greeks to the Roman Empire was played by the trireme is correct, even though references are often found in old texts to ships with more banks of oars, like the quadrireme, quinquereme and even the eptareme (4, 5 and 7 banks of oars). In the light of current knowledge, it is difficult to take the importance of these vessels seriously, as ships with more than three banks of oars would have been almost impossible to manoeuvre. Many scholars have carried out practical experiments – even Napoleon III interested himself in the problem and gave orders for a full-size trireme to be built to determine the clearance of the oars. All have rejected the possibility that ships of four or more banks of oars could have had any practical manoeuvrability. Such being the case, the tales of Polybius must be treated with reservation when he tells of having seen a quinquereme with

A Roman bireme – 50 B.C. In 70 B.C. the Roman Consul, Pompeius, started a full-scale attack against the pirates who infested the waters of the Mediterranean. Of the 500 ships that took part in this venture, it seems that many were biremes – much lighter and more manoeuvrable than the triremes and therefore more suited to this kind of combat. In 31 B.C. at the Battle of Azio, too, biremes were numerous – their chief offensive weapon being the beak. The turret, useful in actual fighting, was dismantled during normal navigation.

Ship from Lake Nemi – A.D. 160. In 1932 Lake Nemi, near Rome, was drained to recover two Roman ships that were known to be lying at the bottom. One of the craft salvaged was 234 ft. long and the other 240 ft., their respective widths being 66 ft. and 79 ft. One was a warship, fitted with a beak, and the other a merchant vessel. No one has ever been able to explain why such large ships should have been built on such a restricted stretch of water.

300 oarsmen and 200 soldiers, and Pliny the Elder who refers to a quinquereme of 40 B.C. with 400 oarsmen. These ships may have existed but they could never have taken to the high seas.

The same fate was to befall the *Syracusia* which belonged to Gerone II, King of Syracuse, about 280 B.C. This ship, built by Achias of Corinth with the co-operation of the famous Archimedes, was to have had 20 banks of oars, 4 masts and 8 gigantic turrets on deck fitted with catapults. If it had actually been fitted out with all these things, it would have had a tonnage of about 3,650! It is said to have been presented to Ptolemy Philadelphus of Alexandria, whose son, Ptolemy Philopatore, King of Egypt from 285-247 B.C., had an even bigger craft built, according to the historian, Callixenus. This was to have been a ship with forty banks of oars! It would have been 430 ft. long, 73 ft. wide and 89 ft. high. The largest oars would have measured 63 ft. and there would have been at least 4,000 oarsmen. The crew would have numbered 8,000 men altogether – that is, nearly double the number carried in the world's greatest aircraft carriers of today! To build it would have taken the same amount of wood as would have gone into the construction of 140 trircmes, and nails weighing 33 lb. each. Even the huge lighter that Caligula had built to carry the Obelisk from Heliopolis to Rome (now in Saint Peter's Square) would have seemed small in comparison.

Let us leave these sea giants in the aura of legend which surrounds them and turn our attention from the Mediterranean to the bleaker coasts of the North Sea where the first Vikings made their appearance.

Roman cargo boat – 3rd century A.D. In order to keep in touch and maintain trade with her Mediterranean colonies, Rome had a large merchant fleet, its ships inspired by those of the Phoenicians. They were very robust and spacious and relied on sail alone, the elimination of oarsmen allowing more room for cargo. There were a number of variations in type, some being designed as grain carriers, others as transports for horses or general merchandise. These cargo boats sailed close to the coast and broke their voyage at night, lying at anchor close offshore. They had no beak and, in case of attack by pirates, could only defend themselves with the weapons wielded by their crew. Drawings of cargo boats have been discovered on ancient tombs in the excavations of Ostia and Pompeii.

FROM VIKING SHIPS TO THE
TIME OF CHRISTOPHER COLUMBUS

AT the beginning of the 2nd century A.D. the Latin historian, Publius Cornelius Tacitus, made a journey to the areas of Northern Europe, which were then inhabited by barbarians but occupied by the Romans. As he relates in his *Historiae*, he was especially interested in the strange craft used by the Suiones, one of the several primitive and independent tribes who were the occupants of what is now Sweden. These boats were narrow and light, equally curved fore and aft and it seems likely that Tacitus had the privilege of seeing the hulls from which, centuries later, the Viking ships were to be derived.

The origins of the Vikings and their boats, with their many-coloured square sails, still remain obscure. But it is reasonable to suppose that the Swedish, Danish and Norwegian peoples who, in the 6th and 7th centuries inhabited the extreme north of our continent, could have traced their descent directly back to the Suiones. These people ought really to be identified more by the name of "Northmen" (Nor'men – later to become Norman) than by that of "Vikings", as it seems certain that the word "Viking" or "Wiking", meaning "king of the sea" was the title given only to the leader of each maritime expedition.

However, it does not seem wholly inappropriate to call all those fair-haired and bearded men from the North "Vikings"; with their exceptional seafaring skill, they can be called "Kings of the sea". Their ships would appear suddenly on the coasts of Germany, France and Britain,

Ship from Gokstad – 10th century. In 1880 the hull of a Viking ship, 79 ft. long and nearly 17 ft. wide, was recovered at Gokstad, Norway. Built of oak planking, she carried 16 oars each side and a square-sail on her single mast. The warriors' shields were carried over the sides.

Kvalsund ship – 7th century. In 1920 the hulls of two ships with stem and stern of identical shape were discovered at Kvalsund in Norway. Of the two ships (of similar period), the larger one was 60 ft. in length and had a width of 10 ft. 6 in. This Viking ship could be sailed or rowed and had 10 oars each side, but was of coastal type, not suitable for long voyages.

and disappear over the horizon with equal speed after their crews had sacked towns and villages, putting them to fire and the sword. There was no force that could oppose the Vikings – and no storm that could keep them in port – just as there were no ships which could compete with theirs.

Very little is known of the habits and customs of the Vikings on dry land, but the recovery of three of their ships dating back to the 7th, 9th and 10th centuries has allowed us to learn something of the means

by which they extended their influence over Europe. The Viking ships were real masterpieces of naval art. Their hulls, with keel and ribs, were covered with light planking. While the sternpost and stempiece, which were alike, were richly and artistically inlaid. The number of oars could be as many as forty each side and the single mast carried a large square sail. Quite deckless, they could take more than 100 men aboard, whose shields, during the voyage, were placed along the sides. Equally capable of going ahead or astern,

Oseberg ship – 9th century. Another interesting example of a Viking ship was that found at Oseberg. It was 70 ft. long, 16 ft. wide and had a mast 43 ft. tall. It was less seaworthy than the Gokstad ship and appears to have been designed for use in sheltered waters as a pleasure boat or yacht.

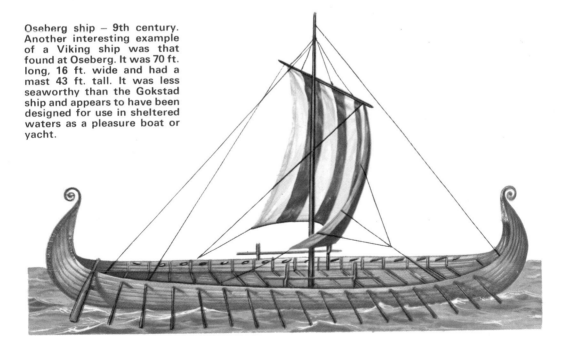

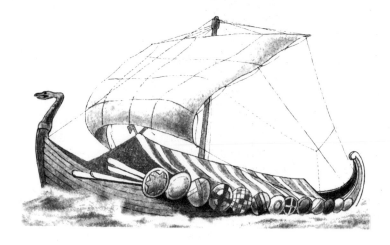

Viking Drakar – 10th century. The Viking long warships or, to be more exact, Nor'man were called "drakars" – or dragon-ships. The hull was light, as were the planks of which it was built, and the mast carried a single square sail. The "drakar" carried up to 40 oars each side, probably used only in combat. The larger types were able to carry as many as 150 men.

they made full use of the force of the wind on long voyages, entrusting to the oars the task of giving them extra speed and manoeuvrability when attacking. There were several different types – coastal, ceremonial and war. Some were called "drakars" (great dragons), or "snekars" (serpents), because of their decorated bows.

It was with these ships that the Norsemen reached Ireland and settled there in the 8th century and with which, one hundred years later, they penetrated into Russia and, from Kiev, went down the Dnieper River as far as the Black Sea, taking Constantinople by siege. With their "drakars" they reached Greenland in 986 and it was from that island that Lief, son of Erik the Red, sailed with 35 companions, in a craft comparable to the proverbial nut-

shell, to embark on a venture that was not to be repeated for five centuries – by Christopher Columbus. In fact, in the year 1000 a Viking ship crossed the Atlantic Ocean, arrived in Labrador, sailed round the island of Newfoundland and ended her voyage on the coast of the continent of America – at the mouth of the Hudson River where today New York stands. In view of the difficulty and inaccuracy with which news could spread in those days, such an astounding adventure was not nearly sufficiently appreciated – doubt was thrown on the whole voyage and in a short time it was forgotten.

It was logical that such sailors, undaunted by any ocean, should be attracted by the riches of the South, and their first objective was the Frankish Kingdom (France), in the time of Charlemagne. A

The Winchelsea ship – 13th century. After William the Conqueror, Duke of Normandy, had won the Battle of Hastings in 1066 and become ruler of England, the Norman style of ship must have been common on the surrounding seas. On the City of Winchelsea's seal, of 1300, it can be seen how radically the "drakar" had changed – gone are the oars, and the fore and aft castles have made their first appearance. These super-structures were not yet a part of the hull. It is logical to suppose that such ships were used by the English Crusaders to make their journey to the Holy Land.

Dover ship – 13th century. Subsequent to the Winchelsea ship, it has larger castles. The crow's nest is seen for the first time on the single mast.

Hanseatic ship ("cog") – 13th century. It is probable that the stern rudder was first used by ships belonging to the cities of the Hanseatic League.

century later the Nor'men were no longer content to sack the areas along the coast but penetrated into the interior by sailing up the Seine, the Loire and the Rhône. In the year 841 they sacked Rouen and in 845 and 856 it was the turn of Paris. No fleet existed that could stop them and, although France was powerful, she ended up by finding herself so much in their power that, in 911, Charles the Simple conceded them land on the Lower Seine provided that they would cease attacking Paris. In fact it was a wise decision. The land took its name from these rough settlers and became Normandy, and in turn the settlers gained by the more advanced civilisation of the original inhabitants.

It was from Normandy that the great invasion fleet set off for nearby Britain which, until then, only Caesar's legion-aries had succeeded in occupying. In September, 1066, William the Conqueror, Duke of Normandy, gathered together a good 3,000 ships (of which 700 were warships) on the coast of France and attempted an action which, many centuries later, neither Napoleon nor Hitler had the courage to repeat. The non-existence of an English navy allowed William to land his army without difficulty and, on 14th October of the same year, he met and defeated Harold, the last Anglo-Saxon king of England, near Hastings, in a battle which has become an epic of British history. William succeeded where an earlier attempt – in 893 – had failed. Then the invaders had found their way barred by the first British fleet, created by Alfred the Great, the man who had unified the country. Those who followed him on the

Adriatic ship – 10th century. Few documents are available to us regarding the Adriatic ships of the 9th, 10th and 11th centuries. This illustration is taken from a medal of 931.

Mediterranean merchant ship – 13th century. Typical of Venetian ships used for the Crusades, it was 120 ft. in length, 43 ft. 6 in. wide, and had a capacity for 600 people.

throne did not understand the need to follow his example and paid for their blindness with their liberty. For centuries, however, Alfred's farsightedness and Harold's culpable negligence showed the British that their safety and power depended on the existence of a fighting fleet capable of maintaining sea power.

While groups of Nor'men who had been on their way south remained in France and England, others pushed on still further and, from the 8th century onwards, appeared in the Mediterranean which, having already been dominated by Rome, was to become witness to many bloody battles.

While the superiority of sail over oar had already been accepted for the ships owned by the Hanseatic cities of Hamburg, Bremen, Lübeck and Danzig, and for

Amalfi galley — 13th century. The 13th century galley already had two masts with lateen sails while still retaining the three-bank system of oars — each oar, that is, being handled by a single oarsman. Two or three men sat on one bench working oars which rested on adjoining rowlocks. The rudder was still lateral. The dreaded "beak" was made of bronze.

Venetian "cocca" or merchant ship – 1380. This type of merchant ship was probably Nordic, but such vessels were built in Venice from 1348. Very rounded, they had a particularly high stern and stem.

A Venetian "buzzo" (pot-bellied ship) – 13th century. From a painting by Carpaccio, it has a large square sail and a second mast aft with lateen sail. Like the "cocca" it had a stern rudder.

French and English vessels, in the Mediterranean the oar was still at the height of its importance. In fact, with a fleet composed of "dromones" and "achelandias" (war galleys with sail and oars), derived from the Roman triremes and biremes, the Byzantine Empire – successor of the Roman Empire – had fought Arab attempts at colonisation which started in the 7th century. The "dromone", smaller than the classical trireme, numbered 25 oars each side and usually carried not more than 100 men. An average vessel of this type was 130 ft. long with a single mast, square sail and with fore- and aft-castles for the bowmen. The Arab ships were not very different.

The first important clash between the Mohammedan and Byzantine fleets took place in 655, off the coast of Lycia – a country in Asia Minor – when the Arabs were the victors.

However, 17 years later, when the Arabs again confronted the Byzantines, their fates were reversed. In a battle near Sicily the Byzantines revenged themselves, thanks largely to the use of their new weapon – "Greek fire". This was actually a jet of liquid fire, able to float, flaming, on the water, discharged a short distance off by a leather "syphon" covered in bronze. "Greek fire" guaranteed the safety of Byzantium for many years and the secret

of its formula was jealously guarded. Even today the exact composition of the liquid – which must have been lighter than water – is not known, although it is thought to have been a mixture of naphtha, resins and camphor.

Although driven back several times more by the Byzantines, the Arabs spread into Africa and as far as the Spanish

A Genoese "usciere" – 13th century. This type, designed to carry horses, measured about 82 ft. in length and 33 ft. in breadth. The horses – up to 50 – were carried in slings.

Danzig ship – 1400. One of the most advanced of its time. Of special interest are the fore and aft castles, both shown as integral parts of the hull.

French ship – 1400. Later than the Danzig vessel, this ship, illustrated in Froissart's *Chronicles,* shows the evolution of the round ship.

Pyrenees, and in 826 they conquered Sicily. In the 12th century they were to be well and truly driven out of this island by the Normans who, by then, were in such a strong position as to be able to consider themselves masters of the whole of Southern Italy. Using their characteristic tactics they first made their appearance in Apulia at the beginning of the 9th century and gradually infiltrated inland until one of them was actually crowned King of Sicily in 1130. These Norman invaders had very little left in common with their Viking predecessors, but for the people of Southern Italy that did not make things any the easier.

While the South passed from Arab to Norman domination, this period, for other parts of Italy – Amalfi, Pisa, Genoa and Venice (all subjects of the Maritime Republics) was one of achievement.

The first to come to the fore, in chronological order, had been Pisa. In 603 this city could already boast a powerful fleet and was subsequently able to free herself from both Byzantine and Lombard rule. Once independent, she not only defended her hard-won privilege by fighting the Byzantines at sea but also stood up to the Saracens and anyone else who opposed her dominion on the Tyrrhenian Sea. It was therefore inevitable that she should be-

come involved in the battles in which the Maritime Republics were enemies and rivals. After moments of great glory, a slow decline started in 1300, and in 1406 she fell under the rule of Florence, so losing touch with the sea.

The Republic of Amalfi, too, was formed out of her people's urge for independence and the resultant rebellion against the Lombards in 839. Amalfi was already a flourishing sea-faring city and the contribution made by her ships, enrolled in the fleet of the Campana League, was a determining factor in the defeat of the Saracens at the Battle of Ostia in 843. The men of Amalfi, first-class sailors and astute traders, forged ahead to conquer the markets of the Near East and, somewhat lacking in scruples, even allied themselves with the Saracens against the Byzantines, to achieve these ends. But the people of the Republic did not succeed in freeing themselves from the vice-like grip that the Normans had on them and ended up by joining them.

If the military qualities of the Amalfi Republic appeared to be fading away, it was certainly not the case with its sea-faring qualities which, through the centuries, remained very much alive. Although it may not be strictly true to say that the Amalfitan, Flavio Gioia, was the inventor of the compass, he nevertheless perfected this instrument, to the point of making it fit for practical use.

Gioia's compass consisted of a magnetised rod fixed to a small piece of wood floated in a container full of water. The instrument was finally perfected in the 14th century by the addition of the compass card, which meant that bearings could be taken at sea, thus making possible long voyages of discovery. In any case, it was the Amalfitans who were the first to use it and to spread the knowledge of its use. It is said that the compass had been known in China since 2634 B.C., but if this is true it seems strange that Marco Polo found no trace of it on his voyage to Cathay.

It was, in fact, three Venetian merchants, Matteo, Nicolò and Marco Polo, who, about 1270, brought home an amazing crop of information on the habits and customs of the Far East. At the same time, the Great Khan of the Tartars learned of the existence of Europe by means of those worthy representatives of the City of Venice, who had reached him under the protective symbol of the Lion of Saint Mark. For centuries that same Lion had been borne on the standards of Venice, a city which grew up in 840 around the nucleus of the Rialto and very soon became powerful and respected. In the 9th century she had had to defend herself from the Slavs and from the Saracens but, by the year 1000, Venice had already reached a period of expansion and was sending her ships, under the orders of the Doge, Orseolo, to conquer Dalmatia and other bases that were to form the foundation for her outstanding commercial growth. For Venice, as for Pisa and Genoa, the Crusades were to be a decisive factor. Jerusalem having fallen into Mohammedan

Portuguese ship – 1450. One of the earliest three-masted ships, she was equipped with cannon. The Genoese first used cannon at sea in 1319.

hands, Pope Urbano II proclaimed the First Crusade in 1099, appealing to all Christian people to send their best men to liberate the Holy Land. Many rallied to give their support under the flag of Geoffrey of Bouillon, leader of the expedition, but to convey soldiers in such large numbers to the areas around the site of the Holy Sepulchre, ships had to be found. The three Maritime Republics had the ships and it was to them that the Crusaders turned.

If the journey by land was long and difficult, the sea voyage was likewise far from easy. The Crusaders were crowded together in their hundreds in the holds and

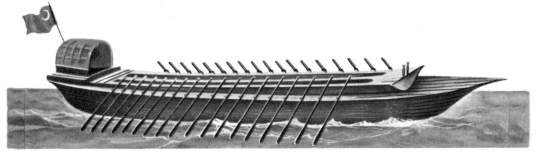

Turkish galley – 13th century. For centuries Turkish ships were the scourge of the Mediterranean and this one was used primarily for acts of piracy. Very fast and manoeuvrable, she was driven by 36 oars, the rowers being prisoners reduced to slavery. Chained to benches and under the whip of the slave-driver, they were forced to work 10 or 12 hours at a stretch.

Dutch merchant vessel – 15th century. Broad, spacious and sturdy, the Dutch round ships of the 15th century started to become well-known on all the sea roads.

For the Crusaders, their greatest reward was the liberation of the Holy Sepulchre – for Venice, Pisa and Genoa it was the incredible strengthening of their military and commercial power.

Naturally, the Genoese and Venetians allowed their ships to be used for subsequent expeditions, when the two Republics were not minding them for other conflicts of their own. To describe the composition of the Venetian fleet in 1202 at the time of the Fourth Crusade, it is enough to recall that it was capable of transporting 4,500 horses and knights, 9,000 equerries and 20,000 soldiers to the Holy Land, under the leadership of Enrico Dandolo. Over 1,200 boats were used, all belonging to the Republic of Saint Mark.

The areas of involvement of two great maritime powers like Venice and Genoa, in those days, were still quite distinct – the first dominated the Eastern Mediterranean while the latter controlled the central zone. But in 1261 the commercial routes of the two Republics overlapped and there was war – a long and bloody war, interspersed with occasional truces and marked by great naval battles. Before finally attacking Venice, Genoa had to free herself from her greatest rival and nearest neighbour, Pisa – this she did on 6th

on the decks of the 120 Pisan, 200 Venetian and 200 Genoese galleys. But nothing seemed too heavy a burden to these Knights of Christ – while nothing seemed more advantageous to the administrators of the Maritime Republics than to collect the charter money and to assure for themselves the rich markets of the Near East.

Carrack – 1460. This type of cargo ship, which was armed sufficiently to defend herself against pirate attacks, seems to have originated in Portugal. The carrack was a sizable vessel, with large fore and aft castles, decks capable of accommodating more than 1,000 passengers, and a fair number of cannon. She carried three masts with two square sails and a lateen.

Dutch carrack – 1470. Rich in detail, this drawing based on a contemporary Flemish painting, shows how well the Nordic people were able to develop the principle of the Portuguese carrack. A protective framework has been introduced on the castles over which, during combat, a cover was spread which gave some protection against the lighter missiles. Unlike the Portuguese carrack, all three masts have fighting tops, these fitted with protective nets and spikes as a safeguard for the mastheadsman in case of boarding. Non-portable armament was fitted on two of these fighting tops. The grapnel suspended from the bowsprit was probably used to hold fast the ship that has been boarded. Ten cannon are ranged on the poop-deck, five on each side. The Dutch maintained that even a cargo vessel should be able to oppose any assailant successfully.

August, 1284, at the Battle of Meloria. There, 90 Genoese ships, under the command of Oberto Doria and Benedetto Zaccaria, overcame 102 Pisan galleys commanded by a Venetian, Alberto Morosini. Doria captured 33 ships, sank the same number and took 1,272 prisoners, among whom was Morosini himself.

The biggest clash between Genoa and Venice took place on 8th September, 1298, near Curzola, and the Venetians, under the command of Andrea Dandolo, were beaten by the galleys of Lamda Doria. Marco Polo was among the prisoners taken. The following year a peace treaty was signed that was to last for fifty years – and then war broke out again. It is not difficult to imagine what the Italian Maritime Republics might have been able to achieve if, instead of fighting among themselves, they had formed an alliance. But there was never a lasting union and only too frequently did the galleys of Saint Mark and Genoa open fire on one another. It is correct to say "opened fire" because, from the beginning of the 14th century, cannon were in widespread use at sea and the Genoese and Venetians were among the first to adopt this new offensive weapon in their ships, in those Italian galleys that had been the mainstay of the Mediterranean fighting fleets for centuries.

The galley, derived from the "dromone" was a long ship, with two banks of oars up to the 12th century, and with only one bank from then on. A medium sized galley was about 165 ft. long, while a small one would have had a length of about 135 ft., a width of 20 ft., with 26 oars 40 ft. long each side. The first Italian galleys had only one mast. Later, two masts were used with a triangular sail called a "lateen", which seems to have made its first appearance in the Mediterranean in the 4th and 5th centuries, although its origins are unknown. In the very early galleys, the disposition of the oars was in treble formation – that is, they were in groups of three, on adjoining rowlocks, each one worked by a single oarsman who shared the bench with two others. Later on the tiéred formation was adopted in which the oars, worked by three to seven men, were much longer and heavier than those of the treble-formation galleys. Until the use of cannon became more widespread, their most feared weapon was the beak.

However, those ships which were used solely for warlike purposes in the Mediterranean carried oars right up to the 16th century. When the galley was required to be used more as a cargo ship, it became a "taride" – more spacious, but heavier and slower. It no longer served as a warship

The *Pinta* – 1492. Was one of Columbus' caravels. According to the learned De Albertis, she was 82 ft. long, almost 24 ft. wide, 11 ft. deep and had a tonnage of 154. She was three-masted and carried two square sails and a lateen. On her great voyage of discovery she was captained by Martino Alonza Pinzon and had a crew of about 30 men.

The *Niña* – 1492. The smallest of Columbus' ships, she was 79 ft. long, 14 ft. wide and had a tonnage of 147. The *Niña* and *Pinta* were caravels, Iberian ships of modest size, unlike the *Santa Maria* which was really a carrack. When she left Palos she had lateen sails – not suitable for an ocean-going vessel – and it seems that, during the voyage, she was forced to hoist square sails. The crew consisted of only 18 men. More fortunate than the *Santa Maria* she completed her voyage and made a safe return to Spain.

and was transformed into the "galleass", its slowness being compensated for by its greater capacity for carrying large numbers of artillery pieces. The round sailing ship that had been so far developed in Northern European seas was also popular in the Mediterranean for trading purposes.

By the year 1300 navigation beyond the Straits of Gibraltar and along the Atlantic coast was made under sail. In Northern Europe ships were being given rudimentary castles – this to improve their fighting power – and they began to increase in size. Their broad-beamed, single-masted "cogs" evolved into two-and three-masted square-riggers. The latter were known as "holks" and during the 15th century they were to become the most important of all North European types. The after rudder, more solid and practical than the lateral one, was invented during the 12th century – probably in Friesland – and its use spread quickly. It seems that the first "cocca" was built in a Venetian

dock-yard in 1348 and was used solely for trading. At the same time, the round ship was also taking on the functions of a warship in the English Channel and North Sea. In fact, when the 100 Years War broke out between France and England, the English found themselves confronted by the French, reinforced by the Spanish and the Genoese, and both fleets were almost exclusively composed of round sailing ships.

On 24th June, 1340, the first clash took place between this type of ship in the Battle of the Ecluse. More than 200 French vessels surprised the British fleet which was under the personal command of Edward III. The battle ended with the utter defeat of the French, almost all Philip VI's ships being sunk and more than 30,000 Frenchmen lost.

While the struggle between France and England dragged on for more than a century, other navies were being formed and with them emerged new types of ships.

The Portuguese had become a maritime power to be respected and the first carracks came from their shipyards, quite large, rounded cargo ships with more decks and very well armed. The principle of the carrack was adopted by the Flemish shipyard workers and even stronger and bigger ships were commissioned. Spain, too, after her centuries' long struggle with the Arabs, achieved national unity and formed a fleet composed mainly of carracks and caravels for navigating beyond the Straits of Gibraltar, and of galleys for use in the Mediterranean.

The time was now ripe for an undertaking that was radically to change the geographical knowledge of our planet. An Italian, Christopher Columbus, who was born in Genoa in 1451, having been sailing the seas for many years and having spent some time trying to make his fortune in Britain and Portugal, found himself in Spain at the court of Ferdinand and Isabella of Castile. Here he found financial support for his plan to open up a new way to the Indies. The world was then as yet unaware of the presence of land between Spain and the Indies. But it had been established that the world was round and Columbus believed that, by sailing towards the West in a straight line, he would reach the Orient – that is, the Indies – without having to sail round Africa. On the 3rd August, 1492, Columbus left Spain and set out towards the unknown and open sea with the *Santa Maria*, which he defines in his diary as a "nau" (nave – ship) – it was probably a carrack – and two caravels, the *Nina* and the *Pinta*. On 12th October, after a long and dramatic ocean crossing, the look-out on the *Pinta* shouted, "Land!" – the cry which was to have undreamt-of significance. Some time later, the great navigator set foot on an island that he called "San Salvador". He believed he had reached the Indies, not knowing that he had, in fact, discovered the New World.

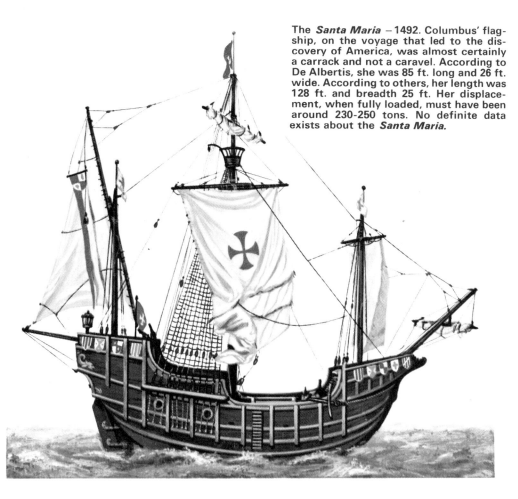

The *Santa Maria* – 1492. Columbus' flagship, on the voyage that led to the discovery of America, was almost certainly a carrack and not a caravel. According to De Albertis, she was 85 ft. long and 26 ft. wide. According to others, her length was 128 ft. and breadth 25 ft. Her displacement, when fully loaded, must have been around 230-250 tons. No definite data exists about the *Santa Maria*.

FROM THE ERA OF DISCOVERY
TO THE SHIPS OF NELSON

HISTORIANS link the end of the Middle Ages with the date 1492 – that is, with the discovery of America. Columbus' great achievement was not, all the same, a single incident to be set apart from the series of voyages into unknown seas which had already started in the first half of the 15th century. In that "era of great discoveries" – from 1450–1550 approximately – men came to learn as much about the planet on which they lived as they had succeeded in doing in thousands of years. Great credit for this was due to the Portuguese, Spanish and Italian navigators who, with their great courage, demonstrated how the ships of those days

– the sturdy carracks and the handy caravels – were already able to contend with the oceans. Henry of Portugal, known as Henry the Navigator, was the patron and instigator of the first expedition into the unknown. Although he, personally, never set foot on board a ship, his nickname was more than deserved since it was he who encouraged Portuguese sailors to go as far as Ceuta in 1415, to Madeira in 1417 and to Senegal in 1445, where they established colonies. Even after his death in 1460, the great Lusitanian carracks continued to sail further and further south, along the coast of Africa.

In 1482 Diego Cao reached Cape Santa

Portuguese carrack – 16th century. Ships like this rounded the Cape of Good Hope, led by Bartolomeo Diaz, thus opening the way to the Indies.

Victoria – 1519. The only one of Magellan's five ships to sail round the world. Magellan died in the Philippines but the voyage was concluded by Sebastiano del Cano.

San Gabriel – 1497. The ship in which Vasco da Gama, having rounded the Cape of Good Hope, reached Calcutta, thus opening the new route to the East Indies. She is defined as a caravel by some experts, but others describe her as a carrack – the *San Gabriel* is a typical example of a 15th century ship. It seems that her tonnage was not more than 120, but the loftiness of her fore and after castles (two and three decks high), and the number of guns mounted on two decks, show that she was roomy enough. Vasco da Gama's discoveries were of enormous importance to the development of trade with the Indies, as were those made later by Ferdinand Magellan.

Maria and, in 1487, Bartolomeo Diaz first struck the Congo and then went on to reach the Cape of Good Hope, to which he gave his name. Five years after Columbus' first voyage to the West in search of a new route to the Indies, Vasco da Gama reached Calcutta having rounded the Cape of Good Hope and crossed the Indian Ocean. The route to the Indies was chartered – on his return to Portugal he had covered 24,000 nautical miles in 630 days and da Gama had shown to his countrymen and to the whole world the way to the land of fabulous wealth. As a result of this urge for exploration, Portugal, by the middle of the 16th century, had

become rich and powerful, with colonies in Africa, Goa, Ceylon, Madagascar and even in Brazil – which Pedro Alvarez Cabral had reached in 1500. Every year, at the end of March, a Portuguese fleet would set sail from Lisbon for the Indies, to return 12 months later laden with gold, jewels and merchandise of all kinds.

All this, of course, had happened with the approval of neighbouring Spain, on the grounds of an agreement drawn up in 1493 under the auspices of Pope Alexander VI who was himself Spanish by birth but was known to be above all rivalries. According to this agreement, all the lands which might ultimately be discovered to

Matthew – 1497. Spurred by the discoveries made by Columbus and the Portuguese, King Henry VII of England decided to finance plans put to him in 1497 by the Venetian Giovanni Caboto (John Cabot). Cabot's idea was to reach the New World by following a very northerly route across the Atlantic Ocean. Cabot left England aboard the *Matthew* a vessel of very modest size. He discovered the island of Newfoundland and then landed in Labrador. He was the first European definitely known to tread the soil of the American mainland – if the still uncertain Viking achievement is excluded. In 1497 Columbus had seen only the islands and it appears that Amerigo Vespucci did not land on the coast of Brazil until 1499.

Great Harry — or **Henry Grace à Dieu** – 1514. Built in record time by Henry VIII of England for his journey to France, she was the greatest ship of her time. Known by the two names of **Great Harry** and **Henry Grace à Dieu,** she was over 200 ft. long with a tonnage of about 1,500. She had two fore and aft decks and two castles above, the after one being of exceptional height. For armament there were 21 great muzzle-loading guns and at least 230 small calibre pieces. The complexity of her four masted sail plan and the excessive weight of her artillery were contributory factors in making the vessel ill-suited for ocean voyages. She ended her days in 1552 when she caught fire.

the west of a hypothetical line drawn from the North to the South Pole, passing 100 leagues to the west of the Azores, were to be Spanish, whilst all those to the east of the line were to be Portuguese. Thus it was

Santa Catarina di Monte Sinai — 1515. Another giant of her times — flagship of the Portuguese fleet, she had six decks and was armed with 200 cannon. She was the last carrack to be built before the era of the galleons.

that Africa and the Indies were the concern of the Lusitanians, while to the Spanish fell the Antilles, Panama, Florida, Mexico and Peru. Here were coffers filled with gold – which were, for the most part, offered to the crown of Castile by Hernando Cortez, the greatest of the Spanish "conquistadores" of the Americas. And it was a Portuguese, unpopular in his own country, who gave to Spain the honour of flying the Spanish flag on the first ship to complete the journey round the world – Ferdinand Magellan. In the service of Charles V, he left with five ships for the East, dropped south along the coast of Brazil, discovered and passed through the straits which were to take his name, emerged into the Pacific and reached the Marianne Islands and the Philippines, where he was killed by a native. But his ship, the *Victoria*, completed the undertaking and so demonstrated the unquestionable roundness of the Earth.

The New World took its name from Amerigo Vespucci who reached there in 1499, also in the service of Spain, whilst the Cabots – under British auspices – were the first to reach Labrador.

In this race for discoveries and the consequent wealth of the Americas and the Indies, France and England remained mere outsiders, largely because they were still exhausted from the Hundred Years' War in which they had been engaged from 1339 to 1453. It was not until 1534, when Jacques Cartier discovered Canada, that

the first French overseas colony was
founded. The two countries, divided by
the English Channel, were too involved
with one another to bother about faraway
conquests. The meeting between Henry
VII (who arrived in France in the finest
ship of the time – the *Great Harry* or
Henry Grace à Dieu) and Francis I did not
improve the situation and war broke out
again in 1522.

England and, to an even greater extent,
France had no big fleets and they were
often short of men and great admirals to
lead them. They were frequently forced to
turn to the Italians – Genoese and Venetians – who had such long-standing maritime traditions. One of the greatest admirals of the 16th century was Andrea Doria.
Genoese by birth, he started by being in
command of his own city's fleet and then
of the French fleet against the Spanish.
Finally he was in the service of Charles V,
on whose behalf he occupied Tunis and in
1541 led an expedition to Algiers. He was
one of the greatest mercenary leaders and
navigators, one who fully understood that,
however important it was to explore across
the oceans, it was no less vital to keep watch
and fight in the Mediterranean.

European civilisation was being carried
by ship to great areas of land which, in return, gave their natural wealth. Meanwhile, in the very heart of Europe, in the
Mediterranean itself, the Turks were

La Grande Francoise – 1533. French rival of
the *Great Harry*. She was so big that she was
unable to enter the port of Le Havre, even
with the help of an exceptionally high tide.

threatening Christianity. After the fall of
Constantinople in 1453, they became even
stronger and challenged Genoese and
Spanish alike, occupying Otranto and
carrying on a ruthless privateering campaign against every Christian ship.

And so it was that, on the 25th May,
1571, the Holy See, the Venetian Republic
and powerful Catholic Spain united in the

Turkish galley – 1571. The
greatest battle between
galleys took place at
Lepanto in 1571 between
Christian and Turkish
fleets. The latter had 208
galleys and 63 ships of
other types. Ali Pasha
was captain of the Otto-
man formation with 87
galleys positioned in the
centre. On the left was
Euldi Ali, the famous
pirate, with 59 galleys,
and on the right was
Mehmet Chaoulak with
54. The clash with the
Christian forces lasted five
hours.

Venetian galley – 1571. One of the Venetian ships which took part in the Battle of Lepanto was under the command of Agostino Barbarigo and Sebastiano Veniero. Led by the 22-year-old Don John of Austria, the Christian fleet comprised over 200 ships, nearly all of them galleys, some Spanish, Genoese, Venetian and Papal. On board they carried more than 80,000 men.

Holy League against the Turks. Don John of Austria, just 22 years old and the natural son of Charles V, was put at the head of the biggest naval formation of those times – 204 galleys (100 Spanish, 80 Venetian, 24 Papal and Genoese) and 6 Venetian galleasses. Opposing him was Ali Pasha with a fleet of 271 ships, 208 of which were galleys. On 7th October, 1571, the battle took place at Lepanto, to the south of the Isle of Oxia, at the mouth of the Gulf of Patras, between Christianity and Mohammedanism. Don John's squadrons were captained by the Spaniard, the Marquis of Santa Cruz; the Venetian, Agostino Barbarigo; the Genoese, Gian Andrea Doria; and the Roman, Marcantonio Colonna. In the forefront of the Christian array, 6 gigantic heavy galleasses, armed with powerful artillery, were drawn up. It was really these new ships designed by Francesco Bressan, which withstood the impact of the Turkish formation of galleys. The battle soon turned into a merciless tussle in which quarter was neither given nor expected. Galleys pressed up against one another for boarding and hand-to-hand fighting, and issues were decided in this way. Ali Pasha's flagship was overcome after two long hours of struggle, the Admiral himself being captured and put to the sword. His head was cut off and raised high on the mast of his own ship, indicating in no uncertain way the complete overthrow of the Turks. 80 Turkish galleys were sunk and many others captured. In all 30,000 Mohammedans were killed and more than 8,000 taken prisoner.

It was the biggest conflict between galleys in history – a decisive victory for Christianity but paid for at a high price with Spanish and Italian blood. Aboard one of the ships under the command of Gian Andrea Doria was a hitherto un-

Papal galley – 1571. One of Colonna's 12 Papal galleys at Lepanto. In the battle which ended with a victory for the Christians, 8,000 Italians and Spaniards lost their lives and about 30,000 Turks. Although 12,000 slaves were set free a great many died, sinking to the bottom with the Turkish galleys.

Spanish galleon — 16th century. The origin of the galleon is generally traced back to Spain and her trade with her colonies in the New World. A merchant ship, the galleon had a more slender hull than the carrack and was also better armed. The galleons of that time were about 135 ft. long and 33 ft. wide; they had three or four masts, were basically square-rigged and had one or more lateens aft to aid steering. Contrary to what the name might seem to imply, the galleon did not derive from the galley but from the carrack or, perhaps, from the Venetian "cocca". Galleons, armed as they were with 60 cannon, came to be regarded as symbols of Spanish power in the Americas.

known Spaniard – Miguel de Cervantes. This man, who was to become the greatest figure in Castilian literature with his *Don Quixote*, lost his right hand in the battle.

If the Battle of Lepanto ended well for the Christian forces, it was due not only to the bravery of those taking part, but largely to the use of a new type of Mediterranean ship, the galleass or large galley. By comparison with the galley, it was a veritable fortress, armed with at least 50 cannon, equipped with a ram and a strong but sharp stem, lethal for smaller vessels. With a complement of 550 sailors and 200 or more soldiers, it was able to make headway against twenty galleys. After Lepanto, the galleass was for long to remain the warship *par excellence* of the Mediterranean, whilst the ocean-going navies found first the galleon and then the full-rigged sailing ship the most efficient vessels for the mastery of the seas.

The Spanish glee at the victory in the Mediterranean was, however, to be short-lived. Although the Spanish had assured for themselves relative peace for their trading, by this crushing of the Turks, the voyages of their great galleons laden with gold from their colonies in the New World to Spain were becoming less and less safe from year to year. The French and the English, in fact, who were almost completely without overseas possessions, wanted to enjoy the fruits of their discoveries just the same, at Spain's expense. They armed quite a number of privateers who, also attracted by personal interest,

attacked the Spanish ships with unparalleled audacity.

Among the many sea-adventurers of the time, one young Englishman in particular stood out – Francis Drake. With the support of the English Queen, who could not

Golden Hind — 1577. She was the flagship of the five-ship squadron with which Francis Drake conducted his war against the Spanish.

Spanish galleon of the Great Armada 1588. Seventeen years after the victory at Lepanto, the Spanish suffered a disastrous naval defeat in the English Channel. The Armada assembled by Philip to vanquish England and restore order to the Low Countries, was first harried and out-manoeuvred by the handier English ships and then scattered by the elements. The Spanish fleet consisted of 130 ships – galleons, galleys, galleasses and others, carrying 2,630 guns and about 30,000 men. Only 65 ships of the Armada ever returned to Spain – all the others being lost.

openly declare war on Spain, he carried out a series of piratical expeditions against Spanish Colonies and harbours. In 1572 he raided the cities of Nombre de Dios and Cartagena, where the riches of the American possessions that were to be sent to Europe were concentrated. He even crossed the Panama Isthmus on foot, with a few companions, to see the Pacific. That sight fired him with enthusiasm to such a point that, having returned to England, he left there again in 1577 with five ships, having decided to circumnavigate South America and launch his attacks on Spanish ships actually in the Pacific. The task was more difficult than anticipated and in order to pass through the Magellan Straits he had to withstand a storm which lasted some 52 days!

However, Drake's *Golden Hind* – which was called the *Pelican* when she had sailed from England – gave the Spanish a lot of trouble and she returned home, via the China Sea and the Indian Ocean, laden with booty. Queen Elizabeth knighted Drake and made him a Vice-Admiral. For his coat-of-arms, Drake chose a picture of the world, encircled with the words, *Tu primus circumdedisti me, divino auxilio.* (You were the first to sail round me, with the help of God). This was fact, for while Magellan had died en route, Drake lived to return.

The Spanish galleons of the "Golden Fleet" and the privateers were great protagonists on the oceans in the 16th and 17th centuries. The galleon was a type which had been developed from the car-

Ark Royal – The first of her name, she was built for Sir Walter Raleigh, who sold her to Queen Elizabeth. She was of 800 tons burden and carried 44 guns, 12 of them suitable for close fighting only. In the Battle of the Armada she was flagship of Lord Howard of Effingham who was in supreme command. The English fleet comprised 32 Queen's ships and 163 armed merchantmen, many of them too small to be of much fighting value. Harried up the Channel and short of ammunition, the Spanish fleet anchored off Calais, but fled in panic before fireships, Caught in disarray and in dangerous shoal waters, the Spaniards were again attacked and pursued up the North Sea.

rack or the Venetian "cocca" – a big, heavy and spacious vessel three or four masted, with square and lateen sails and extremely seaworthy. The confidence of her crew lay not in her powers of man-oeuvre but in her powerful armament – in her cannons that alone could hold off the pirates' attacks. But the daring of the pirates was such as to make them capable of capturing large, well-armed ships in spite of the fact that all they had were small galleons and old carracks. These however were as easy to handle as the galleons were unwieldy.

When the captain of a galleon attacked by a corsair was firing all his guns, after having flung as much grapeshot as he could find in his ship and had finally let fly a last round with his personal silver weapons, he had no way of escape left to him – he was compelled to yield. And the pirates would return to France – or, more often, to England – with rich spoils.

King Philip II of Spain decided this state of affairs could not be allowed to continue. In 1587 Drake, with a squadron of 30 ships, went so far as to sack Cadiz where part of the new fleet was being pre-pared. He sank 18 ships and captured six others. Philip II who, unlike Charles V, had paid too little attention to his navy, then made up his mind to attack England, with the intention of dethroning Queen Elizabeth and, having done that, of turn-ing all his attention to Flanders where, for some time, the Dutch had been getting more and more restless and pugnacious. And so he arranged for a great Armada or fleet, to be prepared, consisting of 132 ships of the national squadron, recalled from the Americas, Naples and Sicily. Some of these ships were of quite large tonnage, like the flagship, *San Martin*, the *Gran Grin*, the *Sant'Anna* and others. The Armada was placed under the orders of a man who had scarcely any seafaring ex-perience, the Duke of Medina Sidonia. He was in command of an inclusive ton-nage of about 62,000, armed with 2,630 guns and carrying 30,000 men. This squadron should have been able to deal with the English fleet, under the command of Howard, Drake and Hawkins. This had a strength of 102 ships, mostly of no great tonnage, which carried a relatively small number of guns and some 15,000 men. The plan was to destroy the English fleet then to despatch from the ports of Dun-kirk and Nieuport to the English coast 150 small boats bearing with them 30,000 soldiers ready for the landing.

But things did not go as Philip II had foreseen, mainly due to the heavy weather

Barents' ship – 1596. William Barents, a Dutchman and first of the Polar explorers, went to seek a route to China across the North Pole. He died after a terrible winter spent amongst the ice.

Mayflower – 1620. The English ship which carried the 102 Pilgrim Fathers to the New World. The *Mayflower* had a tonnage of 180 and was approximately 100 ft. long. She took 75 days to make the Atlantic crossing.

Jupiter – 1626. A Dutch galleon of the East India Company which had been founded in 1602 to trade with the distant Colonies. Like deep sea vessels of her time her bows were low and, although blunt, had a long projecting stem. She carried a huge amount of cargo and was powerfully armed. At the beginning of the 17th century, the Dutch had about 10,000 merchant vessels, of all sizes, in service – most of them products of Dutch shipyards – and a total of more than 100,000 sailors. In that century, the sea power of the Low Countries was unquestioned and increased even more after the founding of the East India Company for trade with the Americas.

at sea, to the lack of preparedness of his people, and to the unsuitability of Mediterranean ships for use in the stormy Northern latitudes. It was more a succession of relatively minor engagements and constant harrying by the smaller and handier British ships rather than a single battle which took place, until a storm finally threw the Spanish fleet into total disorder. Instead of giving orders for the ships to try and find the shortest way back

to their ports of departure, the Duke of Medina Sidonia ordered that the return journey was to be effected by sailing round Britain, and this completed the collapse. Only about 7 Spanish ships had been lost in the clashes with the English but many were badly damaged and so the Armada still had much of its strength when it ventured into the Northern seas. Twenty ships were wrecked there whilst another 35 disappeared in the fog and

Sovereign of the Seas – 1637. The finest ship built in England in the 17th century by the famous shipwrights, Peter and Phineas Pett. She was also one of the first with three decks. She took part in numerous battles, being given the nickname of "The Golden Devil" by the Dutch because of her decoration and fire-power. She was armed with 100 cannon and cost more than £65,000.

Aemilia – 1639. Flagship of Maarten Tromp, Dutch Commander-in-Chief in the Battle of the Downs in which 67 big Spanish ships led by Oquendo and a lesser number of Dutch ships faced each other. After a series of skirmishes, a frontal engagement took place – one of the first in which artillery fire was a determining factor. Twenty Spanish ships ran aground on the English sand-banks and as many sank in flames, 6,000 lives being lost. The *Aemilia,* armed with more than 50 guns, had a very flat bottomed hull which allowed her to manoeuvre better over the dangerous shoals than the Spanish ships.

storms. Only half of their number – later ironically called the "Invincible Armada" by the British and French – made the journey back to the port of Santander. Spanish power had received a severe blow and the Dutch did not hesitate to profit from it.

Since the 14th century, the merchants of the Low Countries had created a powerful mercantile fleet and had started trading on all the routes of the world. But,

two centuries later, a Dutch navy also appeared which was determined to oppose the Spanish in order to give the country independence from Philip II's yoke. The men who had been called "sea-beggers" by the Spanish were destined to give the latter much trouble, especially after the disastrous set-back of the Armada. In June, 1600, 70 Dutch ships went so far as to sack Las Palmas in the Grand Canary Islands, while two years later the East

La Couronne – 1638. Built by Cardinal Richelieu to rival the English *Sovereign of the Seas,* she was one of the finest and biggest warships of the period. Armed with 72 cannon, she was faster and more manageable than the British craft. She was 200 ft. long, excluding her ram. Her mainmast was 185 ft. high and she had a tonnage of 2,000 tons.

GALLEYS, GALLEASSES AND SHIPS FROM 14TH TO 18TH CENTURIES

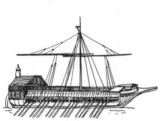

Venetian galley — 14th century. One of the first galleys of which there is documentary evidence.

Venetian galley — 15th century. Still single-masted, with 44 oars in groups of three on each side.

Venetian galley — 17th century. Two masted, with 20 oars on each side with three men to each oar.

Nordic galley — 17th century. More than 165 ft. long and 30 ft. wide. There were 27 oars each side with five men to each oar. Carried up to 500 men.

Royal French galley — 17th century. 170 ft. long, there were 34 oars each side. Armed with five guns and 12 lesser pieces and could carry 800 people.

Venetian galleass — 15th century. The first galleasses, bigger than galleys, appeared in 1431.

Venetian galleass — 16th century. Six craft of this type broke through the Turkish fleet at Lepanto.

Venetian galleass — 17th century. 165 ft. long, with a maximum of 50 oars, each handled by five to seven men.

Venetian galleass — 17th century. 230 ft. long, it had 36 guns and 64 small ones. Three-masted, with lateen sails, she carried up to 32 oars each side.

Papal galley — 18th century. One of the last galleys which used mainly sail, even though equipped with oars. By this time, the galley was disappearing.

Carrack — 15th century. Sailing ship of the high seas, probably of Portuguese origin.

Genoese carrack — 16th century. Although the galley still predominated, Genoa also used carracks.

Mediterranean galleon — 16th century. According to some opinions, derived from the Venetian "cocca".

Dutch galleon — 16th century. The Dutch used this type of ship for trade with the Indies.

Dutch frigate — 17th century. Smaller, lighter and faster than the galleon, it was used for escort duties.

The Dutch flute — 17th century. Of Dutch origin, smaller than the frigate, about 100 tons.

Dutch merchantman — 16th century. Unarmed, for trade in the Channel and North Sea.

Dutch pinnace — 17th century. Derived from and larger than the flute — both a merchant and a war-ship.

Dutch yacht — 17th century. Derived from the river boats, single-masted, it had many uses.

Swedish galleon — 17th century. As the years passed, the galleon became bigger and more heavily armed.

Artillery-carrying galliot or small galley — 17th century, which carried mortars for bombs weighing 200 lb.

Fireship — 17th century. Ship of any type, fit only for breaking-up, sent in flames against the enemy.

Zeven Provincien –1666. Flagship of Admiral de Ruyter, one of the greatest seamen of his time, Commander-in-Chief in the war against England of 1665-67. This struggle came to a head with the Four Days' Battle in the Channel when de Ruyter won a decisive victory over the English fleet which was under the orders of George Monk, Duke of Albermarle. On this occasion the *Zeven Provincien* showed all the qualities of a splendid ship, armed with 100 guns in batteries on three decks. De Ruyter died in an encounter with the French in 1676.

India Company was founded for the purpose of taking the place of the Portuguese in the lucrative trade with the East. But the first, great head-on clash between Spanish and Dutch at sea took place in 1639, at a time when the Low Countries were allied to the France of Cardinal Richelieu. Amongst other things, this eminent statesman was a strong advocate of his country's need to bring its fleet up to date. On 21st October, 1639, in the English Channel, the Dutch Admiral, Maarten Tromp, overcame, with a few ships, a 70-strong Spanish fleet led by Don Antonio de Oquendo, one of Spain's greatest admirals. The Dutch full-rigged vessels had deeper keels and were easier to handle and so could manoeuvre better in the dangerously shallow waters in which the battle took place. The encounter ended with 20 Spanish ships running aground on the coast of England and the same number being sunk or put to flight.

Thus as the sea-power of Spain began its decline so that of Holland was beginning to expand enormously. With the Treaty of Westphalia in 1648, the independence of the seven Flemish Provinces was recognised, but it had to be strenuously defended in a continual naval war.

In the Four Days' War against England in 1655, another great Flemish admiral came to the fore, Michiel de Ruyter, who remained at the head of the fleet until 1676.

French full-rigged ship of the 1st line – 1670. Up to the middle of the 17th century, all ships, however armed, had equal standing in the national fleets. However, in 1653 the British Admiralty laid down that, in battle, ships should be deployed "in line", according to the number of cannon they had, so as to obtain the greatest volume of broadside fire at the same time. In 1670, the Royal French Navy followed the British example and ordered her ships into five classes – 1st line: 3 decks, from 70-120 guns, 165 ft. long, 1,500 tons. 2nd line: 3 decks, from 50-70 guns, 150 ft. long, 1,100-1,200 tons. 3rd line: 2 decks, from 40-50 guns, 135 ft. long, 800-900 tons. 4th line: 2 decks, from 30-40 guns, 120 ft. long, 500-600 tons. 5th line: 2 decks, from 18-20 guns, 100 ft. long, 300 tons.

This was a time in which alliances changed like the phases of the moon – first, the French with the Dutch against the English; then the French with the English against the Dutch; and then again the Dutch, having made peace with the English, against the Spanish and French. De Ruyter's pre-eminence grew with every encounter. He fought against many admirals but his bitterest enemy was the Frenchman Admiral Duquesne. And it was, in fact, in a clash with him that de Ruyter – one of the greatest sailors of all time – was to end his days, in a sea far away from his native waters.

In 1674 the Sicilians rose up against the Spanish. Duquesne's French fleet hurried to their aid and, after having been waylaid by the Iberian fleet, faced de Ruyter's Flemish squadron off the shore of Augusta on 22nd April, 1676. A shot from the enemy's cannon broke the Dutch Admiral's legs and he died soon afterwards.

But the disappearance of de Ruyter from the scene did not bring to an end the clashes between the French and the Dutch, in which the English often took part.

In the meantime, about 1650 the battle fleets of the major countries were reorganised on a completely new basis. The British Admiralty led the way by establishing new naval battle tactics – the biggest ships, better armed, were to face the enemy in line ahead and no longer frontally or in

Swedish frigate – 1691. In origin, the frigate was a small boat towed by the flagship, but with the passing of time it increased in size until it became a three-masted craft, adequately armed, but lighter and faster than the galleon and big full-rigged ship. At the end of the 17th century the Swedish fleet included a sizable number of frigates which proved themselves valuable in the continual skirmishes at sea with Denmark. The Swedes also used frigates for privateering attacks against the Danish ships returning home laden with merchandise.

Dreadnought – 1704. The first British warship to bear the name. The *Dreadnought* of 1704 was a ship of the 3rd line, according to British classification, being armed with 60 guns. In 1653 English ships had been classified in lines and divided into two groups – ships of the line and those that were not of the line. The full-rigged ships "of the line" – i.e. those that were able to do battle in line ahead – were:- 1st line – more than 90 guns; 2nd line – more than 80 guns; 3rd line – more than 50 guns. Then came the division of the rest: – 4th line – more than 38 guns; 5th line – more than 18 guns; 6th line – more than 6 guns. The standards of classification in the various "lines" were modified in time and varied considerably from fleet to fleet.

groups, so that their broadside fire could concentrate on the enemy. The biggest ships were to line up in the first rank and the smaller ones were to be ranged in the second and third, according to the number of their guns. Thus the ships would be divided into ranks and those up to the third rank (i.e. those with more than 50 guns) were to be described as "of the line". By now, the technique of naval construction had made great strides. In England, two shipwrights, Phineas and Peter Pett – father and son – had created the first three-deck full-rigged ships on very elegant lines, powerfully armed and adorned with carved figures and gilding. The English Navy, thanks to them, was about to become the most powerful in the world and Samuel Pepys, Navy Minister from 1660-1688, spared no efforts to achieve this end.

In the French shipyards, too, work went on incessantly on the building of great full-rigged ships. After Richelieu and Mazarin, Colbert – Minister of Finance to Louis XIV – was all in favour of a great fleet for France, and it was due to his work that the French Navy was to know great glory in the last decade of the 17th century.

In Italy, the shipyards of Genoa were becoming increasingly active, but it was Venice that continued to have the highest reputation in the world for the best shipyards. Her designers and shipbuilders alike were so highly thought of that many foreign heads of state, like Peter the Great of Russia, sent their own technical men to Venice to learn the art of shipbuilding. In 1574, on the occasion of a visit to Venice by Henry III, a large galley was assembled before him, consisting altogether of more than 1,000 pre-fabricated pieces. Technical progress in shipbuilding, wherein lay the strength of ships from 1500 onwards, lay in the correct choice and seasoning of the various woods used, on the new prin-

THE SHIPS OF DE BOUGAINVILLE AND COOK

Boudeuse – 1766. The ship in which Louis Antoine de Bougainville, lawyer and mathematician as well as explorer, discovered Tahiti, after he had crossed the Atlantic, passed through the Magellan Straits and sailed for a long time in the Pacific. From "the enchanted island" he returned to France via the East Indies. The **Boudeuse** was a small three-masted sloop, almost unarmed.

Endeavour – 1768. A barque with which James Cook, one of the greatest sailors and explorers of all time, completed his first voyage of discovery by reaching Tahiti. Subsequently Cook discovered New Zealand and Australia and was the first to cross the Antarctic Polar Circle. The **Endeavour** – 97 ft. long – was armed with 22 small guns and carried a crew of 94.

ciples of hull construction and on a deeper understanding of the laws of dynamics. Venice built ships for many countries of the world in addition, of course, to the ships for the Venetian Republic which was constantly involved in a struggle against the Turks and Corsairs. In 1669 Venice had lost Candia. From 1700–1710 she was forced to protect her merchant shipping with military convoys. In the years that followed, she had to wage a war against semi-barbarous people in which no quarter was given until a peace treaty was signed with them in 1763.

These Corsairs, who came from the Barbary ports of Tripoli, Algiers and Tunis, respected no flag, attacking and plundering where they could. As a result, the navies of all European countries – either separately or together – had to engage in constant combat against these dreaded scavengers of the sea.

In the meantime, courageous men were venturing further and further away in their search for new lands, to lift the last veils from the unknown parts of our globe. Cook, the British explorer, went round the world three times. He was the first to cross the Antarctic Circle; he reached Australia, discovered New Caledonia, New Zealand, the Hebridean Islands and finally fell victim to a savage. De Bougainville, the French explorer, discovered Tahiti, and many others who felt the call of the sea revealed hidden corners of the world.

While in Europe, one war came after another, in the New World an event of major importance was to take place in 1781 – the British Colonies in North America claimed their independence and, after a long struggle, obtained it. The French sided with the Americans and numerous clashes occurred between the British and French fleets in the waters of the Lesser Antilles. France then was calculating on snatching for herself the rich possessions of the British crown in Central America.

However, the most memorable duel between the fleets of the two rival nations was to take place as a consequence of the French Revolution. Just as on dry land, the struggle at sea between Britain and France – first with the Revolutionaries and then with Napoleon – was to be fought to the death. On the proclamation of the Republic in 1792, France had a strong fleet of 86 full-rigged ships, 76 frigates, about 100 smaller ships and was altogether an adversary to be feared by the Royal Navy. The first battles took place from 1793–1795 while Napoleon, neglecting the sea, was involving himself on the continent of Europe. The French troops occupied

Ètats de Bourgogne – 1781. One of the most beautiful men-o'-war of her time, she was designed by Jacques Noël Sané, the great French naval architect. This three-decker, armed with 118 cannon, remained in service until 1848.

Pomone – 1804. A French ship with 40 guns she represented the frigate-type ship of the First Empire, characterised by exceptional qualities of handling. When she was under full sail, she was the fastest ship in the world.

Victory – 1778. Britain's most famous warship flew the flag of many famous admirals besides that of Sir Horatio Nelson who was mortally wounded on board during the epic Battle of Trafalgar in 1805. Built in a dry dock at Chatham, the *Victory* was laid down in 1759 and completed in 1778. She was designed as a first rate of the finest type, capable of showing the flag anywhere and was given an extra large store and water capacity to enable her to spend exceptionally long periods at sea. Her tonnage by the old measurement was 2,162. On several occasions she was modernised and had her armament altered, but as built she carried 104 guns. Although damaged at Trafalgar, she still exists, in a dry dock at Portsmouth.

Redoubtable – 1805. A French three-decker with 74 guns. It was one of the many sharp-shooters positioned in her tops who fired the shot which caused Nelson's death at Trafalgar on 21st October, 1805. The *Redoubtable* was sunk the same day.

Venice in the Italian Campaign. The Maritime Republic of Venice died, after centuries of glory, in the flames that engulfed the precious superstructure of the last Bucentaur, or state barge, in Saint Mark's Square.

In 1798 Napoleon sailed for the Campaign in Egypt and experienced his first reverse at sea on 1st August, 1798, at Aboukir, this at the hands of a British Admiral, Horatio Nelson, who had come to the fore the previous year in the Battle of St. Vincent against the Spanish. With about 20 ships, Nelson surprised the French fleet and destroyed it; only two full-rigged ships out of 14 succeeded in escaping his cannon. It was a great victory for a man who, only a year previously, had lost an arm in a naval encounter and who, although deprived of a limb, had wanted to continue the struggle against Napoleon, convinced as he was that Britain's only safeguard against invasion lay in the destruction of the French fleet.

On 21st October, 1805, Nelson was to complete the work started at Aboukir (the battle of the Nile) by defeating a fleet of 33 French and Spanish ships at Trafalgar, not far from Gibraltar. At the end of the encounter, about 15 of Napoleon's vessels had been captured and others, very battered, were in flight. Before the battle, Nelson had signalled the following message to the ships of his squadron: "England expects that every man this day shall do his duty." And England was not to be disappointed – and among those called on to give all was Nelson himself who, having

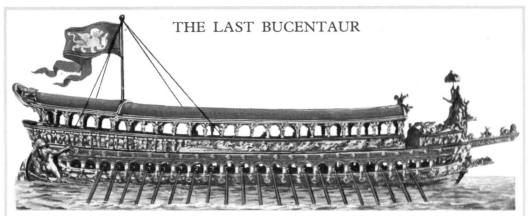

THE LAST BUCENTAUR

Bucentaur – 1729. This great barge used to house the Doge of Venice for the annual ceremony of the marriage between the city and the Adriatic on Ascension Day. The third and last barge was 144 ft. long and 24 ft. wide, with 42 oars handled by 168 oarsmen.

been hit by a ball-shot during the fray, died in the arms of the Commander of the *Victory*, the ship on which his own flag was flying. Before he died he had learned that the battle was won and that England, once more, had been saved.

Twenty-two years later, the implacable enemies, France and England, were to find themselves allies, together with a Russian fleet, in action in the Mediterranean at the Battle of Navarre. After the fall of the

Napoleonic Empire peace had reigned but, in 1827, British, French and Russian public opinion was very strongly against the atrocities being committed by the Turks against the Greeks in their struggle for independence. A naval squadron was therefore formed consisting of 10 ships of the line and 10 frigates, to a total of 1,298 cannon and 18,000 men of the three Powers. On 20th October, this combined fleet annihilated 62 Turkish ships, three of

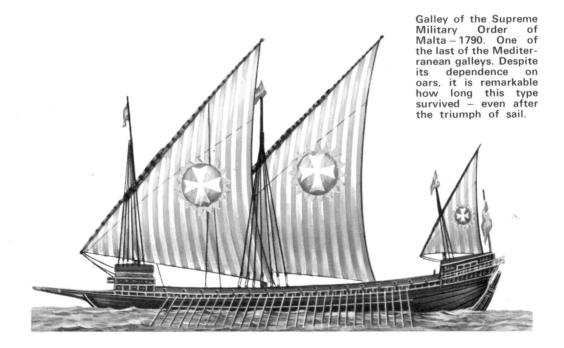

Galley of the Supreme Military Order of Malta – 1790. One of the last of the Mediterranean galleys. Despite its dependence on oars, it is remarkable how long this type survived – even after the triumph of sail.

47

SHIPS AND GALLEYS OF THE 17TH AND 18TH CENTURIES

Full-rigged French ship of the 1st line – 17th century. Three decker with 100 guns. 165 ft. long. 1,500 tons.

Full-rigged British ship of the 1st line – 17th century. *Royal Katherine,* launched in 1664, with 84 guns.

Full-rigged Turkish ship of the 2nd line – 17th century. 80 guns. Classification varied from fleet to fleet.

Full-rigged Russian ship of the 3rd line – 18th century. Flagship of the Baltic squadron, with 74 guns.

British frigate of the 4th line – 18th century. 40 guns. Frigates became bigger as time passed.

Tuscan sloop of the 5th line – 18th century. 18 guns. Sloops acted as escort and patrol vessels.

French frigate-galley – 17th century. This is the *Charles* of 1676, with sail and oars.

Genoese full-rigged ship – 18th century. This is the *Sant' Antonio,* of 1716, with 50 guns.

Genoese half-galley – 18th century. This is *La Beatrice.* She was about 165 ft. in length.

French galleass – 18th century. From 1600 there were no structural modifications to this type of ship.

Spanish Zebec – 18th century. Used by the pirates of Barbary, very similar to the felucca.

Dutch cutter – 18th century. Derived from the yacht, fast and almost unarmed.

British frigate – 18th century. One of the biggest ships of this type, double-decker with 50 guns.

French frigate – 17th century. This is the **Muiron** in which Napoleon travelled to France in 1799.

Sardinian frigate – 19th century. The **Beroldo,** one of the finest ships in the Sardinian navy.

French corvette – 19th century. The **Diligente** of 1803. Smaller than the frigate with 20 guns.

Danish corvette – 18th century. The corvette gradually took over the functions of the frigate.

French corvette – 18th century. This is the **Astrolabe** in which Dumont d'Urville made a voyage of 26 months.

British transport ship – 18th century. The **Bounty,** long remembered for the mutiny of her crew.

Full-rigged ship **Duc de Duras** of the French Indies Company – 18th century.

British transport ship – 18th century The **Swallow,** launched in 1782.

French lugger – 18th century. Similar to Italian brig, armed with two guns.

Danish barge – 17th century. Typical Nordic merchant ship. 50 ft. long.

Mediterranean coastal trading craft – 17th century. 40 ft. long.

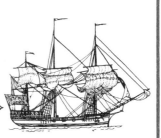

Mediterranean "polacca" – 18th century. For coastal trading.

which were large vessels of considerable tonnage. The battle was not foreseen – the European fleet had only intended to give a show of strength but a gun went off and, in a second, guns were being fired on all sides. It was the last great naval battle before the steamship took over. The mighty full-rigged ships of the line, armed with 100 or more cannon and built in the shipyards of Britain, France, Italy and Holland were the final triumph of sail. Nothing could be imagined more perfect, more powerful, more safe or even more beautiful than those giants of the sea.

From Magellan's *Victoria* to the galleons of the Golden Fleet, from the *Sovereign of the Seas* to the *Valmy*, there had been continued progress in naval construction. From Columbus' carrack to the three-deckers of Nelson, little more than three hundred years had passed – decisive years for navigation and for civilisation, for knowledge of the world and the development of trade. They were years of wars and battles but also years of progress and evolution in all fields. One result of this evolution was to be the invention of the steam-engine and its application in ship-building.

Constitution – 1797. One of the first three frigates belonging to the Confederated States of America: 204 ft. long, 44 ft. wide, with 50 guns, she could develop the exceptional speed of some 13·5 knots.

Valmy – 1847. The last of the big three-decker full-rigged ships built by the French Navy. The enormous wooden hull supported masts some 200 ft. tall. At her sides, 120 guns were arranged in long rows. In her design she represents the peak of development for the great men-o'-war sailing ships at the time when they became outmoded by the emergence of the steamship.

MERCHANT SHIPS FROM THE FIRST DAYS OF STEAM TO 1920

FROM the time when man started to have confidence in water, he was filled with the desire to find something that would release him from the slavery of the oar and from the inconstancy of the winds – something that would enable him to navigate his ship mechanically. Although this idea may seem to be comparatively modern, in fact it has been confirmed that the Chinese and the Romans – according to the *Architectural Treatise* by Marco Vitruvio, who lived in the 1st century B.C. – had already designed paddle-ships. The paddles were worked by men or by animals such as oxen and horses. Naturally it was only a matter of hazy intuition, but by the beginning of the 16th century Leonardo da Vinci was tackling the problem seriously. He produced designs of paddle-boats, one of which was worked by pedals.

According to what has been learnt from certain ancient documents, Blasco de Gerais, a Spaniard, gave a demonstration to Charles V on 17th June, 1543, of how he could make a large boat move by means of a mysterious machine, with neither oars nor sails. Whether this is true or false, it nevertheless demonstrates the existing ferment of ideas and the initiative that was to end in achievement. What finally made possible the fulfilment of so many dreams was the invention of the steam-engine.

Steam tug by Jonathan Hulls – Gt. Britain 1736. Equipped with an "atmospheric" motor by Newcomen. The steam was used to propel the paddle-wheel, which was placed aft.

Steamship by Claude de Jouffroy – France 1783. Barge fitted with steam-engine and paddle-wheels. On 15th July, 1783, it steamed up the River Saône for 15 minutes.

Steam barge by John Fitch – U.S.A. 1787. First tested in Philadelphia. The barge, 45 ft. long, was equipped with a steam-engine that worked six oars on each side.

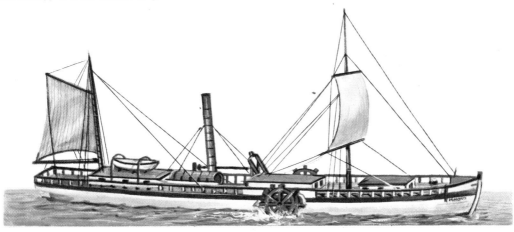

Clermont – U.S.A. 1807. The first steamship to come into public service, produced by Robert Fulton. She started a regular link-up between New York and Albany on the Hudson River. 142 ft. long and 14 ft. wide, she was fitted with a steam-engine that worked two paddle-wheels. Once the first doubts had been overcome, the public started to make use of the *Clermont.*

Charlotte Dundas — Gt. Britain 1802. Probably the first practical steamboat, she towed two canal barges for 20 miles.

FIRST EXPERIMENTS IN ENGLAND AND AMERICA

Comet – Gt. Britain 1812. The first commercially successful steamship built this side of the Atlantic. Length: 43½ ft.

Phoenix – U.S.A. 1808. Designed and built by John Stevens, she was the first steamship to sail on the open sea on her transfer journey from New York to Philadelphia. She went into passenger service on the Delaware River.

One of the earliest experimenters with steam engines was Denis Papin (1647-1714), but Thomas Newcomen's ideas were more practical for instead of heating water in the cylinder, Newcomen – in 1705 – used a separate boiler. But more than a hundred years still had to pass before the principle could be applied practically and on a reasonably large scale. This was thanks to Robert Fulton, an American who had lived for some time in England and France. Amongst other things, he was the inventor of an under-water machine. On 17th August, 1807, he inaugurated the first steam-boat passenger service on the Hudson River from New York to Albany with his *Clermont*. The run, of 150 miles against the current and with a contrary wind, was covered in 32 hours, to the great satisfaction of the guests and of the paying passengers. On that fateful day, steam navigation was born, this through Fulton's ability in combining the ideas of earlier inventors. So the ship was released from the limitations of human energy and of the wind's caprices to gain much greater manoeuvrability, an increase in speed and in safety.

Before Fulton, others had carried out interesting experiments with craft fitted with steam-engines. In 1783 a Frenchman, Claude de Jouffroy d'Abbans, had gone upstream on the Saône for 15 minutes on board the *Pyroscaphe*, the second of his three steamboats. On 27th July, 1786, John Fitch, an American, had tested out a

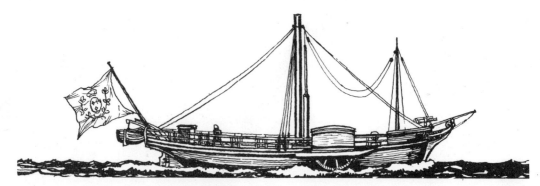

Elise – Gt. Britain 1813. The first steamship to achieve the Channel crossing. The *Elise* left Newhaven on 17th March, 1816, and, after a difficult passage, arrived at Le Havre 17 hours later. She was captained by her owner. The *Elise* had been launched on the Clyde with the name of **Mergery**, and later became the first packet steamer on the Thames. She had a displacement of 70 tons, an engine of 10 nominal h.p. and was 63 ft. long.

Savannah – U.S.A. 1819. The first ship with a steam-engine to cross the Atlantic. She was a three-masted sailing ship with paddle-wheels that could be dismantled and hoisted on to the deck. Under the command of Captain Moses Rogers, who had already had trial runs with the *Clermont* and the *Phoenix* she left America on 26th May, from the Savannah River and had a triumphal arrival in Liverpool on 22nd June. The engine was used for only 85 hours during the crossing.

boat about 50 ft. long, driven by 12 oars worked by a steam-engine. Symington, an Englishman, had built the 56 ft. *Charlotte Dundas* on behalf of Lord Dundas, which could tow two barges each laden with 70 tons of merchandise, for 20 miles in six hours.

All these experiments, although they themselves were not followed up, had been most valuable to Fulton who succeeded in creating the first really commercially successful steam paddle-boat. In company with people who believed in him and in progress, he built other steamships and increased the number of passenger services on the Hudson and Mississippi, opening up new horizons for inland communica-

tions in the great American continent, so rich in navigable rivers.

The honour of having gone to sea for the first time in a steamship belonged, however, to John Stevens, whose *Phoenix* was finally made sea-worthy at the same time as Fulton's *Clermont*. Having obtained the concession for the services on the Delaware River, Stevens had to transfer his ship from New York to Philadelphia, and the voyage went extremely well.

In Europe, too, the development of steam was swift. In 1812, Henry Bell started up a passenger service on the Clyde between Glasgow and Greenock with the *Comet*. On 17th March, 1816, a steamship crossed the English Channel for the first

Curaçao – Holland 1827. Although she sailed under the Dutch Naval flag, she was primarily a merchant paddle-steamer, built in the dock-yards of Dover, England. After the achievement of the *Savannah*, very few further crossings of the Atlantic were made. The *Curaçao* was the first to achieve regularity of service, this with three annual voyages, made 1827-8-9, between Rotterdam, Curaçao and Paramaribo. This 438 ton steamer was very seaworthy and had a long life. Although equipped with sail she generally proceeded under steam.

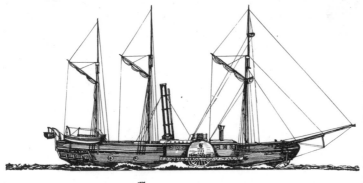

Ferdinando I – Italy 1818. The first steamship from an Italian State – the Kingdom of the Two Sicilies. Pierre Andriel, the same man who made the first Channel crossing under steam, obtained the permission of King Ferdinand I to inaugurate a route between Naples and Marseilles. The *Ferdinando I* was launched from Naples on 24th June, 1818. She had a tonnage of 247 and 16 passenger cabins.

Aaron Manby – Gt. Britain/France 1822. First steamboat with hull made entirely of iron, built in England for service on the Seine.

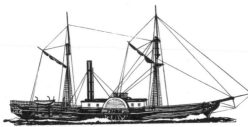

Dante – Italy 1840. One of the first Italian steamships employed on the Mediterranean routes, mainly between Genoa and Sardinia.

Sirius – Gt. Britain 1837. The first steamship to cross the Atlantic under continuous steam power. The voyage lasted 18 days.

Archimedés – Gt. Britain 1839. The first ship to be fitted with Francis Smith's patented propeller. Length 107 ft.

time – the *Elise*, built in England in 1813, had been acquired by a Frenchman, Pierre Andriel, who intended to use her on the Seine. The undertaking was less easy than he thought – to cross the Channel took some 17 hours, partly because of a storm.

As a result, it became generally believed that steam was better on rivers than on the open sea. At dawn on 22nd June, 1819, it therefore seemed incredible to the people of Liverpool to see a steamship come into their port, having crossed the Atlantic from America. This was the *Savannah,* which had completed the voyage in 27 days, although of this time she had travelled under steam for only 85 hours, the rest being under sail alone. A new phase had now been entered upon – steam could even face up to the oceans. In 1825 an Englishman, Captain Johnson, with 23 companions, linked Falmouth to Calcutta – in the *Enterprise* they sailed round Africa in 103 days, making use of engine-power for 64 of them.

In the same year, 170 steamships already existed in Britain alone, some of which were employed on postal services with numerous European ports. The first steamships had already made their appearance from 1818 in Germany, Denmark, Austria and in the Kingdom of the Two Sicilies. Ship-building was making great strides. In 1822 the first steamer with an iron hull had been completed on the Thames, the *Aaron Manby*. In 1838 an Englishman, Francis Pettit Smith, successfully applied his patent propeller for the propulsion of boats to the *Archimedes*, a steam frigate.

Hardly 31 years after the inauguration of the first steam service on the calm waters of a river, a trans-Atlantic passenger liner was to come into being. A new Company, waiting for the completion of its own ship, learnt that the Great Western Railway Company was going to beat them

Great Western – Gt. Britain 1838. The first steamer built specifically as a trans-Atlantic liner, designed by I. K. Brunel and launched at Bristol for the G.W.R. Company. She sailed from Bristol three days after the *Sirius* and arrived in New York 4 hours after her, having completed the crossing in 15 days, 5 hours. Gross tonnage: 1,320. Length overall 236 ft. Passenger capacity: 240.

in starting up a trans-Atlantic service. In order to be first they chartered the Irish cross Channel ship *Sirius* which, with the astonishing number of 94 passengers aboard, duly left England for the United States. The voyage was made entirely under steam but the consumption of fuel was so high that, when the tiny ship was in sight of the American coast, even the ship's furniture had to be thrown into the furnace. In the port of New York, thousands of people were celebrating the arrival of the *Sirius* when the *Great Western* made her appearance on the horizon – the first real trans-Atlantic liner in the world, the first ship designed (by Isambard Kingdom Brunel) specifically for regular service on the Atlantic. With only seven passengers aboard, she had completed the crossing in 15 days 5 hours – three days less than the *Sirius*. Her fuel consumption was 30 tons of coal per day. The *Sirius* suspended service after two trips, as she was too small and quite unsuitable. The *Great Western* continued to run back and forth 17 times

between Bristol and New York until 1846.

By now the public was feeling more and more confident in steam navigation, even if they did continue to like the ships to be fitted with masts and sails for any possible eventuality. In fact, there were never any serious accidents and the achievement of the steamship *Driver* in completing a voyage round the world from 1842-1847 aroused great interest. She had relied solely on her engines to cover the 75,696 or more miles that she had travelled.

After the *Great Western*, Brunel – the greatest ship-builder of the century – produced the *Great Britain*, which was floated out of a dry dock in 1843. She was the first liner to have an iron hull and propeller drive; she had six masts, was capable of carrying 260 passengers and 1,200 tons of cargo. Brunel, still not satisfied, wanted to achieve his ambitious plan of building the biggest ship in the world, five times the size of her contemporaries, a giant of 18,915 tons gross, at one time named *Leviathan*, but finally

Great Eastern – Gt. Britain 1858. This giant ship, Brunel's last, was the only one to be driven by both paddles and propeller. She was 692 ft. in length overall and 118 ft. in breadth over paddle-boxes. She was intended to carry 4,000 passengers and a crew of 400. Her maximum speed was 15 knots and she could set 65,000 square yards of sail. Her gross tonnage was 18,915.

STEAM PASSENGER SHIPS UNTIL 1918

Castor – France 1830. One of the first steamboats in the French merchant navy.

Arcidura Ludovico – Austria 1837. First ship of the Lloyd Triest. 310 tons.

Britannia – Gt. Britain 1840. First steamship built for Cunard. 1,156 tons gross.

Great Britain – Gt. Britain 1843. 3,270 tons. Length: 289 ft. Passengers: 360.

Piemonte – Italy 1852. Used on the Genoa-Naples run by the Rubattino company.

Lombardo – Italy 1841. Mail carrier on the Genoa-Cagliari run.

United States – U.S.A. 1860. First American trans-Atlantic steamer of this name.

Clarendon – Gt. Britain 1853. Passenger ship used on Middle East routes.

Washington – U.S.A. 1864. Opened the French Lines trans-Atlantic service.

La Normandie – France 1883. Owned by the **Cie. Generale Transatlantique** she was a 16-knot ship of 5,962 tons gross.

City of New York – U.S.A. 1888. Built in Britain. She had twin screws and a gross tonnage of 10,499. Speed: 20 knots.

Turbinia – Gt. Britain 1904. Passenger ship for the Great Canadian Lakes – one of the first operated by steam turbines.

Vulcanus – Holland 1910. The first full-powered sea-going motor tanker. 1,179 tons gross. Used locally in the East Indies.

Vaterland – Germany 1914. One of the giant luxury liners built before the First World War. 54,282 tons gross.

Cracovia – Italy 1920. The first turbine driven merchant ship to be built in Italy. 8,052 tons gross.

Persia – Gt. Britain 1856. Clyde built, she was the biggest ship in the world and the first iron paddle steamer on the Atlantic. She won the Blue Riband for the Cunard Line with a record Atlantic crossing of 9 days 1 hour 45 mins. Of 3,300 tons gross, she had an overall length of 398 ft. and an average service speed of 13 knots. She was sold out of Cunard service in 1878. Despite her steam machinery she carried sails.

launched as the *Great Eastern* in 1858. One of her two main engines drove the paddle wheels, whose diameter was 56 ft., the other one the 24 ft. propeller. These gave an average speed of about 14 knots. She was designed to carry 4,000 passengers – 800 of them first class – and for use on the Indian or Australian trades. There were so many technical difficulties that Brunel, ruined financially, died of discouragement, even before she was launched. The purchasers of the *Great Eastern* soon discovered the impossibility of making her pay on the Eastern run, both through the insufficiency of passengers and the great competition from the existing sailing ship services. So, after using her for a few trips between England and the United States in 1860, they were forced to give up. The ship was far too big for any trade and sailed with only a fraction of her designed complement of passengers and so only brought losses to her owners. However, the greatest ship of all in that early period of steam navigation was later to accomplish a task of extreme importance for the whole world – the laying of cables for telecommunication between Europe and America and between Europe and India. The *Great Eastern* was not a failure, as many people maintained – she was merely proof that Brunel was fifty years ahead of progress, his only fault being his optimism.

Meanwhile, from 1847, ships of French and American companies had started regular services in the Atlantic, followed by others flying the German and Italian flags. In 1854 it was possible to go from Le Havre to New York for just 90 francs, meals included, and with the passing of years, the lower class tickets for the crossing became cheaper and cheaper – in 1885 they cost just 65 French francs.

Great impetus was given to the passenger services by immigration. One only needs to consider that, in 100 years (1820-1920) some 72 million people emigrated from Europe. Of these, 34 million went to the United States. Around the year 1900 about 300,000 emigrants a year left from Italy alone, a figure which more than doubled from 1912-1914.

Sir David Scott – Gt. Britain 1821. Whilst steam was making great strides, the East India Company was still making use of these full-rigged ships for trade to and from India.

Flying Cloud – U.S.A. 1850. One of the most famous and fastest clippers in the world, built by Donald McKay of Boston. She covered the distance between New York and San Francisco, via Cape Horn, in 89 days.

It was only logical that the shipping companies should expand in order to meet the continuous, growing needs by gradually providing bigger and bigger and more efficient ships, with greater comfort and luxury for the first-class passengers and better adapted and more roomy accommodation for the emigrants.

From 1850 the steamships no longer made much use of sails, although they were used in a fair wind, for steadying purposes and in case of a broken propeller shaft. Steamers operated across the Atlantic to regular time-tables and there were many services a week between England, Europe and America. In 1874,

when the risk of fire had diminished, smoking was allowed on board and, in 1879, electric light was seen in a liner. By the turn of the century the big ships carried orchestras for the pleasure of their luxury passengers. Technical progress, too, was making great strides. Hulls had started to be made of steel, much lighter and more resistant than iron. About 1900 the first steam-turbine appeared, less cumbersome, lighter and more powerful than the old steam reciprocating engine. In the turbine, which was invented by an Englishman, Charles A. Parsons, in 1894, the steam made a multi-bladed shaft turn, this being directly connected to the propeller, instead of driving pistons. The first turbines turned in only one direction; therefore, in order to go astern, an auxiliary turbine had to be brought into action – one which drove a propeller in the opposite direction. This invention had enormous effects on navigation and was very soon adopted on many passenger ships, giving them, more than anything, greater speed.

The diesel engine, invented by Rudolf Diesel in 1893, followed a long series of experiments with internal combustion engines – made by a number of inventors – which started about 1807. It was about the middle of the 19th century that the design of the cargo ship – then built of iron – diverged from that of the mainly passenger-carrying ship. They were mostly of small size and even by 1914 few were of more than 5,000 tons gross. In 1886 the first refrigerated ship was produced and in 1896 the first really successful oil-tanker, the *Gluckauf*, appeared. The steam freighters, however, had a hard struggle against the competition offered by sailing ships, which seemed in no hurry to disappear.

In fact, in the 19th century, at the same time as steam was becoming widely used,

Cutty Sark – Gt. Britain 1869. The most perfect example of a merchant sailing ship, before the steamship finally took its place, was the clipper, with her slim bows, graceful lines and great spread of sails. The American ones were followed by others built in Britain and of these the *Cutty Sark* was one of the most famous. She was one of the last of the tea clippers and was later used on the Australian wool trade. Of a length of 212 ft. and a breadth of 36 ft., she carried 32,000 square feet of canvas and had a crew of 28. Her maximum speed was just over 17 knots. She is still preserved at Greenwich.

Thomas W. Lawson – U.S.A. 1902. Steel built hulls which were much lighter and tougher than wooden and iron ones gave the technical men the chance to work on large schooners like the ***Lawson*** She was launched from a shipyard in Massachusetts with a gross tonnage of 5,218, when steam was already gaining the upper hand. After having been employed for five years as a collier she was acquired by the Sun Oil Company who converted her into a tanker.

the sailing ship reached its peak of perfection, above all with the clippers which were American in origin. With slim-lined hulls and enormous sails, they were capable of taking advantage of the least breath of wind and they sailed all the seas of the world, beating every other ship for speed. In 1855, when Brunel started building his *Great Eastern*, the British clipper, *Lightning*, was one of those maintaining a regular service between London and Australia, sailing round via the Cape of Good Hope, with cargo and several hundred passengers. On one occasion she did the homeward voyage in 64 days.

The ships which were used to bring the tea from China to Europe were real clippers and amongst the fastest. In 1866 a group of these took part in a keen race from the Chinese port of Foochow to England. The *Taeping* won, having completed the voyage – with all sails set – in just 99 days, preceding the second ship's arrival by only 28 minutes! Trade between the Orient and

Europe, however, was to be speeded up enormously when the Suez Canal was opened. This was done in 1869 by a Frenchman, Ferdinand de Lesseps, from the designs of the Italian civil engineer, Negrelli.

The technical progress made in the dockyards revolutionised concepts of shipbuilding, even of the sailing ship, and at the end of the 19th century the greatest schooners were seen. These were five, six and even seven-masted, with steel hulls and greatly increased tonnages of up to 5,000 gross measurement. Nevertheless, by 1905 the struggle between sail and steam had resolved itself in favour of the latter. According to data from Lloyds' Register, 19,153 steamships were at sea that year against just 10,603 sailing ships – 29,963,392 tons of steam shipping against 6,037,501 tons of sail. And that just 98 years after the first voyage of the *Clermont*.

At the beginning of the 20th century, the revolution of steam had completed its

Mississippi – U.S.A. 1850. One of the famous Mississippi river boats that traversed the length of the great United States waterway. The service was started up in 1812 between New Orleans and Natchez by the ***New Orleans***, belonging to a company founded by Roosevelt, Livingston and Fulton. By 1812 there were already 35 boats, from 40-450 tons, one the ***Mississippi***. By 1840 there were more than 1,000 of these splendid colourful boats.

American clipper – 1853. The *Great Republic* employed on Oriental routes.

British clipper – 1870. The *Torrens,* a fine example of these very fast vessels.

German five-masted barque *Potosi* – 1895. A giant of 4,026 tons gross.

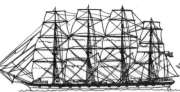

British four-master *County of Linlithgow*–1887. Ship-rigged. 2,202 tons gross.

German four-masted barquentine – 1904. The *Beethoven*, 2,005 tons. Length: 271 ft.

Italian four-masted barque – 1903. Gross tonnage of 2,464, she was 293 ft. in length.

Italian three-master *Cosmos* – 1865. The square sails denote ship rig. Tonnage: 1,715.

Brigantine. Two masts, with square sails on foremast and fore and aft sails on both.

Three-masted barque. Distinguished by lack of square sails on mizzen.

Barquentine. This rig carried square sails on the foremast only.

Brig. Had only two masts, square rigged on both, with trysail aft.

Two masted schooner. Unlike the topsail schooner this had no square sails.

Large racing yacht. Cutter rig, with deep keel.

Cutter rig smaller than yacht. Deep keel.

Mediterranean lateen-rigged for domestic trading.

Local type used for coastal trading in the Adriatic.

Ariel and *Taeping* – Gt. Britain 1866. These were two of the many "China Clippers" which, each year, brought to England the new season's tea from China. Besides the bonus paid for being the first home there were other incentives for making fast passages. On 30th May, 1866 the most famous of all these races started, as the *Ariel, Taeping* and *Serica* left Foochow. On the way home they repeatedly caught sight of one another and finally docked at London on the same tide – late on 6th September – the *Taeping* beating the *Ariel* by a mere 28 minutes.

miracle. To travel by sea was no longer an adventure in which one had to be ready to face up to risks and discomforts and, what is more, pay a high price. In 1905 an emigrant to the United States would have paid a relatively modest fare. The first-class traveller certainly paid much more but he was offered every comfort, rapidity of service and a degree of safety that, up to only a few decades before, would have seemed Utopian. In 80 years the liner had undergone a profound and radical trans-formation – no comparison was possible between the *Great Western* and the splendid *Mauretania, Lusitania, Aquitania, Olympic* and *Vaterland*. Whereas Brunel's ship travelled at 14 knots, the *Mauretania* crossed the Atlantic at 25 knots, in less than 5 days. She was awarded the famous "Blue Riband", the symbol of the fastest liner in the world, which she retained for twenty-two years. Whilst the old ships had

offered small cabins to their passengers, crude sanitary arrangements, oil lights and one single dining saloon, the new ships put at their passengers' disposal cabins with running water, electric light and tele-phone, sheltered decks and large public rooms more or less like those of any large hotel on dry land.

The tonnages of the big passenger liners had progressively increased from about 20,000 tons to 54,000 tons during the first fourteen years of the 20th century, yet only 50 years or so earlier the 19,000 tons of the *Great Eastern* had been considered sheer madness.

The next invention which was to bring even greater security to sea voyages was Guglielmo Marconi's telegraphy without wires. The first installation in a British liner was in 1901. It enabled any ship so equipped to keep in radio contact both with other ships and with land. The sea-

Titanic – Gt. Britain 1911. Launched in 1911, she left Southampton on 10th April, 1912, on her maiden voyage to New York. She had 1,316 passengers on board and a crew of 892. But, at 11.40 p.m. on the 14th April, the gigantic ship collided with an iceberg that tore a hole in her, some 300 ft. in length. She sank two hours and 40 minutes later and 1,503 persons lost their lives. She had a tonnage of 46,328 tons, was 852 ft. in length and had a service speed of 21-22 knots.

Aquitania – Gt. Britain 1914. The last great trans-Atlantic liner to be launched from British ship-yards and brought into service before the First World War. This splendid Cunard liner, of 45,647 tons, was 865 ft. long and 97 ft. in breadth. After a very few voyages, she was requisitioned and served as a troop-carrier and hospital ship. She continued in service until 1950, covering in all three million miles and carrying some 1,200,000 passengers.

man was no longer alone, left to his lucky star, but was supported by others like himself who, on receiving a short signal in Morse Code, would speed to his aid. The value of radio was driven home when, on 15th April, 1912, the world's largest liner, the *Titanic*, collided with an iceberg in the dead of night on her maiden voyage. A spur of ice tore open the hull below the waterline, for some 300 ft., so causing the loss of the splendid ship in less than three hours. Thanks to radio, other ships hurried to her position to pick up survivors. Even so, 1,503 lives were lost.

The *Titanic* tragedy was steam shipping's worst disaster prior to the outbreak of the First World War. All the same, it did not prevent ever growing numbers of people from crossing the Atlantic, or the other oceans, either on business trips or just simply as tourists. The steamship had reduced to almost nothing the enormous distances that used to separate the Five Continents; it had given a very great impetus to maritime trade and had opened up new horizons on the world. Very valuable in peacetime, it was fated to be exploited, too, for waging war at sea and it enabled traditional tactics to be revolutionised. At the outbreak of the First World War, sail had already been relegated to an adventurous and romantic past.

Lusitania – Gt. Britain 1907. She and her sister *Mauretania* were the first express liners to be turbine-driven. The *Mauretania* won the Blue Riband from the *Kaiser Wilhelm II* in 1907 and held it for 22 years. She was scrapped in 1935, but the *Lusitania's* career was cut short, for on 7th May, 1915, she was torpedoed without warning by a German submarine and sank in 20 minutes. Of those on board 1,198 lost their lives. 31,550 tons gross. Length: 762 ft. Service speed $25\frac{1}{2}$ knots.

NAVAL FORCES FROM STEAM SHIPS
TO THE FIRST WORLD WAR

SIX small Turkish sailing ships were the first to realise the significance of what steam was going to mean to ships of war, this in the Summer of 1826. They had the bad luck to encounter the steamship *Karteria*, which had been presented by the United States to the Greek patriots who were then calling for the recovery by Greece of all Greek-speaking areas.

Despite the complete lack of even a breath of wind, the *Karteria* powered by steam was able to manoeuvre at will against the Ottoman sailing ships. She sank them one by one with the fire from her 8 guns, which were of quite light calibre, and had been mounted on improvised positions on deck. However, another 25 years were to pass before steam made a decisive impact on warships.

The great admirals considered the new system of propulsion absolutely unsuitable for combat vessels owing to the heaviness and bulk of the engines and fuel, the vulnerability of the great paddle wheels, and the difficulty of ensuring supplies of coal wherever the fleet might have need of them. But other inventions arrived on the scene to disturb the already unquiet sleep of the military authorities. There was the

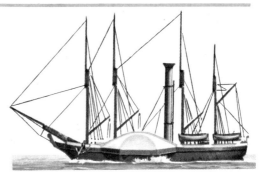

Karteria — Greece 1826. The first steamship to be involved in combat. Armed by Greek patriots, she defeated six Turkish ships.

Agamemnon — Gt. Britain 1852. The first ship of the line with 100 guns to be equipped with steam machinery and screw propulsion.

Napoleon — France 1852. First ship of the line, 2nd rate, with 92 guns, to have steam and propeller. One of the French Navy, she was built from a design by the famous naval architect, Dupuy de Lôme. With a 900 h.p. engine, she developed 13·8 knots. 5,057 tons. Length about 235 ft.

ARMOURED BATTERIES

Tonnante – France 1855. First example of an armoured battery. She took part in the Crimean War. 1,600 tons. 4 knots. 16 × 2½ in. guns.

Monitor – Federal States of America 1861. Armoured battery, with 2 × 11 in. guns placed in a revolving turret. She was the **Merrimac's** rival.

Merrimac – Confederate States of America 1861. Converted steam-frigate of the same name, armoured with metal plating and offcuts of rails.

Onondaga – France 1863. Built in America and bought by France. Her armour-plating was 6 in. thick. Displacement: 2,500 tons. Speed: 5 knots. 4 × 9½ in. guns in two turrets.

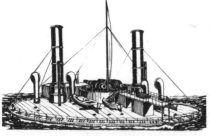

Novgorod – Russia 1873. Nicknamed **Popoffka,** she was circular in shape and 101 ft. in diameter. She mounted 2 × 12 in. guns and was quite unmanageable at sea.

howitzer, which was evolved from the old-time mortar. There was the rifling of gun barrels invented by a Piedmontese General, Giovanni Cavalli. The former gave much greater powers of destruction whilst the latter made for more precise aiming. This, of course, demanded new thinking as to the use of artillery, which had remained rather behind the times. In the early part of the 19th century, a 16-inch calibre gun was still loaded from the muzzle and could just fire one ball every five minutes at a distance of not more than 4,300 yards.

The great sailing men-o'-war with 100 and more old-type guns were very soon to be discarded, under pressure of progress. The first use of a steam-engine in warships took place in 1829 when the *Sphinx* became part of the French fleet. She was a paddle-drawn corvette of 777 tons and was seen for the first time in action during the conquest of Algiers. But it was not until 1850 that the first ship-of-the-line came to be built with steam and a propeller. This was the *Napoleon,* the brain child of a talented young French naval engineer, Dupuy de Lôme. This ship, quite revolutionary in many respects, carried 92 guns. Two years later, in 1852, the British replied with the *Agamemnon,* which was of the same type but larger.

It was the Crimean War that sparked off the great transformation in naval forces when, from 1854 to 1856, Russia was involved against Turkey, whose Allies were France, Great Britain and Piedmont. This War convinced the last remaining sceptics that steam was of practical value, since it was through the use of such ships that the transport and provisioning of great contingents of troops from Europe to the East was made possible. In addition, it demonstrated the need to cover ships with armoured plating as a protection against gun fire. In fact, Napoleon III had some "floating batteries" built – the *Tonnante, Lave* and *Devastation,* equipped with steam-engines and covered with iron armour to a thickness of 8 in. On 14th October, 1854, a short distance away from the fort of Kinburn, ships such as this, while they razed the enemy emplacements to the ground, were repeatedly hit by Russian howitzer shells without suffering any damage. The first "ironclad" came on the scene as a result of this experience – the armour-plated frigate, *Gloire,* designed and built by Dupuy de Lôme in 1859. Armour-plating 8¾ in. thick had been put over the wooden hull, from 6 ft.

Alabama – Confederate States of America 1862. Privateer with steam and sail, built in Britain. She ranged the Atlantic and Indian Oceans for two years, capturing 38 ships. She was sunk by the *Kearsage*.

Florida – Confederate States of America 1860. Privateer, she scoured the Atlantic for 26 months, enjoying the plunder from 37 attacks before being torpedoed by a Federal cruiser in the neutral port of Bahia.

below the waterline to the upper part of the battery. Her armament consisted of 6 × 9.4 in. and 2 × 6.4 in. guns, of the modern breech-loading type. A year later, the *Warrior* was launched from a British shipyard – the first British ironclad – which was remarkable for having an iron hull, which was protected in the same way with armour-plating.

The first encounter between two ironclads took place on 8th March, 1861, at Hampton Roads during the American Civil War, between the Southern *Merrimac* and the Northern *Monitor*. The former was really a converted screw-driven frigate, from which the superstructure had been removed, armed with ten guns and a ram, whilst the latter was an armoured lighter with a rotating turret equipped

with two heavy 11 inch guns, built to original designs by the Swedish inventor, Ericsson. At first the *Merrimac* played havoc with the Northern fleet, but when the *Monitor* engaged her in a duel with equal weapons, the battle lasted for four hours during which time the two ships rained blows upon one another without sustaining any damage whatever. The American war therefore confirmed the value of armour-plating, besides marking the appearance of what was in effect the ancestor of the battle-cruiser – a very fast and well armed ship, employed by the North to hunt down the privateers of the South.

The first important battle between warships of the modern concept – that is, propelled by steam and armour-plated, all

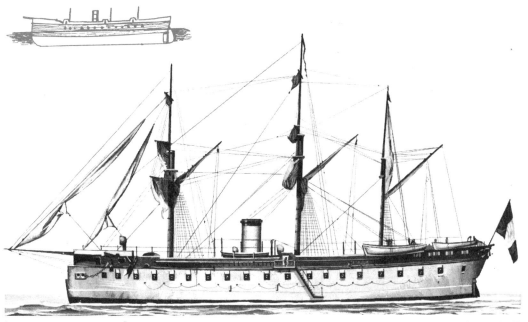

Gloire – France 1859. The first "ironclad" in the world, built by Dupy de Lôme. Her wooden hull was covered with armour-plating, consisting of two layers of iron plating which extended from the deck to 6 ft. below the waterline. Displacement: 5,675 tons. Length: 253 ft. Speed: 12 knots. Armament: at first 30 × 36-pdr. smooth bore guns, later 6 × 9.4 in. guns.

Warrior – Gt. Britain 1861. First British armoured ship, built in reply to the *Gloire.* Unlike the French ship, the *Warrior's* guns were still muzzle-loaders. She had an iron hull and the midship part, for a length of some 200 ft., was further protected by armour-plating. Displacement: 9,210 tons: Length: 380 ft. Speed: 12·5 knots. Armament: 28 × 7 in. guns.

derived from the *Gloire* or from the *Warrior* – took place in the waters of the Adriatic at Lissa. At the outbreak of the Third Italian War of Independence, the Italian Navy – which had recently been created on the lines of the Sardinian Navy – was formed almost exclusively of armoured ships, acquired from British and French shipyards. It was superior, both numerically and in firing strength, to the Austrian Navy. All the same, the Commander-in-Chief of the Italian Fleet, Admiral Pellion di Persano, wanted to avoid a frontal engagement and preferred to undertake the occupation of the island of Lissa. The attack – in which the Commander of the frigate, *Formidabile,* Simone di Saint Bon, showed his courage – was conducted in

a hesitating and tardy manner by Persano, so much so that his squadron ended up by being taken by surprise by their Austrian counterpart under Admiral Tegetthoff. The Italian fleet consisted of an armoured vessel with very strong ram, seven armoured frigates, four armoured sloops and some smaller ships, totalling 74,000 tons, 612 new type guns with rifled barrels, and 10,800 men. The Austrian fleet comprised seven armoured frigates and smaller ships to a total of 47,000 tons, 531 guns which were still smooth-bored and 7,700 men. Tegetthoff's attack was conducted with such decision and violence, with both guns and rams, that the order of the Italian ships was broken up and, after three hours, the battle came to an end with the sinking

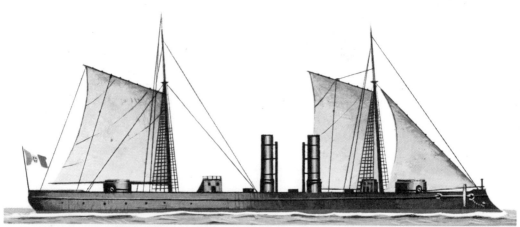

Affondatore – Italy 1865. This warship, designed for ramming purposes, was built in Britain. Suffered severe damage at Battle of Lissa in 1866 when attacked by the Austrian ship *Kaiser;* this in spite of being protected by armour-plating. As a result, she was entirely modernised in 1883. Displacement: 4,376 tons. Length: 325 ft. Speed: 12 knots. Armament: 2 × 10 in. guns and iron ram. Crew: 309.

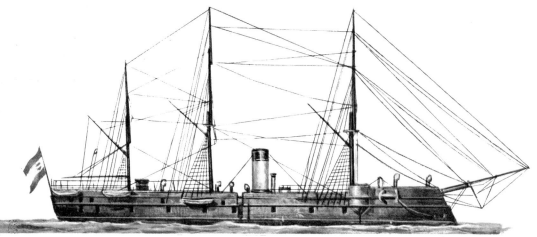

Ferdinand Max – Austria 1865. Was Admiral Tegettoff's flagship at the Battle of Lissa, during which she rammed and sank the Italian frigate *Re d'Italia* The *Ferdinand Max* had a wooden hull with armour on the sides only, the deck being unprotected. Displacement: 5,140 tons. Length 262 ft. Speed: 10·3 knots. Armament: 14 × 7 in., 4 × 3·5 in. and 2 × 2·75 in. guns. Crew: 480.

of the frigate *Re d'Italia* and of the gun-boat *Palestro,* whilst other ships sustained very serious damage. If for the young Italian Navy, Lissa was a gory baptism of fire which evoked wonderful deeds of valour by both officers and sailors, it was nevertheless a disaster, and it added little to naval knowledge that was not already known.

The battle had, however, confirmed the obvious, that even armoured ships could be overcome by gunfire and that they were not yet sufficiently protected. Later, after 1866, there started a race to increase the calibre of guns, this to get the better of armour-plating, which was getting thicker

and thicker; also to increase the thickness of the plating and so stand up to howitzer shells of very large calibre. From the 10 in. guns in the *Gloire* which were in fixed emplacements, we have arrived at the gigantic 17 inch guns, weighing 100 tons apiece, mounted in the rotating turrets of the Italian ironclads *Lepanto* and *Italia.* From the 4 inch thick plating of the *Gloire,* we end with that of the English Turret ship *Inflexible,* of 1876 which was some 2 ft. thick. To put a brake on this merry-go-round, steel was starting to replace iron for the building of hulls. The use of light and particularly tough steel made it possible to start reducing the thickness of armour-

SHIPS AT LISSA

Re d'Italia – Italy 1864. 5,700 tons. 276 ft. 12 knots. 2 × 4 in., 30 × 6.25 in., 4 × 3 in. guns. Crew: 550.

Palestro – Italy 1866. 2,200 tons. 200 ft. 8 knots. 4 × 8 in., 1 × 6.5 in. guns. Crew: 250.

Formidabile – Italy 1862. 2,725 tons. 210 ft. 10 knots. 16 × 6.5 in., 4 × 3 in. guns. Crew: 370.

Kaiser – Austria 1858. 5,815 tons. 254 ft. 11.9 knots. 10 × 9 in., 6 × 3.5 in., 2 × 2.75 in. guns. Crew: 500.

Don Juan d'Austria Austria 1865. 3,588 tons. 240 ft. 11 knots. 14 × 8.25 in. guns. Crew: 300.

Salamander – Austria 1861. 3,110 tons. 230 ft. 10 × 7 in., 4 × 3.5 in., 2 × 2.75 in. guns. Crew: 400.

Devastation — Gt. Britain 1873. First British ironclad without sails and a signal mast only. Iron hull, well armoured. Twin screws. Displacement: 9,330 tons. Length: 285 ft. Speed: 14 knots. Armament: 4 × 10 in. guns. Two torpedo tubes.

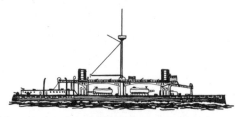

Duilio — Italy 1876. Displacement: 11,200 tons. Length: 341 ft. Speed: 15 knots. Original armament: 4 × 17·7 in. guns in two turrets, 3 × 4·7 in. and many smaller guns. Crew: 420.

Maine — U.S.A. 1890. Armoured ship of the line. On 15th February, 1898, she blew up at Havana, thus sparking off the Spanish-American War. Displacement: 6,682 tons. Armament: 4 × 10 in. guns. Crew: 420.

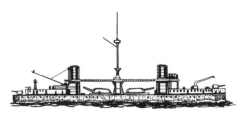

Andrea Doria — Italy 1885. The first ship of the line with this name, she was built at La Spezia, with a steel hull, partially protected by armour of up to 17·7 in. thick.

Royal Sovereign — Gt. Britain 1892. Special features were their high freeboard and twin funnels. Steel hulls, displacement 14,150 tons. 380 ft. 17 knots. Main armament: 4 × 13·5 in. and 12 × 6 in. guns.

Charles Martel — France 1893. An example of the French ironclad of that period. Displacement: 11,882 tons. Speed: 18 knots. Armament: 2 × 12 in., 2 × 10·6 in. guns.

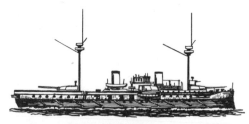

Pelayo — Spain 1887. One of the finest Spanish battleships. Displacement: 9,900 tons. Length: 330 ft. Speed: 16 knots. Main armament: 2 × 12·5 in. and 2 × 11 in. guns. Crew: 580.

Kaiser Barbarossa — Germany 1900. With four sister ships, she made up the core of a powerful fleet. Displacement: 10,600 tons. 400 ft. Speed: 18 knots. 4 × 9·4 in., 14 × 5·9 in. and 12 × 3·4 in. guns.

plating. During the last decade of the 19th century, the design of battleships continued to advance by a process of trial and error. Then, to create new problems and revolutionise the principles of naval gunnery, came the invention of a new kind of gun-powder which enabled guns to be fired with great rapidity.

In the meantime, a new sort of small offensive craft was establishing itself – the torpedo-boat. Its first appearance had been during the American Civil War, with an especially fast steam sloop, which had a long boom forward-at the end of which was fixed an explosive charge called a torpedo. By taking advantage of its speed, the sloop would approach the target to the point of causing an explosion of the charge by impact against the hull. After torpedo-boats had further demonstrated their efficiency during the Russo-Turkish War of 1887, all the Navies in the world adopted this new type of ship – which gained further offensive possibilities through the invention of the self-propelled torpedo. It was in 1866, at Fiume, that an engineer, Robert Whitehead, tested this device, which weighed 300 lb. and carried 18 lb. of dynamite. Fired from a special tube, it travelled at a speed of six knots towards the target, propelled by a compressed air engine.

Torpedo-boats were built ever faster until they exceeded speeds of 30 knots. Their numbers likewise increased and the logical consequence of this was the creation of a new type, the torpedo-boat destroyer. At the same time, battleships were equipped with light, quick-firing guns to drive off or sink the attackers before they could get close enough to fire their self-propelled torpedoes.

In only 50 years, from 1850-1900, combatant fleets had undergone radical change. The real test of ships and of weapons, as well as of the new theories of naval tactics, came with the Russo-Japanese War. At the end of the 19th century, Britain possessed the greatest naval fleet in the world, followed by France, Russia and Italy. Japan was ninth in the list. But only five years were enough for the latter, helped by ships bought from Great Britain, to be ready to confront the Russian colossus and so establish her supremacy in Eastern waters. At dawn on 27th January, 1904, just before the official declaration of war, three squadrons of torpedo-boats penetrated into Port Arthur, torpedoing three large Russian ships at anchor there. Admiral Togo, Commander-in-Chief of the Japanese

TORPEDO BOATS

Torpedo-sloop – Confederate States 1861. The explosive device struck the ship being attacked.

Russian torpedo-boat – 1890. The torpedo, by then self-propelled, was launched from a special tube forward.

French torpedo-boat – 1898. One torpedo-tube was mounted forward, above the waterline, a second being aft.

Lancier – France 1900. Sea-going torpedo-boat, capable of a speed of 26 knots, equipped with three torpedo-tubes.

Audacieux – France 1901. Sea-going torpedo-boat. 185 tons. Speed: 30 knots. Three torpedo-tubes.

Viper – Gt. Britain 1899. First turbine-driven torpedo-boat destroyer. 447 tons. Speed: 37 knots. Two torpedo-tubes.

Mikasa – Japan 1899. Admiral Togo's flagship in the Battle of Tsushima in 1905, during the Russo-Japanese War. The excellence of the Japanese preparations and the blunderings of the Russians led to the overwhelming defeat of the latter's fleet. Displacement: 15,200 tons. Max. speed: 18 knots. Armament: 4 × 12 in., 14 × 6 in. and 20 smaller guns. Crew: 770.

Navy, aimed at bringing the balance of force in his favour, just as Yamamoto did nearly 40 years later at Pearl Harbour. At the outbreak of hostilities, the Russian Fleet in the Pacific consisted of eight battleships, five armoured cruisers, nine smaller cruisers and light craft, whilst Togo's fleet consisted of seven battleships, nine armoured cruisers, 16 cruisers and a large number of torpedo-boat destroyers and torpedo-boats. In only one year of war, the Russian squadron in the Pacific was completely destroyed and the Russian commanding Admiral, Makarov, lost his

life when he went down with the *Petropavlovsk* after she struck a mine. This was a new weapon which was extensively used by the Japanese and had been invented 100 years before by Fulton.

While the Russians were experiencing alternate good and bad luck on land, the Tzar decided to send his best naval squadron to the Pacific. This was the Baltic Fleet which, in order to arrive in the operational area, had to sail round Africa, a long voyage which was a strain to both men and ships. Under the command of Admiral Rojestvenski, the squadron con-

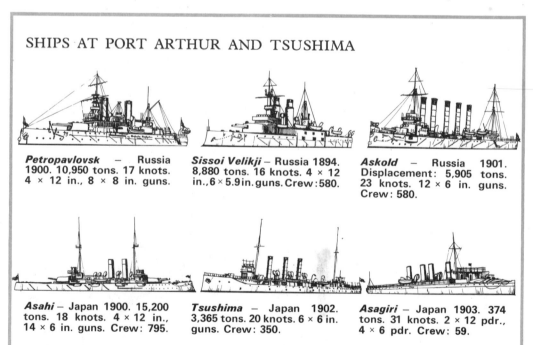

SHIPS AT PORT ARTHUR AND TSUSHIMA

Petropavlovsk – Russia 1900. 10,950 tons. 17 knots. 4 × 12 in., 8 × 8 in. guns.

Sissoi Velikji – Russia 1894. 8,880 tons. 16 knots. 4 × 12 in., 6 × 5.9 in. guns. Crew: 580.

Askold – Russia 1901. Displacement: 5,905 tons. 23 knots. 12 × 6 in. guns. Crew: 580.

Asahi – Japan 1900. 15,200 tons. 18 knots. 4 × 12 in., 14 × 6 in. guns. Crew: 795.

Tsushima – Japan 1902. 3,365 tons. 20 knots. 6 × 6 in. guns. Crew: 350.

Asagiri – Japan 1903. 374 tons. 31 knots. 2 × 12 pdr., 4 × 6 pdr. Crew: 59.

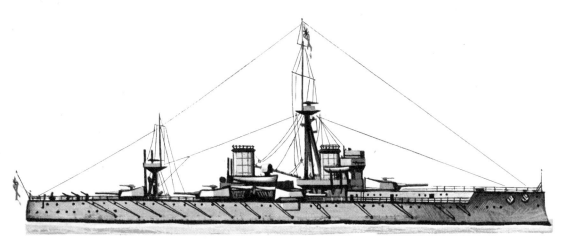

Dreadnought – Gt. Britain 1906. The prototype from which all battleships derived. Built for long range combat, she could fire a broadside from eight of her 10 × 12 in. guns and was equipped with five torpedo tubes. She was the first battleship in the world to be turbine driven. Displacement: 17,900 tons. Length: 526 ft. Speed: 21 knots. Armament: 10 × 12 in. and 24 × 12 pdr. guns. Crew: 730.

sisted of 12 ironclads (four of which were very modern), four cruisers and some smaller ships. But Togo was lying in wait for his opponent in the Korean Strait, between the island of Tsushima and the Korean coast. On the 27th May, 1905, the Japanese opened fire at a distance of some 7,500 yards, concentrating it on the leading battleships. It was a massacre. A great many Russian ships sank and about 7,000 men lost their lives, against about 800 Japanese. It was a triumph for Togo who, even though he had fewer guns, owed his success to the rapid fire and greater range of his guns.

A direct consequence of the Battle of Tsushima, otherwise known as the "Battle of the Japanese Sea", was the appearance of the *Dreadnought*. This was a British all-big-gun battleship, launched in 1906, on which all the ships of the line that came after were to be modelled and which were to be perfected in the battleships of the Second World War. On the basis that big naval battles would, in future, take place with the protagonists at greater and greater distances from each other, thanks to the perfecting of gun-laying methods, the *Dreadnought* was without medium calibre guns. She was equipped with 10 × 12 in. guns in five twin-turrets and 24 × 12 pdr. quick firing guns and 5 maxims. With armour-plating up to 11 in. thick, she combined powerful armament with exceptional speed – 21 knots – thanks to her steam turbines, which were the first ever fitted in a battleship. The dreadnought had arrived, in the true sense of the word. From 1907-1914 all the major powers were involved in a new naval armaments' race.

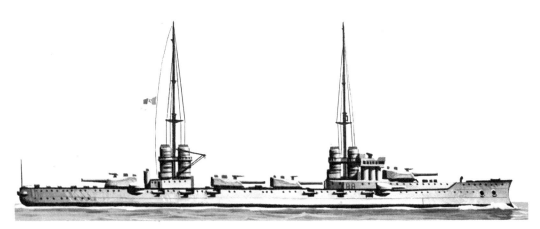

Dante Alighieri – Italy 1913. Built at the Castellamare Dockyard. She was the first Italian ship of Dreadnought type and the first in the world to have triple-gun turrets. She could bring all her 12 × 12 in. guns to bear in a broadside. Displacement: 20,500 tons. Length: 520 ft. Speed: 22 knots. Armament: 12 × 12 in. and 38 smaller guns, 3 torpedo tubes. Crew: 970.

THE SUBMARINE FROM THE FIRST EXPERIMENTS TO 1915

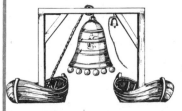

Catalan bell – 1600. Used for the recovery of wreckage. It was made of wood, bound with iron.

De Son's boat – 1653. Built in Rotterdam in the shape of a spindle, it was supposed to submerge.

Borelli's machine – 1680. According to the description it would have been propelled by oars.

Turtle – 1775. Submarine designed by an American, Bushnell. It was used by Sergeant Lee.

Nautilus–1801. Designed by Fulton and made of copper, it had a tank for ballast while submerged.

Bauer's submarine – 1850. The propeller was revolved by two members of the three-man crew.

El Ictineo– Spain 1862. By a Spaniard, Monturiol, it was the first submarine of modern conception.

Holland No. 1 – U.S.A. 1875. The first submarine designed by the American inventor John Holland.

Nautilus–Gt. Britain –1887. One of the first British submarines. She carried a crew of three.

Plunger – U.S.A. 1897. The first of Holland's submarines to be ordered by the U.S. Navy.

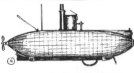

Argonaut– U.S.A. 1898. Designed by Simon Lake to rest on the ocean bottom and move about on wheels.

Delfino – Italy 1890. The first submarine of the Marina Militare Italiana.

Class "A" – Gt. Britain 1904. 180 tons. Speed: 11 knots on the surface, 7 knots submerged.

"B I" – U.S.A. 1907. 150 tons. Speed: 9.5/8.5 knots. Two torpedo tubes. Crew: 10 men.

U-boat 46 – Germany 1915. One of the submarines with which Germany launched her offensive.

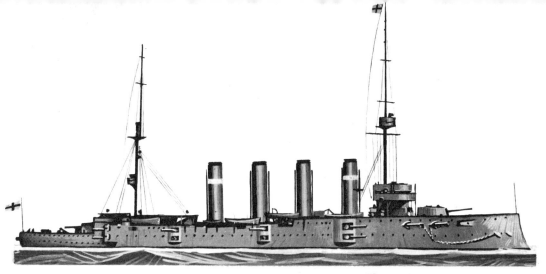

Good Hope – Gt. Britain 1902. "Drake" class cruiser. The **Good Hope** and **Monmouth** were both sunk at the Battle of Coronel on 1st November, 1914, but the smaller **Glasgow** and the armed liner **Otranto** escaped, although the former incurred some damage. Displacement: 14,100 tons. Length: 535 ft. Speed: 24 knots. Main armament: 2 × 9·2 in. and 16 × 6 in. guns. Crew: 900.

From the slipways of the dockyards came a steady stream of ships like the *Dreadnought*, battle-cruisers (battleships in which part of the protective armour had been sacrificed to reduce weight and so increase speed), light cruisers, torpedo-boat destroyers, torpedo-boats and, finally, submarines.

For more than a century, research had been going on into the possibility of producing a ship that was capable of navigating under the surface. In fact, it was in the early 17th century that the first recorded submarine boat – hand rowed – was demonstrated on the Thames before James I. After several American experiments some primitive boats called "Davids" were used by the Confederate forces in 1863. In Europe further designs by Goubel and Nordenfelt were more promising, but it was the "Holland" type, named after its American inventor, which was adopted by the U.S. and Royal Navies. The first British order was placed in 1901 but by 1914 the Royal Navy had 96.

The world was to have the opportunity of becoming very aware of it in the course of the First World War, which, in the Summer of 1914, broke out between Great Britain, France and Russia allied against Germany and Austro-Hungary. Turkey went into the war at Germany's

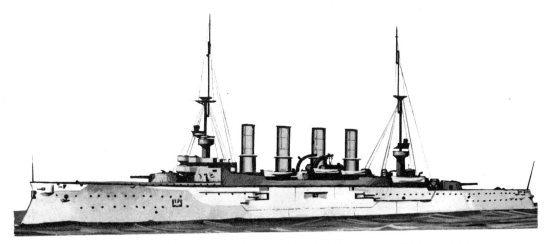

Scharnhorst – Germany 1907. Armoured cruiser. On 8th December, 1914, a British Squadron, comprising five cruisers and two battle cruisers, avenged the losses of Coronel by sinking the **Scharnhorst, Gneisenau** and two other ships. Displacement: 11,600 tons. Length: 474 ft. Speed: 22½ knots. Armament: 8 × 8·2 in., 6 × 5·9 in. and 20 smaller guns. Crew: 765.

SHIPS OF THE BATTLES OF CORONEL AND FALKLAND

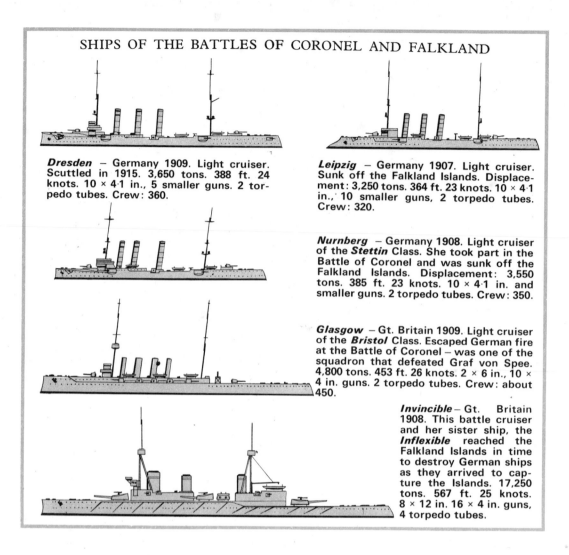

Dresden – Germany 1909. Light cruiser. Scuttled in 1915. 3,650 tons. 388 ft. 24 knots. 10 × 4·1 in., 5 smaller guns. 2 torpedo tubes. Crew: 360.

Leipzig – Germany 1907. Light cruiser. Sunk off the Falkland Islands. Displacement: 3,250 tons. 364 ft. 23 knots. 10 × 4·1 in., 10 smaller guns, 2 torpedo tubes. Crew: 320.

Nurnberg – Germany 1908. Light cruiser of the **Stettin** Class. She took part in the Battle of Coronel and was sunk off the Falkland Islands. Displacement: 3,550 tons. 385 ft. 23 knots. 10 × 4·1 in. and smaller guns. 2 torpedo tubes. Crew: 350.

Glasgow – Gt. Britain 1909. Light cruiser of the **Bristol** Class. Escaped German fire at the Battle of Coronel – was one of the squadron that defeated Graf von Spee. 4,800 tons. 453 ft. 26 knots. 2 × 6 in., 10 × 4 in. guns. 2 torpedo tubes. Crew: about 450.

Invincible – Gt. Britain 1908. This battle cruiser and her sister ship, the **Inflexible** reached the Falkland Islands in time to destroy German ships as they arrived to capture the Islands. 17,250 tons. 567 ft. 25 knots. 8 × 12 in. 16 × 4 in. guns, 4 torpedo tubes.

side in 1914. Italy (in 1915) and the United States (in 1917) joined the Allies.

The make-up of the Fleets at the outbreak was as follows: Great Britain – 62 battleships, 8 battle-cruisers, 87 cruisers, 227 destroyers, 109 torpedo-boats, 75 submarines. Total: circa 2,100,000 tons; Germany – 46 battleships, 5 battle-cruisers, 42 cruisers, 152 destroyers, 45 torpedo-boats, 30 submarines. Total: circa 900,000 tons; France – 24 battleships, 24 cruisers, 80 destroyers, 90 torpedo-boats, 75 submarines. Total: circa 600,000 tons; Italy – 19 battleships, 19 cruisers, 52 destroyers, 48 torpedo-boats, 33 submarines. Total: circa 300,000 tons; Austria – 12 battleships, 15 cruisers, 18 destroyers, 54 torpedo-boats, 6 submarines. Total: circa 200,000 tons.

The first naval battles of any importance between British and German ships took place thousands of miles from the theatre of war on land – on 1st November, 1914, in the Pacific, off Coronel, on the Chilean coast, and in the Atlantic off the Falkland Islands on 8th December of the same year. In the first clash, a squadron of four German cruisers, under the command of Admiral Graf von Spee, nearly wiped out the British fleet sinking two of the three cruisers commanded by Admiral Cradock. In the second, Spee was to be defeated by a group of two British battle-cruisers, five cruisers and one armed liner under Admiral Sturdee's command. Four German ships were sunk, amongst which was the *Scharnhorst*, Admiral von Spee's flagship. The only important operation in the Medi-

74

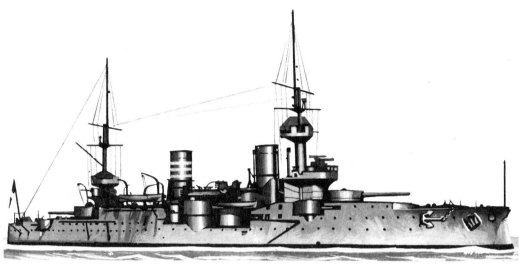

Bouvet – France 1896. Battleship of the French squadron which, on 18th March, 1915, tried, with a group of British ships to force the Dardanelles Straits. The ship was sunk by a mine there and 670 people lost their lives. The British battleships *Irresistible* and *Ocean* were also sunk and others damaged. Displacement: 12,205 tons. Length: 401 ft. Speed: $17\frac{1}{2}$ knots. Armament: 2 × 12 in., 2 × 10.6 in. and smaller guns, 4 torpedo tubes.

terranean, before Italy went into the War, was the attempt which was carried out on 18th March, 1915, on the part of an Anglo-French squadron to break through the Dardanelles in order to effect a link-up with the Russian ships in the Black Sea. The operation ended tragically. One French battleship was blown up by a mine while two elderly British ones, the *Irresistible* and *Ocean*, also fell victim to the mines which had been laid to block the Straits.

When Italy entered the war, it fell to her Fleet to make sure that the Austro-Hungarian Fleet was prevented from emerging from the Adriatic, where their ships would have been a danger to the carrying of troops and supplies in the central Mediterranean. For months, nothing of importance happened – the Austrian Fleet avoided direct contact with the Italian

Fleet, restricting its activities to firing their cannon on the Adriatic coast, which was done by one or two ships which were always ready to take themselves off at the rapid approach of Italian ships. The Italian Navy particularly distinguished itself at the end of 1915 and during the early months of 1916, first in the arduous task of provisioning the Serbian army, and then in its evacuation, for which 81 steamships were employed. They made 560 trips, carrying 183,000 men and 10,000 horses from Albania to Corfù, Marseilles, Bastia, Bizerta, Ponza and Asinara.

Meanwhile, on 4th February, 1915, the Kaiser had proclaimed under-water war and the German submarines, positioned in the Atlantic, reaped a harvest of victims among the merchant ships that were bringing supplies from the United States to Great Britain and France. And so the

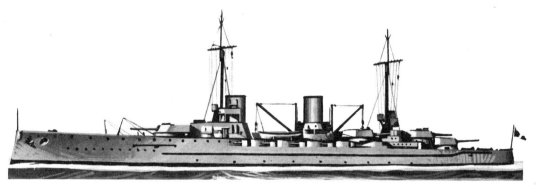

Goeben – Germany 1911. Battle cruiser. The outbreak of hostilities found her in the Mediterranean with the cruiser, *Breslau,* with the task of attacking British convoys coming from the Orient. Displacement: 22,640 tons. Length: 610 ft. Speed: 25 knots. Armament: 10 × 11 in., 12 × 5.9 in. guns, 4 torpedo tubes. Crew: 1,100.

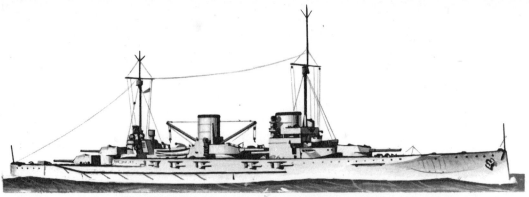

Moltke – Germany 1911. Battle cruiser, Admiral von Hipper's flagship. Von Hipper was Commander of the German cruiser squadron in the biggest naval battle of the First World War – the Battle of Jutland. The German Fleet, under the command of Admiral Scheer, consisted of 22 battleships, 5 battle cruisers, 11 light cruisers and 72 torpedo-boats. The *Moltke,* sister ship of the *Goeben,* was damaged during the engagement.

submarine war gathered momentum. Amongst other things, it brought about the necessity for merchant ships to sail in convoy, under the strong escort of destroyers and smaller ships. The major naval battle of the whole war, the biggest clash of battleships in history, occurred on 31st May, 1916, in the North Sea off Jutland. It was the Kaiser's wish, during the first part of the operation, that the German Fleet should be exposed as little as possible, in spite of the fact that Grand Admiral von Tirpitz, was of the opposite opinion. But when Admiral von Scheer was appointed Commander-in-Chief, he succeeded in imposing his own ideas and in getting permission for a general sortie from their bases to carry out a powerful bombardment of the English coast. The British Admiral of the Fleet, Admiral Jellicoe, having had warning of the attack, unhesitatingly set out with the British fleet to meet the enemy. The German squadron consisted of 22 battleships, 5 battle-cruisers, 11 light cruisers and 72 destroyers, whilst the British had 28 battleships, 9 battle-cruisers, 33 cruisers, 79 destroyers and a ship which had been adapted for use as an aircraft-carrier (the first in history!).

At 15.48 on 31st May, von Hipper's company of battle-cruisers made contact with Admiral Beatty's heavy cruisers. After only ten minutes of heavy gun fire, two British battle-cruisers were sunk whilst almost all the other ships were seriously damaged. The clash between the main bulk of the two fleets took place about 18.30. It was an inferno! By sundown, the Battle of Jutland was over and the British had lost 3 battle-cruisers, 3 cruisers and 8 destroyers, while the Germans had lost 1 battleship, 1 battle-cruiser, 4 cruisers and 5 destroyers. It is still debated today as to

Iron Duke – Gt. Britain 1914. Flagship of the Grand Fleet at Jutland, which comprised 28 battleships, 9 battle cruisers, 33 cruisers, 79 destroyers and the world's first aircraft carrier – one of whose planes was used for spotting. Displacement: 25,000 tons. Length: 620 ft. Speed: 21 knots. Armament: 10 × 13·5 in. and 12 × 6 in. guns, 4 torpedo tubes. Crew: about 1,000.

Lion – Gt. Britain 1912. At Jutland this battle cruiser carried the flag of Admiral Beatty. Under her command were six battle cruisers, and four battleships, which met von Hipper's ships on 31st May, 1916. The encounter between the two larger squadrons followed that of the cruisers. Displacement: 26,350 tons. Length: 700 ft. Speed: 28 knots. Armament: 8 × 13·5 in., 16 × 4 in. guns, 2 torpedo tubes. Crew: 1,000.

who were really the victors at the Battle of Jutland. There are those who say it was the Germans who did more damage and claimed more victims; nevertheless it was the Germans who retreated and lacked the courage to leave their bases again – and that inactivity led to mutiny. Certainly, never again in history did so many armoured ships confront one another: Jutland represented the triumph of new naval gunnery techniques.

In the sector of the Adriatic where the Austro-Hungarian Fleet was forced to remain confined in their fortified ports, the Italian Navy took the initiative by making assault attacks, which were carried out by courageous men in motor torpedo-boats which were both very fast and silent – the M.A.S. (*Motoscafo Anti-Sommergibile:* English equivalent – M.T.B.) On 10th December, 1917, Captain Luigi Rizzo penetrated into the port of Trieste and sank the battleship, *Wien.*

On 10th June, 1918, while an Austrian

SHIPS OF THE BATTLE OF JUTLAND

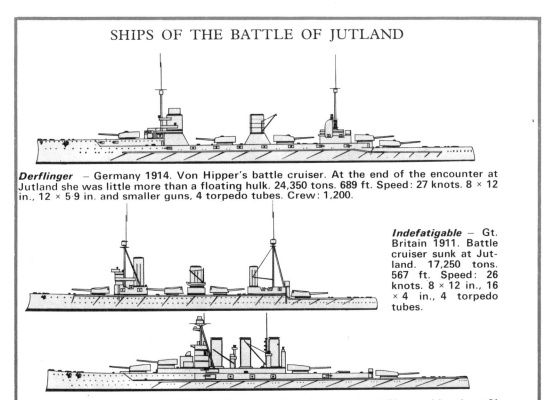

Derflinger – Germany 1914. Von Hipper's battle cruiser. At the end of the encounter at Jutland she was little more than a floating hulk. 24,350 tons. 689 ft. Speed: 27 knots. 8 × 12 in., 12 × 5·9 in. and smaller guns, 4 torpedo tubes. Crew: 1,200.

Indefatigable – Gt. Britain 1911. Battle cruiser sunk at Jutland. 17,250 tons. 567 ft. Speed: 26 knots. 8 × 12 in., 16 × 4 in., 4 torpedo tubes.

Tiger – Gt. Britain 1914. One of the battle cruisers in action at Jutland. She was hit at least 21 times. Displacement: 30,000 tons. 704 ft. Speed: 28 knots. 8 × 13·5 in. and 12 × 6 in. guns, 4 torpedo tubes. Crew: 1,185.

Szent Istuaw – Austria 1915. Battleship of the Dreadnought type, of the same class as the *Viribus Unitis, Tegetthoff* and *Prinz Eugen*. The pride of the Austrian Fleet, she was sunk on 10th June, 1918, just off Premuda by the MAS (Motor torpedo boats) 15 and 21. Displacement: 20,000 tons. Length: 520 ft. Speed: 21 knots. Armament: 12 × 12 in., 12 × 5·9 in. and 22 smaller guns, 4 torpedo tubes. Crew: 1,050.

squadron was approaching an engagement near the Otranto Channel, the battleship *Szent Istuaw* was torpedoed and sunk. On 11th February, 1918, Costanzo Ciano went to taunt the enemy in the Bay of Buccari. On 14th May, 1918, Mario Pellegrini, with an "acrobatic" midget submarine, called the *Grillo*, penetrated the port of Pola – the same port where, just before the end of the War, Raffaele Rossetti and Raffaele Paolucci swam to the *Viribus Unitis*, mined and sank her.

The First World War was finally brought to an end on land. On 21st November, 1918, the German High Seas Fleet surrendered and gathered in the sheltered waters of Scapa Flow, in the Orkneys. What had been the pride of the Kaiser and of von Tirpitz was now riding at anchor, awaiting the enemy's pleasure, in all – 14 battleships, 7 cruisers, and 49 destroyers. But on 21st June, 1919, on orders from Admiral von Reuter, the entire armada was scuttled. The world looked on at this sad end to a fleet whose crews had mutinied and had refused final action with the Royal Navy. It was several decades before the remains of these ships were finally raised and broken up. The hope that it would be a long time, if ever, before ships and war were spoken of in the same breath was not to be realised.

MAS (MTB) – Italy 1917. Created as a *Motoscafi-Anti-Sommergibile* (Anti-submarine craft) – hence the initials – they were used for surprise torpedoing expeditions. Fast and silent, due to their electric motors, the "MAS" taunted the Austrian fleet in its own bases. Displacement: 20 tons. Speed: 28 knots. 2 torpedo tubes and anti-submarine bombs.

OCEAN PASSENGER LINERS

DURING the First World War most of the various merchant fleets suffered very heavy losses. Ships of the belligerent nations were sunk without warning by torpedoes and gunfire from German submarines and by mines; so too were those of the neutral nations whose vessels, not unnaturally, were often engaged in carrying goods and supplies for the opposing nations. During the four years in which the Great Powers were at war, 12,804,902 tons of merchant shipping went to the bottom. Their individual losses were: United States 397,059 tons. France 899,358 tons (46% of her merchant fleet). Great Britain 7,759,090 tons (42% of her merchant fleet). Italy 872,341 tons (equal to 49% of her pre-war fleet). German, Belgian, Greek and Scandinavian losses accounted for most of the remaining 3 million tons. Italy's losses represented 238 steamships and 395 sailing-ships and were heavy indeed, due largely to the fact that the Italian trans-Atlantic fleet (which totalled some 210,000 tons in 1914) transported the second largest number of American soldiers to France (Great Britain carried the most), while due to enemy submarines, navigation in the Atlantic was undoubtedly the most dangerous.

In 1917, the Allies found themselves faced with a terrible scarcity of cargo ships, aggravated by the fact that steel was being used for purposes more closely connected with the war, and was very largely absorbed in this way. And so ships were built once more with wooden hulls and the point was even reached when some cargo vessels were produced from reinforced concrete. Although they were, perhaps, of some wartime use, they were quickly laid aside when peace returned as being impractical and quite uneconomic. It was the vastly reduced numbers of pre-1914 ships which formed the backbone of the major merchant fleets when, about 1918, the build-up of large numbers of standard type cargo ships in Great Britain, America and Japan got under way. These were of simple, straight-forward design and were built at speeds never before deemed possible. Nevertheless, they

Giulio Cesare — Italy 1923. With her sister-ship *Duilio* (built at Genoa) she was among the first big passenger liners to join the Italian merchant fleet after the First World War. Gross tonnage: 21,657. Length overall: 633 ft. Quadruple screws. Turbines. Speed: 19 knots. Builders: Swan, Hunter & Wigham Richardson, Newcastle.

Ile de France – France 1927. Flagship of the *Compagne Generale Transatlantique* up to 1935 when the *Normandie* was commissioned. She operated on the Le Havre – Southampton – New York route and was one of the most luxurious liners of her time. Her best crossing was made at an average speed of 23·5 knots. Gross tonnage: 43,450. Length overall: 792 ft. Propulsion: steam-turbines. Crew: 800. Passengers: 1,800. Shipyard: St. Nazaire.

served the world well and even now a handful remain in service. These were followed by a great output of more sophisticated vessels, tankers, cargo liners, tramps and passenger ships in such numbers that by 1939 the world total of merchant tonnage was raised to a level never before attained – 62 million tons.

These ships built between the wars incorporated many new features, notably as regards propulsion. The days of coal-fired boilers were numbered and the use of steam itself was fast declining in favour of the diesel engine which, despite a somewhat greater initial cost, was more economical as regards fuel consumption and, not needing boilers, occupied less space, so leaving more for cargo.

Another important technical breakthrough was the perfection of turbo-electric and diesel-electric drive, in which the main engines supplied power to drive electric motors, which in turn were coupled to the propeller shafts. This meant a great

saving of space, for the electric motors could be placed right aft, where the hull was too cramped to receive the main engines. Again, where the different legs of a voyage called for different speeds, this was easily met by many but small prime-movers, some of which could be shut down when full power was not required. Likewise, the use of smaller units meant lower engine rooms – and so more space for passengers or cargo. But electric drive was not intended for the ordinary cargo ship, rather for the more sophisticated liner or warship.

It is clear that post-war ships were, in general, greatly superior to those launched up to 1914. Cargoes slowly increased in size and the average size of cargo ships rose from about 3,000 tons in 1914 to 5,000. The number of tankers multiplied in order to meet the increased needs for transporting both crude and refined oil – mainly the latter, for in those days it was customary to have the refineries close to the oil fields.

Bremen – Germany 1928. Flagship of the Norddeutscher Lloyd, Bremen. On her maiden voyage she made a record Atlantic crossing at an average of 27·83 knots, thereby regaining the Blue Riband which, since 1907, had been held by the Cunard Line's *Mauretania*. Gross tonnage: 51,731. Length overall: 938 ft. Propulsion: steam-turbines. Crew: 950. Passengers: 2,500.

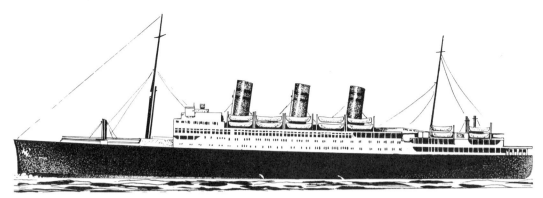

Statendam – Holland 1929. Flagship of the Holland-America Line, she arrived in New York at the end of her maiden voyage on 11th April, 1929 – the 300th anniversary of the arrival of the first Dutch ships in America at the mouth of the Hudson. Gross tonnage: 29,511 tons. Length overall: 698 ft. Propulsion: steam-turbines. Speed: 18 knots. Crew: 600. Passengers: 1,670. Builders: Harland & Wolff, Belfast.

Relative increases in merchant tonnage between 1920 and 1930 were as follows: Great Britain 20,582,652 tons to 23,381,614 tons. Germany 672,671 tons to 4,229,235 tons. France 3,245,194 tons to 3,530,879 tons. Italy 2,242,393 tons to 3,331,226 tons. It must be realised that such increases were brought about despite the fact that, as modern ships came into service, the older ones were withdrawn and scrapped.

Many very difficult problems faced the shipping companies which participated in the trans-Atlantic passenger trade. Soon after the War U.S. restrictions had brought the migratory flood from Europe to the States to an abrupt end and so deprived the many companies of one of their main sources of income. This led to the withdrawal of many older ships and companies. After a period of depression, it became clear about 1925 that another type of trans-Atlantic commerce was emerging, that of tourism. Nearly a million Americans had

come to Europe with the Expeditionary force of 1917-18. When they went home, they had talked so much of the Old World that, in later years, the greatest wish of the middle and upper class American was to visit Paris, London and Rome: so the accommodation standards of trans-Atlantic passenger ships underwent great change. Pre-war vessels had been built to carry large numbers of emigrants or steerage passengers with or without accommodation in the more comfortable higher grade classes. While some ships were altered many others were built in which the accommodation, while it still catered for the luxurious first class, had the bulk of its space allocated to the cabin, tourist or second class passengers, persons of modest means who would not travel rough but could not afford to go first class.

Of the new generation of great trans-Atlantic liners which came into service during the 'twenties one of the first was the *Ile de France*, with a tonnage of 43,100 tons,

Empress of Britain – Gt. Britain 1931. The largest liner ever built for service to Canada, she was designed for the Southampton – Quebec service. In 1932 she established a record by crossing the Atlantic 12 times in 12 weeks. Gross tonnage: 42,348. Length overall: 758 ft. Propulsion: steam turbines. Speed: 24 knots. Crew: 700. Passengers: 1,100. Builders: John Brown & Co.

OCEAN PASSENGER LINERS 1926 TO 1935

Roma – Italy 1926. Built for the **Navigazione Generale Italiana,** she and the very similar **Augustus** helped to build up the prestige of Italian passenger services between Italy and New York. Turbine driven. Speed: 19 knots. 32,583 tons gross.

Vulcania – Italy 1928. Was built for the Cosulich Line's Trieste – South American trade. Given more powerful diesels in 1935 and speed raised from 19 to 23 knots. 23,970 tons gross. 630 ft. overall. Latterly the Siosa Line's **Caribia.**

Conte Grande – Italy 1928. Owned in turn by the Lloyd Sabaudo and Italia Lines and for long well known on the Genoa – South American run. 25,661 tons gross. Length overall: 665 ft. Twin screw turbines. 20 knots. Passengers: 1,700.

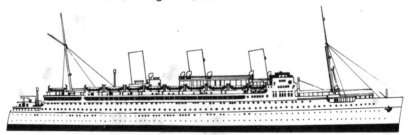

Empress of Japan – Gt. Britain 1929. Later renamed **Empress of Scotland** and used on the U.K. – Canada run. As the German **Hanseatic** was scrapped in 1967. 26,032 tons. Length overall: 666 ft. Turbines. 21 knots. Passengers: 1,200.

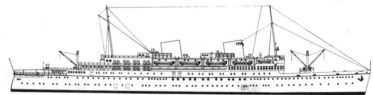

Victoria – Italy 1931. This 22 knot motorship was built for the Lloyd Triestino and used on the Genoa – Suez – Bombay route. Sunk 1942. Gross tonnage: 13,068. Length overall: 540 ft. Propulsion: Quadruple screw diesels. Passengers: 900.

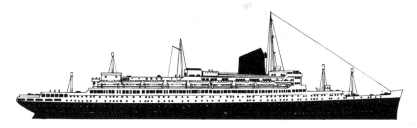

Champlain — France 1932. Built for a secondary cabin class service between Le Havre and New York. 28,094 tons. 641 ft. Twin screw, turbines, 20 knots. Crew: 560. Passengers: 1,050. Sunk off French coast in 1940.

Conte di Savoia — Italy 1932. Operated on the Italia Line's Genoa — New York service. Passage time 6½ days. Was sunk during Second World War. 48,502 tons. Length overall: 860 ft. Quadruple screw turbines. 28 knots. Passengers: 2,000.

President Hoover — U.S.A. 1932. She and the *President Coolidge* were designed for the Dollar Line's service between San Francisco and the Orient. Gross tonnage: 21,936. Length overall: 654 ft. Twin screws. 20 knots. Passengers: 470.

Neptunia — Italy 1932. Of the pre-war Italian liners on the South American run, she and her sister, the *Oceania,* were amongst the most popular. Torpedoed 1941, while bound for Libya. 19,475 tons. 562 ft. Quadruple screw diesels. 19 knots.

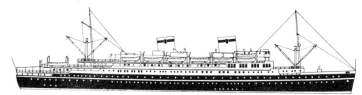

Pilsudski — Poland 1935. With sister ship *Batory* was built in Italy for the Gdynia-America Line. 14,294 tons gross. Length overall: 525 ft. Twin screw diesels. Speed: 17 knots. Passengers: 370 tourist, 400 third class.

Rex – Italy 1932. When launched was the world's fourth largest ship. Was owned by the Italia Line and completed her maiden voyage from Genoa to New York on 27th September, 1932. In August 1933, she won the "Blue Riband" from the *Bremen* with a crossing from Gibraltar to the Ambrose Lightship of 4 days, 13 hours, 58 minutes at an average of 28·92 knots. Gross tonnage: 51,062 Length overall: 880 ft. Quadruple screw turbines, speed 28 knots. Passengers: 2,200.

and a passenger carrying capacity of over 1,500. She used to make crossings from Le Havre to New York in six days and was the first commercial ship to be experimentally fitted with a catapult to launch an aircraft. On the fourth day out, a seaplane would be launched from aft and this would arrive in New York in less than four hours with a load of mail and a maximum of one passenger.

With air travel still in its infancy, the speed of each new passenger ship was a subject of wide interest. Besides the many modestly priced, medium speed passenger vessels there was also a top flight of more luxurious, high-speed liners and there was keen international competition to win the "Blue Riband" of the Atlantic. Quite apart from the aspects of national and company prestige, the record breaker could be assured of heavy bookings for years ahead.

In 1900 the liner *Deutschland* won the "Blue Riband" with a crossing of 5 days, 7 hours, 38 minutes. In 1907, when the

Lusitania and *Mauretania* were commissioned, the record passed to the former, but soon the *Mauretania* proved to be fractionally the faster and, with an average speed of 26.02 knots, she held the record until 1929. Then the brand new *Bremen* achieved an average of 27.83 knots and soon bettered this with 28.51 knots.

However, in 1933, on a more southerly route, an Italian liner for the first time won the Atlantic speed record, the *Rex* making the crossing from Gibraltar to New York at an average of 28.92 knots.

In view of the great outward flow of migrants from Italy to Latin America it was natural that for long most of the Italian lines should concentrate their attention on the South American rather than the North American services. On the latter the build-up was somewhat unassuming, but the position changed during the early 'thirties when the *Rex* and *Conte di Savoia* were building. Then the several main Italian lines operating on both the South and North Atlantic merged to form

Washington – U.S.A. 1933. With her sister ship, the *Manhatten*, also of the United States Lines, was the largest liner in North America. Operated on the New York – Plymouth – Hamburg run and was one of the first ships to have air-conditioning. Gross tonnage: 24,289. Length: 668 ft. Twin screw turbines, speed 20 knots. Built by New York Shipbuilding Corporation.

Normandie – France 1935. The biggest of the pre-war liners and owned by the *Cíe Générale Transatlantique*. She made her first Atlantic crossing in 4 days, 3 hours, 2 minutes and so took the "Blue Riband" from the *Rex*. As the U.S. *Lafayette* she caught fire and sank at New York 1942. 82,799 tons. Length overall: 1,029 ft. Quadruple screw turbo-electric machinery, service speed 29/30 knots. Crew: 1,300. Built by Penhoet Shipyard, St. Nazaire.

one great organisation – the Italia Line. Its creation remains as one of the lasting achievements of Mussolini, who appreciated the prestige value of a first class liner fleet and its value in encouraging tourism. Now, as then, the Italia, together with the Adriatica and Lloyd Triestino Lines – whose respective spheres are the Eastern Mediterranean and waters East of Suez – possess magnificent ships of a calibre only made possible by large subsidies.

On the North Atlantic, competition for the prized "Blue Riband" had, meanwhile, become more fierce. In May 1935 the *Normandie* proved herself to be not only the largest liner afloat but also the fastest, and on her maiden voyage eclipsed the *Rex's* performance by crossing from the Bishops Rock to the Ambrose Lightship in 4 days 3 hours 2 minutes – an average of 29.98 knots. A few months later the *Queen Mary* beat this with a voyage average of 30.01 knots. Within months these two had bettered their performances,

the *Normandie* with 31.2 knots and the *Queen Mary* with 31.69 knots.

In 1939, at the beginning of the Second World War the total tons of shipping for the principal merchant fleets were as follows: Great Britain 21,215,000 United States 12,003,000. Germany 4,835,000. Italy 3,448,000. France 2,953,000. Soon, however, many of these vessels had been sent to the bottom by torpedo, mine or aerial bomb. Not even the giant *Normandie* was to be spared. Taken over to become the U.S. troopship *Lafayette*, she caught fire and sank at New York in February 1942. Once again the merchant navies took on a first line importance and had to face up to hazards and stresses just as great as those of the combat navies. The great liners, once symbols of gaiety and good living, had been transformed into troop transporters and carried men in their thousands to the various battlefronts, to play their part in the biggest conflict in history – the Second World War.

Queen Mary – Gt. Britain 1936. In 1938 she finally won the "Blue Riband" from the *Normandie*, her fastest (eastward) crossing lasting 3 days, 20 hours, 42 minutes – an average of 31.69 knots. Sold to U.S.A. 1967 and now berthed at Long Beach, California, 80,774 tons gross. Length: 1,019 ft. Quadruple screw turbines, service speed 29 knots. Crew: 1,100. Passengers: 2,100. Builders: John Brown & Co.

85

SHIPS OF THE SECOND WORLD WAR

AT the end of the First World War, mankind cherished the hope that war would not occur again for generations. Agreements between the five major World Powers to restrict the arms race, at least in the field of fighting ships, seemed to support this hope. On 12th November, 1921, the first Naval Conference took place at Washington. Taking part were Great Britain, the United States, Japan, Italy and France. Russia, who was still suffering from the effects of the Bolshevik Revolution, was not involved. During the course of the discussions, which lasted for three months, it was decided that Great Britain, the U.S.A. and Japan should put no new battleships on the stocks for ten years, whilst Italy and France would not do so for five years. When this "naval holiday" was over, it would be permissible to build battleships to a maximum displacement of 35,000 tons, provided that the total tonnage of combatant ships of each single nation did not exceed the agreed limits which were: Great Britain and U.S.A. 525,000 tons, equal to 15 vessels. Japan 315,000 tons equal to 9 vessels. Italy and France 175,000 tons equal to 5 vessels. As for aircraft-carriers, whose value had not yet been fully realised, the total tonnage limit for them was fixed at: Great Britain and U.S.A. 135,000 tons. Japan 81,000 tons. Italy and France 60,000 tons.

Even during the "naval holiday", the signatory countries were to be able to build cruisers, provided that their displacement was not more than 10,000 tons and their guns did not exceed eight inches. In point of fact, Great Britain's and the United States' rights of naval supremacy were recognised at Washington, because of their colonial and commercial interests in all waters. Japan's predominance in the Pacific was also sanctioned. It was decided that the best guarantee of France and Italy being good neighbours lay in their equality of forces.

In 1930 a second Conference took place in London, in which the U.S.A. and Great Britain established that their inclusive tonnage for cruisers would be 339,000 tons and for Japan 237,300 tons, whilst the three countries pledged themselves not to create an underwater fleet totalling more than 57,200 tons. France no longer wanted to acknowledge the right of parity with Italy and, as a result, the two nations claimed liberty of action in this field, but at the same time accepting an extension of the "naval holiday" until 1936 for the three Major Powers, and up to 1933 for the other two.

While vague ideas for general disarmament were being uselessly discussed at Geneva, these naval agreements could not be warmly welcomed by public opinion in all countries. But when a new conference took place in London in 1935/36, the waters of peace were no longer so calm. In 1934, Japan had denounced the Washington agreement. In 1935, Germany – already under Hitler's influence – had declared that she no longer wanted to respect the Peace Treaty of Versailles which put restrictions on her Fleet. Italy, for her part, was on bad terms with Britain and France who had proclaimed sanctions at her expense so as to hinder her activities in Ethiopia. The Conference therefore ended in failure – Japan retired and Italy refused to sign. The other three countries were in agreement, provided that the newly-built battleships did not exceed a displacement of 35,000 tons, the aircraft-carriers of 23,000 tons, the cruisers of 10,000 tons and, finally, the submarines of 2,000 tons.

But storm clouds were appearing on the world's political horizon and from 1937 production of naval armaments was resumed in full in all countries. It was already too late – the Second World War broke out before the greater part of the programmes had time to be realised. The ships available were therefore, for the most part, those which had been produced according to the agreements reached at the Naval Conferences – the battleships of 35,000 tons, the cruisers of 10,000 tons – which were aptly called "Washington type". These ships were to have been a guarantee of peace but instead they played leading parts in the gigantic conflict which commenced in 1939.

Richelieu – France 1940. The first of France's three largest battleships. Was launched January 1939 at Brest. She escaped to Dakar 1940 and was there damaged by British depth charges. In 1943 she joined the Allies and saw service in the Pacific as a unit of the British Eastern Fleet. Displacement: 35,000 tons. Length: 794 ft. Speed: 30 knots plus. Armament: 8 × 15 in., 9 × 6 in., 118 A.A. guns. Crew: 1,670.

FRANCE

THE Second World War, which broke out on 3rd September, 1939, caught the French Navy with only two modern battleships and another six dating back to the First World War. Four big ships of 35,000 tons were still on the stocks, building only having started in 1936 in accordance with the Agreements of the Naval Conferences. Only one of these, the *Richelieu*, came into service before 1945. But France's naval ships were hardly able to get involved before the Anglo-French reverses on land brought the Armistice with Germany and Italy on 22nd June, 1940. In less than 10 months of operations, the activities of her fleet had been limited to participation in the Norwegian campaign, a bombing attack on the Ligurian coast when Italy entered the War, and co-operation with a few ships in the evacuation of the 300,000 men trapped in the Bay of Dunkerque by the rapid advance of the German divisions. On the signing of the Armistice, a strong squadron that was lying at anchor at Mersel-Kebir was attacked by guns of British battleships and torpedo-bombers; the battleship *Bretagne* was sunk and the *Dunkerque* and *Provence* were damaged. The British Admiralty feared that the French fleet might side with the Germans. But proof of French anti-Nazi-ism was clearly shown when, on 27th November, 1942, German troops surrounded the port of Toulon preparatory to occupying it. (According to the Armistice conditions, it was at Toulon that the French Fleet of more than 100 ships was to be moored.) The sailors sank their own ships, amongst them the battleships *Strasbourg* and *Dunkerque* and so prevented them from falling into enemy hands. After 1943 the French Navy – consisting of a few vessels left overseas – later augmented by 155 ships lease-lent from America, contributed by great deeds of valour to the liberation and subsequent rebirth of France.

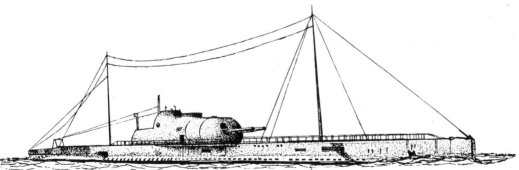

Surcouf – France 1934. The biggest submarine of the Second World War of the "cruiser" type. She was armed with non-slewing 8 in. guns and equipped with a reconnaissance plane which was stowed in a hanger when the craft submerged. Displacement: 2,880 tons. Length: 361 ft. Speed: 18 knots on the surface, 10 knots when submerged. Armament: 2 × 8 in. guns, 10 torpedo-tubes. Crew: 150.

FRENCH NAVAL FORCES AT OUTBREAK OF SECOND WORLD WAR						
Battleships	A/carriers	Heavy cruisers	Light cruisers	Destroyers	Submarines	Total tonnage
8	1	7	11	71	78	564, 108

BATTLESHIPS

Dunkerque – France 1938. At the outbreak of war she and her sister ship, the ***Strasbourg*** were the largest of France's battleships. Damaged by British gunfire and beached at Mers-el-Kebir 1940. Scuttled on 27th November, 1948. 26,500 tons. Length: 702 ft. Speed: 31 knots. Armament: 8 × 13 in., 16 × 5.1 in., A.A. guns. Catapult with 4 aircraft. Crew: 1,381.

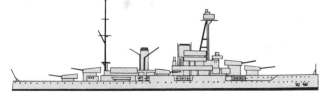

Courbet – France 1913. Was used to form part of breakwater at Arromanches, June 1944. 22,189 tons. 551 ft. 20 knots. 12 × 12 in. and 22 × 5.5 in. guns. Crew: 1,100.

CRUISERS

Tourville – France 1928. Part of the Mediterranean squadron when Italy entered the War. 10,000 tons. 626 ft. overall. 33 knots. 8 × 8 in., 8 × 3 in. and smaller A.A. guns, 6 torpedo tubes. Crew: 605.

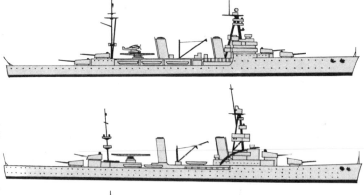

Suffren Class – France 1930. The ***Colbert*** took part in the shelling of Genoa. 10,000 tons. 643 ft. overall. 31 knots. 8 × 3 in. guns, 6 torpedo tubes. Crew: 605.

Duguay-Trouin Class – France 1927. The ***La Motte-Piquet*** distinguished herself in Indo-China. 7,249 tons. 595 ft. overall. 33 knots. 8 × 6.1 in., 4 × 3 in. A.A. guns, 12 torpedo tubes, 1 aircraft. Crew: 578.

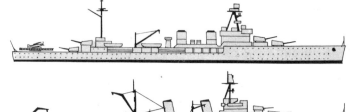

La Galissonniere Class – France 1936. Several of these ships operated with the Allies. 7,600 tons. 581 ft. overall. 31 knots. 9 × 6 in., 16 A.A. guns, 4 torpedo tubes.

DESTROYERS

Chacal Class – France 1926. Six ships. One of them, the ***Jaguar,*** was sunk at Dunkerque. 2,126 tons. 393 ft. 34 knots. 5 × 5.1 in. guns. 8 A.A. guns. 6 torpedo tubes.

Aigle Class – France 1932. Twelve ships, seven scuttled at Toulon. 2,441 tons. 424 ft. 36 knots. 5 × 5.5 in. guns. 4 A.A. guns. 6 torpedo tubes. Mines. Crew: 220.

Bismarck – Germany 1939. With her sister the *Tirpitz*, she was Germany's largest and most modern warship. On 18th May, 1941 she left the Baltic for the Atlantic; was intercepted by British units, and sank the *Hood* Attacked by aircraft from the *Victorious* and *Ark Royal* she was sunk by the *King George V* and the *Rodney*. 41,700 tons. Length: 791 ft. Speed: 31 knots. Armament: 8 × 15 in. guns. Crew: 2,200.

GERMANY

THE Peace Treaty of Versailles contained precise clauses on what the German Fleet should consist of for the future. A maximum of six cruisers of 10,000 tons, six light cruisers of 6,000 tons, 12 destroyers and 12 torpedo boats. The Treaty denied Germany any battleships or submarines.

In fact, Germany never accepted such conditions. Immediately after the War, naval technical experts went to work on building submarines in Baltic shipyards and by 1935 Germany already had a modest submarine fleet. In the same year, she signed an agreement with Great Britain and obtained permission to assemble a surface and an underwater fleet equal to 35% and 45% respectively of Britain's. The agreement also included a clause which Great Britain was to regret bitterly. This stated that, should Germany consider the international situation particularly grave, she would be able to bring her underwater fleet up to the same strength as the British, on condition that the British Admiralty was kept informed. This may have been the agreement but the reality was very different. Since 1933 very little came to be known officially about the state of preparedness of the German Fleet, and especially its underwater strength. On 3rd September, 1939, barely nine hours after the declaration of war, the first British merchant ship was sunk, torpedoed by a German submarine. This was followed 14 days later by the aircraft-carrier, *Courageous* and, 41 days later, by the battleship, the *Royal Oak*, which went to the bottom in those very same waters of Scapa Flow which had seen the scuttling of the German Fleet in 1919.

In point of fact, the German surface navy was not in a position to stand up to the allied British and French – Hitler's attention had been turned more to the army and the air force. Apart from some chases – in one of which the main part was played by the pocket-battleship, *Admiral Graf Spee* – a few marauding cruises against Allied shipping and support action in the occupation of Norway, the German surface Fleet had to be on the defensive rather than attack. One of the two big battleships launched in 1939, the *Bismarck*, was sunk on her first attempt to leave the Baltic, after an almost incredible duel. The *Tirpitz*, her sister ship, ended

Admiral Graf Spee – Germany 1936. On 13th December, 1939, this pocket battleship was attacked by British cruisers off the estuary of the River Plate. Seriously damaged, she took refuge in Montevideo harbour and was scuttled. 12,100 tons. Length: 609 ft. overall. Speed: 26 knots. Armament: 6 × 11 in., 8 × 5·9 in., 14 A.A. guns. 8 torpedo tubes. 2 aircraft. Diesel-driven.

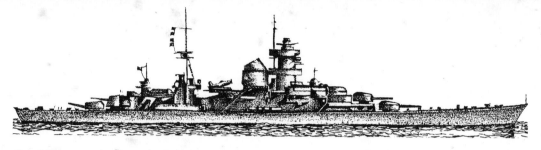

Prinz Eugen – Germany 1940. The most modern and powerful type of German heavy cruiser – comparable to a pocket battleship. She escaped sinking in the engagement which led to the loss of the *Bismarck,* but met her end in the bikini atomic test of 1946. Displacement: 14,800 tons. Length: 654 ft. Speed: 30 knots. Armament: 8 × 8 in., 12 × 4·1 in. and smaller A.A. guns. 12 torpedo tubes. 3 aircraft. Crew: 1,600.

up at the bottom of Tromsoe Fjord, after having been hit by 15 aerial bombs, without actually having taken part in any battles at all. It was only due to the lack of an adequate Fleet to overwhelm the British Navy that Hitler did not try to invade Britain in September, 1940. He had given orders for an armada to be prepared consisting of some 1,900 lighters, 400 tugs, 1,000 motor-boats and 150 transports.

Instead Germany threatened her great rival, with her submarines in what was to become the Battle of the Atlantic, sometimes making it extremely difficult to get supplies through from the United States and the Commonwealth countries. The underwater offensive reached its peak in

1942, the year in which the U-boats sank 6,145,000 tons of merchant shipping bound to or from Britain. Admiral Doenitz applied "wolf pack" technique – groups of 20 or 30 submarines would attack a convoy simultaneously, from all directions, for several successive nights, with exceptional results. The Royal Navy was forced to engage in underwater tactics, concentrating on the perfection of devices for seeking out and locating submarines amongst which were asdic and radar, the latter an invention which could locate U-boats when they rose to the surface to charge their electric motors – and by the introduction of many small escort aircraft-carriers which had been converted from

GERMAN NAVAL FORCES AT OUTBREAK OF SECOND WORLD WAR						
Battleships	A/carriers	Heavy cruisers	Light cruisers	Destroyers	Submarines	Total tonnage
5	—	2	6	42	56	225,000

BATTLESHIPS

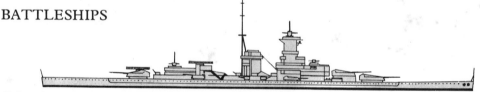

Scharnhorst – Germany 1938. Sister ship: *Gneisenau.* The first real battleships to be built in Germany since the First World War. They were used as support ships in the invasion of Norway 1940 and for the destruction of merchant ships in the Atlantic. 26,000 tons. Length: 775 ft. Speed: 30 knots. Armament: 9 × 11 in., 12 × 5·9 in. and 30 A.A. guns. 4 aircraft. Crew: 1,460.

CRUISER FOR NAVAL RAIDS

Kormoran – Germany 1938. A converted auxiliary cruiser, launched in 1939 as the cargo liner *Steiermark;* sunk off the Australian Coast 19th December, 1941. 8,736 tons gross. 515 feet. 18 knots.

DESTROYERS

"Z" Class – Germany 1937. Twenty-seven ships. Typical destroyer of the German Fleet. From 2,200 to 2,600 tons. Around 384 ft. 36 knots. 5 × 5 in. guns. 8 torpedo tubes. Crew: about 320.

U-33– Germany 1937. One of an ocean-going 625-ton type submarine, she was sunk off the Clyde in February 1940. Germany used more than 1,000 submarines during the war and these caused the loss of over 15 million tons of Allied shipping. About 600 were lost. The submarines of 1945 had tonnages of up to 1,600 tons and were fitted with "schnorkels" which enabled batteries to be recharged without the vessels coming to the surface.

cargo ships. Although Allied shipping losses were enormous, it is only fair to say that over 600 of the 1,100 submarines which Germany flung into the battle were sunk.

Germany, who had put her faith in submarines, clearly showed that she did not believe in aircraft-carriers. Two had been launched in 1939 but never went into active service due to the delay in fitting them out and the damage caused by continuous bombardment. If the German surface Fleet had also been able to count on these two carriers, the results of some of the engagements might have been different. We must not forget that the *Bismarck* had been able to sink a large battle-cruiser

like the *Hood* in five minutes, but her way was blocked and she was powerless before a British naval squadron, after being hit by three torpedoes fired from aircraft of the *Victorious* and *Ark Royal*. Had she had adequate fighter protection supplied by an escorting aircraft-carrier, she would probably have succeeded in entering the Atlantic and forced the already over strained British Fleet to protect her convoys with even larger ships.

Admiral Raeder was right when, in 1938, he told Hitler that the German Fleet would not be ready until 1945. He was not listened to and Doenitz's "Wolf packs" were not successful in changing the course of History.

CRUISERS

Emden – Germany 1925. First combat ship on which electric welding was used. 5,400 tons. 508 ft. overall. 29 knots. 8 × 5.9 in. and 3 × 3.5 in. A.A. guns.

Leipzig – Germany 1931. 6,000 tons. 580 ft. overall. 32 knots. 9 × 5.9 in., 6 × 3.5 in. A.A. and 8 smaller A.A. guns. 12 torpedo tubes. 2 aircraft. Crew: 600.

Admiral Hipper – Germany 1939. 10,000 tons. 640 ft. 32 knots. 8 × 8 in., 24 A.A. guns. 12 torpedo tubes. 3 aircraft.

Königsberg Class – Germany 1929. The *Karlsruhe* was sunk by a British submarine, the *Köln* by the R.A.F. 6,000 tons. 570 ft. overall. 32 knots. 9 × 5.9 in. guns.

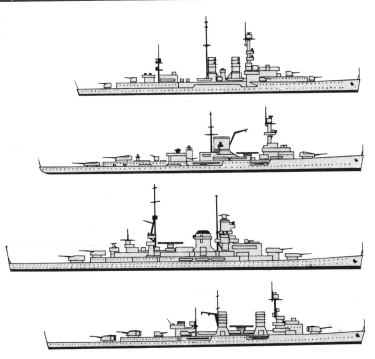

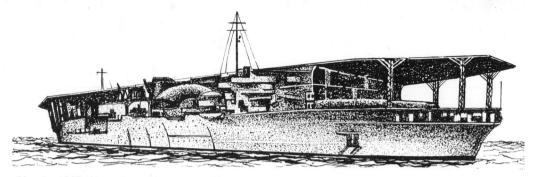

Akagi – 1927. Aircraft-carrier and flagship of the squadron which carried out the surprise attack on Pearl Harbour on 7th December, 1941. The *Akagi*, an ex-battlecruiser of 26,900 tons, was converted immediately after her launching. She was sunk on 4th June, 1942, in the Battle of the Midway Islands. Displacement: 26,900 tons. Length: 766 ft. Speed: 28·5 knots. Armament: 60 aircraft, 1 catapult, 10 × 8 in. guns, 36 A.A. guns.

JAPAN

THE war which broke out in December, 1941, between Japan and the United States, also involving Great Britain, was not very surprising – it was the logical consequence of the Japanese policy of supremacy in the Far East that had started in the early nineteen hundreds with the Sino-Japanese and Russo-Japanese wars. The United States deluded themselves, in the period immediately after the First World War, that the Empire of the Rising Sun would not go so far as directly to menace the U.S.A. It seemed that proof of this lay in the fact that Japan had participated in the Naval Conferences and had accepted having a fleet inferior to those of the Americans and the British. But this should not have raised false hopes since it was clear that Japan did not feel she was yet ready, involved as she was in a war with China, waged primarily on land. However, from 1934 she claimed her independence from every restriction and started preparing for what, at the opportune moment, was to prove so valuable, this at a time when the United States had still not made provision to bring her Fleet up to date and Britain and France could do nothing in defence of their Asian territories.

And so it was that, at 7.57 a.m. on Sunday, 7th December, 1941, the first wave of over 100 aircraft – torpedo-carriers, bombers and fighters – swooped on Pearl Harbour where more than 90 ships of the American Fleets were lying at anchor. The planes had taken off from six Japanese aircraft-carriers, accompanied by two battleships, three cruisers, a destroyer division and several mother submarines carrying two-man submarines, three sub-submarines and had succeeded in arriving close to the objective without being sighted. After a second larger wave of aircraft had attacked Pearl Harbour, the only ships which remained were severely damaged. Ten battleships, three cruisers, two destroyers and many other ships received direct hits; nearly 200 aircraft were destroyed on the runways of the airports;

Yamato – Japan 1942. The biggest and most powerful battleship ever built. She flew the flag of Admiral Yamamoto, Commander-in-Chief of the Japanese naval forces at the Battle of the Midways. She was sunk by American aircraft in 1945. Displacement: 64,000 tons. Length: 863 ft. Speed: 27·7 knots. Armament: 9 × 18·1 in., 6 × 6·1 in. and smaller guns. 7 aircraft.

Kaga – Japan 1928. The first bombers to bomb Pearl Harbour came from the flight-deck of this aircraft-carrier, which was a converted battleship. The planes dropped 138 tons of bombs and torpedoes, sinking or damaging several ships and destroying 188 aircraft. The *Kaga,* like the *Akagi,* sank at the Battle of the Midways. Displacement: 26,900 tons. Speed: 23 knots. Armament: 10 × 8 in. guns. 80 aircraft.

almost 2,400 Americans lost their lives. Out of 354 Japanese aircraft that took part in the raid, which wiped out the United States' naval power in the Pacific in one blow, only 29 failed to return.

With this surprise attack – which could have had even more dramatic effects if the three U.S. Pacific Fleet aircraft-carriers had also been in Pearl Harbour – the Japanese gave a grim demonstration to the world of the vast offensive possibilities of aircraft-carriers. On 15th February, 1942, Japanese troops entered Singapore and had already occupied all the key points in the Pacific and South-East Asia.

Whether the leading characters in the struggle – first for the defence and then for the reconquest of the islands – were the soldiers or the Marines, the War really took place in a series of aero-naval battles – the Battle of the Coral Sea, of the Midway and Marianas Islands and of Leyte. In these gigantic engagements it was not the guns of the battleships which decided the results but the aircraft from the carriers of both Fleets. In 1941, Japan possessed eight such ships but during the course of

the War she lined up another 24 for attack and the rest for escort duties, which she got by converting merchant ships into aircraft carriers was balanced in her favour. The make headway against the American Marines while the number of aircraft-carriers was balanced in her favour. The two largest battleships in the world, the *Yamato* and *Musashi,* 64,000 tons, armed with nine guns of the incredible calibre of 18.1 in. were of little use and were relegated to the role of escort duty. When the Japanese Navy was no longer master of the sea, and above all of the sky within the fuel range of her squadrons, the bases that the Japanese soldiers had occupied in the Pacific fell one by one until even their homeland was threatened. Even without the dropping of the two atomic bombs on Hiroshima and Nagasaki, the results of the War were already clear. It would perhaps have gone on for years but without hope for Japan, the nation that had had such a clear vision of the importance of aircraft-carriers in naval warfare and, because of them, was to know the dishonour of defeat.

I.55 – Japan 1927. A deep-sea submarine which was sunk on 27th July, 1944, by American ships. Although underwater war was important in the Pacific area, it did not reach the proportions of the Battle of the Atlantic. Displacement: 1,142 tons. Length: 360 ft. Speed: 16 knots on the surface – 7.5 knots submerged. Armament: 1 × 5.5 in. gun. 4 torpedo tubes, mines.

JAPANESE NAVAL FORCES AT OUTBREAK OF SECOND WORLD WAR						
Battleships	A/carriers	Heavy cruisers	Light cruisers	Destroyers	Submarines	Total tonnage
10	8	18	29	134	66	1,015,975

AIRCRAFT CARRIERS

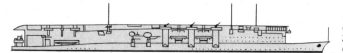

Ryujo – Japan 1933. Light aircraft-carrier. 7,100 tons. 548 ft. 25 knots. 24 aircraft. 12 × 5 in., 24 anti-aircraft guns. Crew: 600.

Hosho – Japan 1922. Modernised 1939-40. 7,470 tons. 552 ft. overall. 25 knots. 26 aircraft. 4 × 5·5 in., 4 A.A. guns, Crew: 550.

BATTLESHIPS

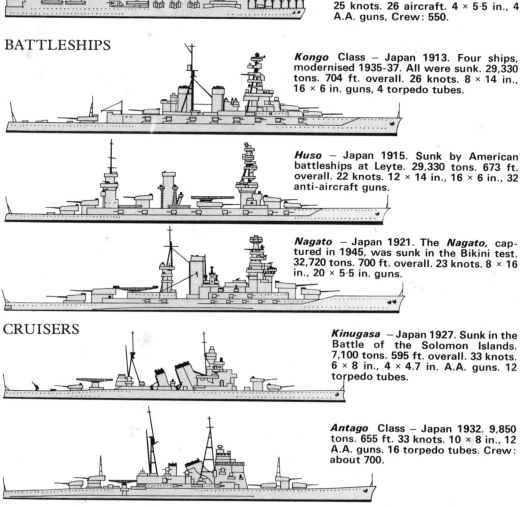

Kongo Class – Japan 1913. Four ships, modernised 1935-37. All were sunk. 29,330 tons. 704 ft. overall. 26 knots. 8 × 14 in., 16 × 6 in. guns, 4 torpedo tubes.

Huso – Japan 1915. Sunk by American battleships at Leyte. 29,330 tons. 673 ft. overall. 22 knots. 12 × 14 in., 16 × 6 in., 32 anti-aircraft guns.

Nagato – Japan 1921. The **Nagato**, captured in 1945, was sunk in the Bikini test. 32,720 tons. 700 ft. overall. 23 knots. 8 × 16 in., 20 × 5·5 in. guns.

CRUISERS

Kinugasa – Japan 1927. Sunk in the Battle of the Solomon Islands. 7,100 tons. 595 ft. overall. 33 knots. 6 × 8 in., 4 × 4.7 in. A.A. guns. 12 torpedo tubes.

Antago Class – Japan 1932. 9,850 tons. 655 ft. 33 knots. 10 × 8 in., 12 A.A. guns. 16 torpedo tubes. Crew: about 700.

Mogami Class – Japan 1935. 8,500 tons. 640 ft. overall. 33 knots. 15 × 6·1 in., 8 × 5 in. A.A. guns. 12 torpedo tubes. 4 aircraft. 2 catapults.

Illustrious – Gt. Britain 1940. Twenty torpedo-bombers took off from this aircraft-carrier on 11th November, 1940 and attacked the Italian Fleet at Taranto. The *Littorio* was hit by three torpedoes, the *Cavour* sank, and the *Duilio,* the cruiser *Trento* and the destroyer *Libeccio* were damaged. Displacement: 23,000 tons. Length: 753 ft. Speed: 31 knots. Armament: 40 aircraft, 16 × 4·5 in. and 64 A.A. guns. Crew: 1,400.

GREAT BRITAIN

THE beginning of the 1900s had seen Britain fully involved in her effort to remain the major naval power in the world. After the First World War, however, she accepted limitation of naval armaments, even though this required division of supremacy with the United States. She accepted this state of affairs for two main reasons: to avoid further financial sacrifices and because she foresaw a long period of peace ahead. And so, from 1926 to 1935, she spent an average of £45 million annually on her Navy. This became £55 million in 1936, £60 million in 1937, £95 million in 1938 and £114 million in 1939. This progression shows how the British Admiralty, as the great crisis approached, tried to take cover, but was beaten on time by the precipitation of events. And so, in 1939, the British Fleet consisted of only 17 battleships, 13 of which had been launched before 1918. The number of her aircraft-carriers, too, was low in comparison with the needs of a war that was to be conducted on almost all the seas in the world. To aggravate the situation, the aircraft-carrier *Courageous* and the battleship *Royal Oak* were torpedoed in the early days of the War, and their loss was certainly not compensated for by the elimination of the battleship, *Admiral Graf Spee,* by British cruisers.

1940 was a very hard year for Britain and, in particular, for her navy. In April, during the evacuation of Norway the aircraft-carrier, *Glorious,* was sunk by two German battleships. In June the drama of Dunkerque took place. This was not a complete defeat simply because the British sailors managed so wonderfully in carrying 300,000 men to safety from the surrounded beach. Also in June, Italy came into the War and France signed the Armistice. The Royal Navy now found itself absolutely alone against the German and Italian Fleets, and its first confirmation of this was to be at the latter's expense. On 11th November, a group of torpedo-bombers from the aircraft-carrier *Illustrious* surprised a squadron of ships lying at anchor in Taranto harbour, causing great damage. This was the first occasion in which an aircraft-carrier came on the scene as a means of attack – a year later the Japanese were to make use of the results of experiences learnt from it.

In May, 1941, Britain had another great success at sea with the sinking of the *Bismarck,* the largest and most modern German battleship. Even though the German surface Fleet was inferior to that of the British, if the battleships had only

Ark Royal – Gt. Britain 1938. Two torpedoes dropped by planes from the *Ark Royal* hit the *Bismarck,* and caused serious damage. The aircraft-carrier was herself sunk on 14th November, 1941, by a German submarine. Displacement: 22,000 tons. Length: 800 ft. overall. Speed: 30·7 knots. Armament: 72 aircraft, 2 catapults, 16 × 4·5 in. and 48 A.A. guns, 8 multi-machine guns. Crew: 1,575.

Valiant – Gt. Britain 1916. One of the five very successful *Queen Elizabeth* class, the first battleships to mount 15 in. guns and burn only oil fuel. Took part at Jutland and in 1941 – at Cape Matapan – helped sink two Italian cruisers. 31,000 tons. Length: 640 ft. overall. Speed: 25 knots. Armament: 8 × 15 in. 12 × 6 in. guns, 4 torpedo tubes. Shown after first reconstruction, secondary armament later modified.

been concentrated there, they would have been able to create a very dangerous striking force indeed in the Atlantic, where the submarines were already operating intensively. The British Fleet may have shown itself alert and resolute on that occasion, but the contrary was the case when, nine months later, it let the battleships *Scharnhorst* and *Gneisenau*, the cruiser *Prinz Eugen* and six destroyers slip through its fingers as they were in transit from Brest to Wilhelmshaven. They passed through the whole length of the English Channel unchallenged.

In the Mediterranean, the British Navy had to compete with the Italian Navy, after the operation against the French squadron at Mers-el-Kebir. The encounters followed one upon the other at Stilo Point, Cape Teulada and Cape Matapan, with loss of cruisers on both sides. The Italian assault boats caused major damage

BATTLESHIPS

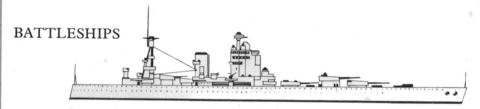

Nelson – Gt. Britain 1925. It was aboard this ship that Eisenhower, Bedell Smith and Badoglio signed the Armistice between Italy and the Allies. 33,950 tons. 510 ft. overall. 23 knots. 9 × 16 in. 12 × 6 in. 70 A.A. guns. 2 torpedo tubes. Crew (wartime): 1,640.

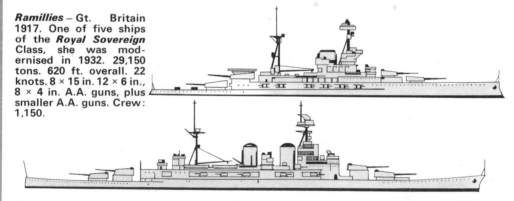

Ramillies – Gt. Britain 1917. One of five ships of the *Royal Sovereign* Class, she was modernised in 1932. 29,150 tons. 620 ft. overall. 22 knots. 8 × 15 in. 12 × 6 in., 8 × 4 in. A.A. guns, plus smaller A.A. guns. Crew: 1,150.

Hood – Gt. Britain 1920. This battlecruiser was modernised in 1930. On 24th May, 1941 she intercepted the *Bismarck* in the North Atlantic and was sunk. 42,100 tons. 860 ft. overall. 31 knots. 8 × 15 in., 12 × 5·5 in. guns. Crew: 1,341.

King George V – Gt. Britain 1940. Her 10 × 14 in. and the 9 × 16 in. guns of the ***Rodney*** reduced the ***Bismarck*** – which had already been hit by two torpedoes from ***Ark Royal*** aircraft – to a flaming wreck. So the crew of the ***Hood*** was avenged; only three men had survived the attack. 35,000 tons. Length: 745 ft. overall. Speed: 29 knots. Armament: 10 × 14 in., 16 × 5·25 in. A.A. guns. 4 aircraft. Crew (wartime): 1,900.

as they forcibly entered the Bay of Suda and the port of Alexandria, so much so that, at a certain moment, the position of the British forces became very difficult. All the same, Italy did not take advantage of her situation in order to try a landing on Malta since she was already too involved in the North African operations.

The Japanese attack on Pearl Harbour on 7th December, 1941, brought the United States into the War at Great Britain's side.

If, for the British, this was a great comfort it also brought with it the worry of a new Front, on which operations had started with the sinking of the only two British battleships out East – the *Prince of Wales* and the *Repulse*.

The struggle against German submarines, meanwhile, became more and more pressing and demanded enormous sacrifices of ships and of men before the Allies could consider themselves the vic-

AIRCRAFT CARRIERS

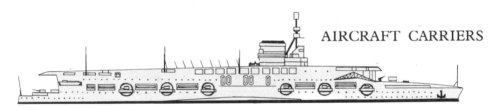

Courageous – Gt. Britain 1917. Modernised in 1930. One of the first victims of German submarines and sunk on 17th September, 1939. 22,500 tons. 786 ft. overall. 30 knots. 48 aircraft. 2 catapults. 16 × 4·7 in. guns (dual purpose) and smaller A.A. guns.

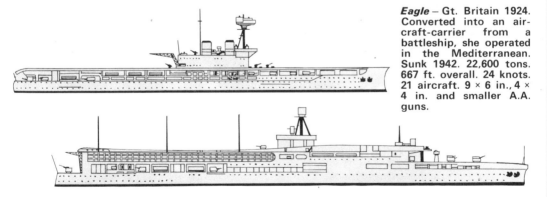

Eagle – Gt. Britain 1924. Converted into an aircraft-carrier from a battleship, she operated in the Mediterranean. Sunk 1942. 22,600 tons. 667 ft. overall. 24 knots. 21 aircraft. 9 × 6 in., 4 × 4 in. and smaller A.A. guns.

Furious – Gt. Britain 1925. Converted from a cruiser. It was her planes which, with others from the ***Victorious***, dropped bombs on ***Tirpitz*** in the Tromsoe Fiord. 22,450 tons. 786 ft. overall. 31 knots. 33 aircraft. 10 × 5·5 in., 3 × 4 in. A.A. and smaller A.A. guns.

tors of the Battle of the Atlantic. In 1942, in the same year that the German submarines broke the record of British shipping sunk, offensive actions started in which the Navy's contribution was to be the deciding factor – in November, 1942, the landing in Morocco; in July, 1943, the landing in Sicily; and, at last, on 6th June, 1944, the landings in Normandy. For this last operation, 4,000 British and American ships assembled, preceded by 200 minesweepers and escorted by six battleships and dozens of cruisers and destroyers. They effected the landing of 250,000 men in 24 hours.

Victory in Europe was not long delayed.

The price paid by the Royal Navy was extremely high. Five battleships and ten aircraft-carriers were sunk, 30 cruisers out of 97, 238 destroyers out of 406, 32 escort ships out of 164 that were in service during the course of the War, were also sunk. Nevertheless, the British Fleet was stronger in 1945 than it had been in September, 1939, and had four battleships, 29 aircraft-carriers, and a number of undefined smaller vessels on the stocks, or on the point of completion. This shows how, even in the most difficult moments, Great Britain found an exceptional capacity for recovery in her unshakable faith in her Navy.

BRITISH NAVAL FORCES AT OUTBREAK OF SECOND WORLD WAR						
Battleships	A/carriers	Heavy cruisers	Light cruisers	Destroyers	Submarines	Total tonnage
17	7	15	73	241	56	1,692,302

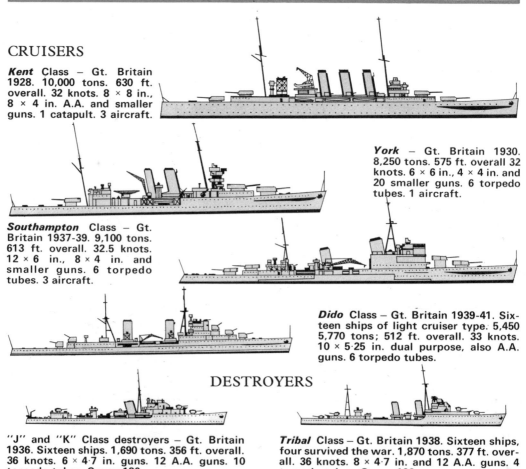

CRUISERS

Kent Class – Gt. Britain 1928. 10,000 tons. 630 ft. overall. 32 knots. 8 × 8 in., 8 × 4 in. A.A. and smaller guns. 1 catapult. 3 aircraft.

York – Gt. Britain 1930. 8,250 tons. 575 ft. overall 32 knots. 6 × 6 in., 4 × 4 in. and 20 smaller guns. 6 torpedo tubes. 1 aircraft.

Southampton Class – Gt. Britain 1937-39. 9,100 tons. 613 ft. overall. 32.5 knots. 12 × 6 in., 8 × 4 in. and smaller guns. 6 torpedo tubes. 3 aircraft.

Dido Class – Gt. Britain 1939-41. Sixteen ships of light cruiser type. 5,450 5,770 tons; 512 ft. overall. 33 knots. 10 × 5.25 in. dual purpose, also A.A. guns. 6 torpedo tubes.

DESTROYERS

''J'' and ''K'' Class destroyers – Gt. Britain 1936. Sixteen ships. 1,690 tons. 356 ft. overall. 36 knots. 6 × 4.7 in. guns. 12 A.A. guns. 10 torpedo tubes. Crew: 180.

Tribal Class – Gt. Britain 1938. Sixteen ships, four survived the war. 1,870 tons. 377 ft. overall. 36 knots. 8 × 4.7 in. and 12 A.A. guns. 4 torpedo tubes. Crew: 190.

Vittorio Veneto – Italy 1940. Her sister ships, and the *Vittorio Veneto,* took part in the Battle of Cape Teulada; the *Littorio* took part in the first and second battles of the Syrtes, off the Libyan coast; and the *Roma* was hit by German bombs and sank with all hands while being transferred to Malta after the Armistice. 35,000 tons. Length: 775 ft. overall. Speed: 30 knots. Armament: 9 × 15 in., 12 × 6 in., 12 × 3·5 in., 30 A.A. guns. 3 aircraft. Crew: 1,900.

ITALY

ON 10th June, 1940, when war was declared against Britain and France, the Italian Navy was powerful, modern and prepared, even though she had respected the agreements of the "naval holiday". Nevertheless, she was compelled to fight at a disadvantage to the British due to three basic facts – absence of aircraft-carriers, shortage of fuel and lack of radar. Government opinion held that Italy did not need aircraft-carriers due to her elongated geographical position in the Mediterranean – this proved to be a serious error of judgment because the Italian naval squadrons lacked adequate aircraft and air protection.

In 1941, when the lack became only too clear, it was decided to convert the liners *Augustus* and *Roma* into aircraft-carriers, and they were re-named the *Sparviero* and *Aquila*. But it was already too late and the two vessels did not have time to go into

service. As for fuel, at the outbreak of the War, Italy had a stock of 2,000,000 tons of diesel oil – hardly enough for one year. Supply difficulties were so great that, from the end of 1942, her big ships were forced to remain at base. The fact that the British already had radar in 1941, whereas the Italians did not, was a decisive factor on more than one occasion – as, for example, at Cape Matapan.

On 28th March, 1941, a British naval formation sank three cruisers and four destroyers in only seven minutes, at dead of night, thanks to the help of radar, without the Italians having any means at all of locating the enemy in order to defend themselves.

With the scales weighted so heavily against them, it can be said that the Italian Navy functioned to the limit of its potential in carrying out its protective duties and in escorting convoys of troops destined for

ITALIAN ASSAULT CRAFT

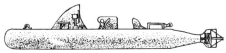

Maiale – Italy 1940. A tiny submarine, of a slow speed, whose head contained 660 lb. of explosive. It was piloted by two men equipped with diving-suits and breathing equipment.

Explosive Midgets Boats – Italy 1940. Having penetrated into harbours, they were launched at the objective like torpedoes. They were used at Suda, at Malta and in the Black Sea.

Trieste – Italy 1930. With her sister ships, the *Trento* and *Bolzano,* and with 4 units of the *Zara* Class, she was one of the heavy cruisers which were the pride of the Italian Fleet. She took part in the Battle of Stilo Point and in convoy escorting operations. She was sunk at La Maddalena on 10th April, 1943. Displacement: 10,000 tons. Length: 645 ft. overall. Speed: 35 knots. Armament: 8 × 8 in., 12 × 3·9 in. A.A. guns, 8 torpedo tubes, 2 aircraft.

overseas, in disrupting communications and British supply lines and in defending its national coastline.

The Italian Fleet was called on to give protection to 1,200,000 men being carried to Libya, Tunisia, Albania, Greece and the Islands of the Aegean, with quite negligible losses. It cut off the strong air-naval base of Malta for many months and caused havoc in the heavily fortified ports of Alexandria and Gibraltar.

The surface Fleet clashed many times with the British – on 9th July, 1940, at Stilo Point; and in 1942, in the mid-June operation, it made every effort to prevent the arrival of two convoys to Malta. In spite of the strength of the battleships which were confronting each other, neither the Italian nor the British squadrons suffered seriously as a result of these battles.

Major damage was caused to the Italians, however, in torpedo-bomber raids from the aircraft-carrier, *Illustrious* in Taranto harbour and to the British in the Bay of Suda where a cruiser was sunk as a result of surprise attacks from assault craft and in the port of Alexandria where two warships were seriously damaged. The explosive

midget craft and the slow torpedoes called "pigs" constituted a constant irritation to the British who could not really feel at ease even in fortified bases such as Gibraltar and La Valletta.

Just as dangerous and dreaded by the Allies were the Italian submarines which operated both in the Mediterranean and in the Atlantic. Her squadron of 32 ocean-going submarines cost the enemy more than 100 ships to a total of 579,000 tons. Of the 133 underwater craft employed during the War, 88 failed to return.

On 8th September, 1943, when Italy signed the Armistice with the Allies, her surface navy was still in a position to fight, as far as numbers of battleships and cruisers were concerned, if only she had had the oil fuel to get them out of their bases. When the order was received to hand them over to those who, up to the previous day, had been the enemy, the Italian crews would have liked to scuttle their fine and powerful ships. But, once again, the navy did its duty to the end. Nevertheless, in British ports Italian ships were not forced to strike their flags – a gallant recognition by the enemy of their courage.

Barbarigo – Italy 1938. One of the *Marcello* Class, of which there were nine ships. She accomplished two missions in the Mediterranean and ten in the Atlantic, sinking many ships. Was sunk in the Bay of Biscay, 1943. Displacement: 941 tons. Length: 239 ft. Speed: 17 knots on the surface, 8·5 knots when submerged. Armament: 2 × 3·9 in. guns. 8 torpedo tubes.

ITALIAN NAVAL FORCES AT OUTBREAK OF SECOND WORLD WAR						
Battleships	A/carriers	Heavy cruisers	Light cruisers	Destroyers	Submarines	Total tonnage
6	—	8	14	160	100	672,750

BATTLESHIPS

Giulio Cesare – Italy 1915. Rebuilt 1933-37. 23,622 tons. 611 ft. 28 knots. 10 × 12.6 in., 12 × 4.7 in. guns. Crew: 1,200.

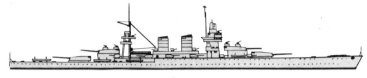

Caio Duilio – Italy 1915. Modernised in 1933-37. 23,622 tons. 611ft. 27 knots. 10 × 12.6 in., 12 × 5.3 in. guns. Crew: 1,200.

CRUISERS

Zara – Italy 1931. 10,000 tons. 599 ft. 32 knots. 8 × 8 in., 30 A.A. guns. 1 catapult. 2 aircraft. Crew: 705.

Raimondo Montecuccoli – Italy 1935. Displacement: 6,941 tons. 598 ft. 37 knots. 8 × 6 in., 22 A.A. guns. 4 torpedo tubes. 3 aircraft. Crew: 522.

Giuseppe Garibaldi – Italy 1937. 7,874 tons. 614 ft. 35 knots. 10 × 6 in., 24 A.A. guns. 6 torpedo tubes. 4 aircraft. Crew: 600.

Bartolomeo Colleoni – Italy 1931. One of a class of six cruisers. 5,069 tons. 555 ft. 37 knots. 8 × 6 in. guns. 4 torpedo tubes.

Eugenio di Savoia – Italy 1936. 7,283 tons. 613 ft. 26.5 knots. 8 × 6 in., 22 A.A. guns. 3 aircraft. Crew: 551

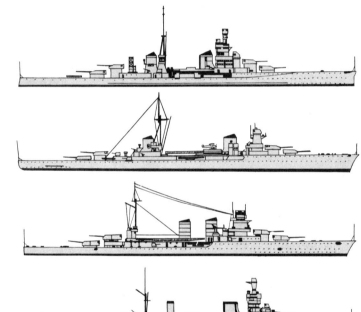

DESTROYERS

Navigatori Class – Italy 1929-31. Twelve ships. The **Luca Tarigo** sank the destroyer **Mohawk** off Malta in 1941. 1,917 tons. 353 ft. 38 knots. 6 × 4·7 in. 18 small A.A. guns. 4 torpedo tubes. Mines. Crew: 170.

Artigliere Class – Italy 1938. Twelve ships. The most modern Italian destroyers in the Second World War. 1,620 tons. 350 ft. 39 knots. 4 × 4·7 in. 16 A.A. guns. 6 torpedo tubes. Mines. Crew: 165.

Yorktown – U.S.A. 1937. This aircraft-carrier, together with the *Enterprise* and the *Lexington,* played a leading part in the first air-naval battles in the Pacific in 1942 – the battle of the Coral Sea and of the Midways. The *Yorktown* was sunk in the second battle, after her aircraft had damaged the *Akagi.* Displacement: 19,000 tons. Length: 809 ft. Speed: 34 knots. Aircraft: 85. Armament: 8 × 5 in. A.A. and smaller guns. Crew: 2,000.

UNITED STATES OF AMERICA

AFTER the failure of the Naval Conference in London in 1935, the United States were the last to take up naval armaments again. In fact, even after the outbreak of war in Europe, many Americans still hoped to remain on the outside and so were not in favour of President Roosevelt's intense efforts to bring the U.S.A. up to a high level of preparedness. It was not until 14th June, 1940, that he succeeded in getting the "Two Oceans Bill" approved. This legislation provided for the immediate building of some 1,400,000 tons of shipping for war purposes. But it took more than two years to get either a battleship or an aircraft-carrier launched, which was why, at the moment of the treacherous attack on Pearl Harbour on 7th December, 1941, the Americans could still not call on even one of their new ships, whose construction had only been started the year before.

At Pearl Harbour, the United States lost all her Pacific Fleet at one blow, excluding three aircraft-carriers which, by chance, had not yet returned to base. After the attack, the only United States ships of the Pacific Fleet that were in a position to fight were the three aircraft-carriers, three cruisers, 13 destroyers and 29 submarines. On these ships rested the entire effort aimed at stemming Japanese expansion in the Pacific Islands and in South-East Asia.

The first encounter between a strong Japanese squadron and an American one took place between 7th-8th May, 1942, in the Battle of the Coral Sea. For the first time, two naval squadrons did not come into direct firing range but attacked each other with the aircraft from their respective aircraft-carriers. In this first air-naval battle in history, one Japanese and one American aircraft-carrier, the *Shoho* and *Lexington*, were sunk. Some weeks later the Japanese decided to occupy the Midway Islands and they headed towards them with a fleet of five aircraft-carriers, nine battleships (among which was the *Yamato*), nine cruisers and 29 torpedo-boat-destroyers. Defending the archipelago were three aircraft-carriers, seven heavy cruisers, 24 destroyers and 25 sub-

Mississippi – U.S.A. 1918. With the rest of this Class, the *New Mexico* and *Idaho,* this battleship carried out a great number of actions, after her modernisation in 1932, virtually all her war service being in the Pacific. Displacement: 33,400 tons. Length: 624 ft. Speed: 21 knots. Armament: 12 × 14 in., 14 × 5 in. and smaller A.A. guns. Aircraft: 3; 2 catapults. Crew: 1,320.

Lexington – U.S.A. 1927. Aircraft-carrier of the Pacific Fleet, she escaped the massacre of Pearl Harbour. Having been hit by at least three torpedoes and two bombs in the Battle of the Coral Sea, she was destroyed by internal explosion due to ruptured petrol lines. Sister ship – *Saratoga.* Displacement: 33,000 tons. Length: 888 ft. Speed: 33 knots. Aircraft: 83; 1 catapult. Armament: 16 × 5 in. A.A. and smaller A.A. guns. Crew: 2,120.

marines – all American. The torpedoes and the bombs of the 240 Japanese and the 160 United States aircraft caused the Battle of the Midways to end with the sinking of four Japanese and one American aircraft-carrier. Admiral Yamamato, left without aerial support, gave up his attempt to land and gave the order to retreat. It was the first great American victory – the start of the counter-offensive that was to develop, four months later, with the occupation of Guadalcanal.

However, the biggest engagements between aircraft-carriers took place in the Battle of the Mariana Islands. From 18th to 21st July, 1944, nine Japanese aircraft-carriers found themselves confronted by 16 American attacking aircraft-carriers and more than 20 escort vessels. This, in effect, marked the end of the Japanese aircraft-carrier fleet which was almost entirely sunk by American aircraft. In contrast, the United States squadron suffered very little damage and lost only 157 aircraft against 757 Japanese.

The last big naval battle in the Pacific broke out in October, 1944, when the Americans were preparing to occupy the Island of Leyte, the central point of the Japanese defence system. The United States gave a support force to the landing-craft of ten aircraft-carriers, 18 escort carriers, 14 battleships, eight cruisers and smaller craft. Against such a formidable concentration of ships, a single aircraft-carrier, seven battleships and 15 cruisers could do nothing. For the Empire of the Rising Sun, the War in the Pacific was definitely over.

Although the aircraft-carriers were the key to victory, of considerable importance, too, were the 100,000 or more landing-craft of every size employed by the United States for the reconquest of the islands.

The American Navy, which also made such a great contribution to the final operations of the War in Europe, had been caught unprepared. But it was able to reinforce itself during the actual course of hostilities, thanks to the vast industrial power behind it. After 1941, the U.S.A. put into service eight battleships, 36 aircraft-carriers for attack, more than 100 escort carriers, 14 cruisers and an incredible number of light craft. In the Second World War, the United States won for themselves the right to be the biggest and most powerful naval force in the world.

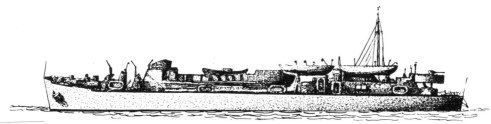

LST 332 – U.S.A. 1942. The necessity of having to make numerous landings in the Pacific and in Europe meant that the United States had to build thousands of landing craft. The L.S.T. (Landing Ship, Tank), was one of the biggest, its length being 327 ft. Generally their displacement was around 1,500 tons; they made 10 knots, had a crew of about 100 men and carried several A.A. guns.

U.S. NAVAL FORCES AT OUTBREAK OF SECOND WORLD WAR						
Battleships	A/carriers	Heavy cruisers	Light cruisers	Destroyers	Submarines	Total tonnage
15	7	18	18	220	100	1,344,870

BATTLESHIPS

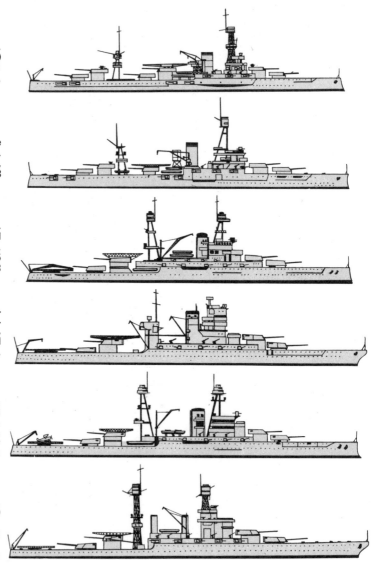

Arkansas – U.S.A. 1912. Modernised in 1927. 26,100 tons. 562 ft. 19 knots. 12 × 12 in., 16 × 5 in. 8 A.A. guns. Crew: 1,330.

Texas – U.S.A. 1914. Twice modernised. 27,000 tons. 573 ft. 19 knots. 10 × 14 in., 16 × 5 in., 10 A.A. guns. 3 aircraft. Crew: 1,300.

Oklahoma – U.S.A. 1916. Battleship, sunk at Pearl Harbour. 29,000 tons. 583 ft. 20 knots. 10 × 14 in., 12 × 5 in., 8 × 5 in. A.A. guns. 3 aircraft. Crew: 1,300.

New Mexico – U.S.A. 1918. 33,400 tons. Length: 624 ft. Speed: 21 knots. 12 × 14 in., 6 × 5 in., 8 × 5 in. A.A. and smaller guns. 3 aircraft. Crew: 1,320.

Arizona – U.S.A. 1916. Modernised in 1931. Sunk at Pearl Harbour. 32,600 tons. 608 ft. 21 knots. 12 × 14 in., 16 × 5 in. A.A. and smaller A.A. guns. 3 aircraft. Crew: 1,360.

California – U.S.A. 1921. Modernised in 1942. 32,600 tons. 624 ft. 21 knots. 12 × 14 in., 16 × 5 in. A.A. and other smaller A.A. guns. 1 catapult. 4 aircraft. Crew: 1,480.

DESTROYERS

"Flush Deck" Class – U.S.A. 1919. 1963 ships of this type, although due for demolition, were used in the Second World War. 1,190 tons. 35 knots. 4 × 5 in. 1 × 3 in. guns. 12 torpedo tubes.

Mahan Class – U.S.A. 1936. Sixteen ships. Destroyer used in Second World War. Displacement: 1,450 tons. Length: 341 ft. speed: 36·5 knots. 5 × 5 in. A.A. guns and smaller A.A. guns. 12 torpedo tubes. Crew: 230.

U.S. NAVAL FORCES AT END OF SECOND WORLD WAR						
Battleships	A/carriers	Heavy cruisers	Light cruisers	Destroyers	Submarines	Total tonnage
21	102	26	45	745	205	—

AIRCRAFT CARRIERS

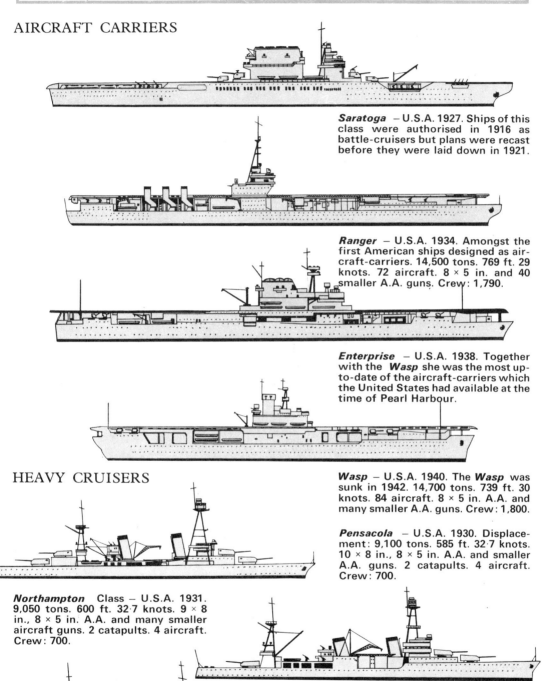

Saratoga – U.S.A. 1927. Ships of this class were authorised in 1916 as battle-cruisers but plans were recast before they were laid down in 1921.

Ranger – U.S.A. 1934. Amongst the first American ships designed as air-craft-carriers. 14,500 tons. 769 ft. 29 knots. 72 aircraft. 8 × 5 in. and 40 smaller A.A. guns. Crew: 1,790.

Enterprise – U.S.A. 1938. Together with the **Wasp** she was the most up-to-date of the aircraft-carriers which the United States had available at the time of Pearl Harbour.

HEAVY CRUISERS

Wasp – U.S.A. 1940. The **Wasp** was sunk in 1942. 14,700 tons. 739 ft. 30 knots. 84 aircraft. 8 × 5 in. A.A. and many smaller A.A. guns. Crew: 1,800.

Pensacola – U.S.A. 1930. Displacement: 9,100 tons. 585 ft. 32·7 knots. 10 × 8 in., 8 × 5 in. A.A. and smaller A.A. guns. 2 catapults. 4 aircraft. Crew: 700.

Northampton Class – U.S.A. 1931. 9,050 tons. 600 ft. 32·7 knots. 9 × 8 in., 8 × 5 in. A.A. and many smaller aircraft guns. 2 catapults. 4 aircraft. Crew: 700.

New Orleans Class – U.S.A. 1934. Three ships of this class were sunk during the Battle of Savo Island. 9,950 tons. 588 ft. 32 knots. 9 × 8 in., 8 × 5 in. A.A. and smaller A.A. guns.

U.S.S.R.

IN the Second World War, the U.S.S.R. was engaged mainly on land while her modest Navy, which mostly dated back to the First World War, proved to be of little practical use. According to the sparse news available on the state of the Soviet Forces' preparedness, from the establishment of the Bolshevik Revolution to the outbreak of the Second World War, it seems that the problem of naval forces was not seriously faced until 1930. In fact, it was a case of starting from nothing and of re-establishing a fleet on an entirely new basis.

The greatest difficulty that stood in the way of this programme being realised was the dearth of naval technical experts, an insufficiency of shipyards and the immaturity of their heavy industries. As a result, even though Russia spent milliards of roubles from 1933-1940 in her attempt to create a fleet which could be compared to those of the major European Powers, the forces that she was able to rally at the be-

ginning of hostilities were completely inadequate to the needs of a war which was to extend to both the North Sea and the Black Sea. So, in the main, the activities of Russian ships were limited to defending the supply convoys coming from the United States and from Britain, once these had succeeded in reaching the neighbourhood of the Russian ports and in making their way through the minefields which seriously obstructed the approach to their coasts. In the theatre of operations in the Black Sea, they also had to deal with the Italian assault craft used in the blockade of Sebastopol.

To sum up, the naval activities of the Soviet Union were almost negligible when compared with those of her other armed forces, which waged war over a vast area of the land. The Russian naval crews fought well, but the means at their disposal were such that they had little chance of contributing to victory.

U.S.S.R. NAVAL FORCES AT OUTBREAK OF SECOND WORLD WAR						
Battleships	A/carriers	Heavy cruisers	Light cruisers	Destroyers	Submarines	Total tonnage
3	—	4	4	46	153	270,489

BATTLESHIPS

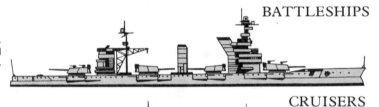

Pariskaya - Kommuna — U.S.S.R. 1914. Modernised in 1931. 23,016 tons. 619 ft. 23 knots. 12 × 12 in., 16 × 4.7 in. guns. Crew: 1,230

CRUISERS

Kirov Class — U.S.S.R. 1937. 8,800 tons. 613 ft. 33 knots. 9 × 7.1 in., 16 A.A. guns. 6 torpedo tubes. 4 aircraft.

Krasni - Kavkaz — U.S.S.R. 1932. Displacement: 8,030 tons. length: 530 ft. 26 knots. 4 × 7.1 in. guns, 26 A.A. guns. 6 torpedo tubes. 100 mines. 1 aircraft.

Krasni Krim — U.S.S.R. 1925. Displacement: 6,934 tons. Length: 508 ft. 29 knots. 15 × 5.1 in., 4 × 4.7 in. and 14 A.A. guns. 6 torpedo tubes. 100 mines. 2 aircraft.

SHIPS
TODAY

A review of all types of ships in the world's fleets, from the
tug to the nuclear-powered aircraft carrier.

ONLY twenty years or so, about the same number that have
passed since the end of the Second World War, have been
enough to bring profound changes to the make-up of the world's
principal merchant and naval fleets. During the last war, hundreds of
ships, cargo and passenger, were sunk and this, coupled with growing
competition, also the need for improved efficiency – to cope with
ever rising costs – is why every country has had to face up to the
problem of the renewal of its mercantile marine, with ships which
incorporate the most up-to-date mechanical techniques, aimed at
satisfying the particular requirements of their individual trades. The
latest cargo ships are quite unrelated to the "Liberty" and "Victory"
ships mass produced by the United States during the final war years.
The oil-tankers of today are giants of ten or more times the capacity
of those of 1950. This too is the age of the specialist ship, the container
carrier, the roll-on-roll-off ferry, and the liquid gas carrier. The
passenger liners have characteristics of comfort and speed far
superior to those of 1938, yet except for those cruising or catering for
the motorist the majority are disappearing before the competition of
the jet air liners. As far as the Merchant Navy is concerned, then, we
can talk of a "new" fleet, even though some very old "tubs" are still
owned by the smaller firms and are employed in the less exacting
trades on which new and specially designed ships would be too
costly.

The change has, perhaps, been even greater as far as naval forces
are concerned – the experiences of a war conducted almost entirely
at sea; utilisation of nuclear energy whether as a deterrent or as a
motive force, progress in missile and radar techniques – all these
factors have contributed to revolutionising tactics and traditional
ideas, and inevitably condemning certain types of ships in favour of
others.

The most sensational shipping development has been the advent
of nuclear propulsion which has now been applied to many naval
vessels and a few merchant ships. It is an extremely important step
forward which, although still in its initial phase, will undoubtedly be
developed more fully in the ships of tomorrow.

THE WORLD'S NAVIES

	ARGENTINA	AUSTRALIA	BELGIUM	BRAZIL	CANADA	CHILE	CHINA, PEOPLES' REPUBLIC	DENMARK	FRANCE	GERMANY, EAST	GERMANY, WEST	GREAT BRITAIN	GREECE	INDIA
AIRCRAFT CARRIERS	I	I	—	I	I	—	—	—	3	—	—	5	—	—
COMMANDO, HELICOPTER AND OTHER CARRIERS	—	I	—	—	—	—	—	—	I	—	—	6	—	—
SUBMARINES	2	I	—	4	4	2	34	4	23	—	13	48	3	
CRUISERS	3	—	—	2	—	2	—	—	2	—	—	I	8	2
DESTROYERS	11	16	—	12	—	2	4	—	18	—	10	22	—	
FRIGATES AND CORVETTES	13	—	2	16	25	3	15	10	30	4	31	71	9	1
MINESWEEPERS AND MINELAYERS	10	6	46	4	6	—	19	34	101	109	72	107	16	
M.T.B.s AND PATROL VESSELS	9	20	—	3	4	4	267	25	14	99	70	14	16	1
MISCELLANEOUS	36	17	24	44	54	30	483	—	159	156	130	484	66	1

NAVAL FORCES

WHEN the United States and the Soviet Union introduced intercontinental missiles with atomic tests, there were many people who thought this meant the end of big traditional naval forces, and that they might be liable to find themselves, within the space of a few hours, the only surviving creatures of whole nations which had been completely razed to the ground, wrapped in a radio-active cloud. At most, the atomic missile-launching submarine might be useful, perhaps even being able to give the decisive blow for victory. Although this argument would be quite true in the case of a total nuclear war, it falls down if one refuses to believe that men can really desire to bring an end to the greater part of humanity. And so the naval forces come very much into the foreground again in that, in a traditional localised outbreak of violence, domination of the sea would be of major importance to

ensure that the vital traffic lanes remained open.

To this end, the United States have built up the largest naval force in the world. Alongside the Polaris submarines – a nuclear retaliation force – is ranged an amazing collection of aircraft-carriers, assault troop-ships, cruisers, destroyers and submarines, accompanied by numbers of auxiliary vessels to keep them supplied and operative in every part of the world. Champions of the Western World, the U.S.A. have created the only really "complete" Fleet of our times, ready to intervene at the right moment on any front from the Pacific to the Mediterranean.

Obviously every nation has its problems, connected with the position that it occupies among the other countries of the world, in relation to financial considerations and to its specific geographical situation.

The Soviet Union has the second largest

NETHERLANDS	NEW ZEALAND	NORWAY	PAKISTAN	PERU	POLAND	PORTUGAL	SPAIN	SWEDEN	TAIWAN	TURKEY	U.S.A.	U.S.S.R.	YUGOSLAVIA	THE WORLD'S NAVIES
I	—	—	—	—	—	—	—	—	—	—	28	—	—	AIRCRAFT CARRIERS
—	—	—	—	—	—	—	I	—	—	—	30	—	—	COMMANDO, HELICOPTER AND OTHER CARRIERS
6	—	15	I	4	11	3	8	22	—	10	207	400	4	SUBMARINES
2	—	—	I	2	—	—	I	I	—	—	47	20	—	CRUISERS
12	—	—	5	2	5	I	19	8	6	10	365	120	3	DESTROYERS
24	4	5	2	5	—	13	20	12	21	218	294	400	3	FRIGATES AND CORVETTES
62	4	14	8	2	19	18	25	43	15	19	73	350	41	MINESWEEPERS AND MINELAYERS
5	13	33	6	6	50	51	19	67	24	56	177	450	119	M.T.B.s AND PATROL VESSELS
40	4	15	8	30	31	60	48	64	152	16	2251	—	36	MISCELLANEOUS

fleet in the world but it does not include any aircraft-carriers – which are felt to be of no use to them in view of the proximity of her land bases. Nor do they pay much attention to surface ships, in which other countries are more advanced. The Russian Navy is primarily founded on a nucleus of 400 underwater craft – 50 of them nuclear propelled – a form of offensive weapon that is particularly to be feared.

Great Britain and France who, at the beginning of the Second World War, were the first and fifth naval powers respectively as far as tonnage went, have had to revise their ideas of reconnaissance for their Fleets, adapting them for the defence of merchant shipping from submarine attack, capable of police operations, and keeping enough ships to maintain contact with their Colonies. These fleets are smaller than in the past but much more modern and efficient, being composed of light aircraft-carriers, cruisers and fast anti-submarine craft.

Italy has rebuilt her naval forces from the ashes of war so that they are well suited to carrying out their duties of defence in the Mediterranean, within the limits of NATO, with very modern ships which are technically well advanced.

The German and Japanese Fleets are coming into being again now, with light anti-submarine craft, while the naval forces of Sweden, Holland, Norway and Denmark, like the Commonwealth countries, keep in step with the times in a continuous process of modernisation. The naval forces of other countries are all rather reduced in importance, being mainly composed of antiquated ships. More than anything, their value is for prestige and to give the countries concerned some political weight.

Today a warship costs, on an average, approximately £2,500 per ton – a frigate, therefore, costs about £6 million. No country can think of rivalling the U.S.A. and U.S.S.R. in this field. It is just, therefore, and a guarantee of peace, that every country should have naval forces in proportion to its defence needs, and that these should always be kept technically up-to-date and able to provide the first protective bulwark for their country.

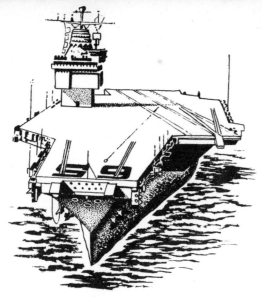

Enterprise – U.S.A. 1961. The first nuclear-powered aircraft-carrier, she is also the world's largest naval vessel. She cost more than £185 million.

AIRCRAFT CARRIERS

THE events of the morning of 7th December, 1941 at Pearl Harbour convinced even the last sceptics of the rôle that aircraft-carriers would be able to play in a modern war, when aeronautical progress had made such giant strides. The Japanese aircraft-carriers played a leading part in an event which could possibly have decided the fate of the whole war, had the three American aircraft-carriers of the Pacific Fleet not escaped the attack and been able to form the basis on which the beginning of the great counter-attack was to rest.

The Second World War fully revealed the uses of this type of ship which had, up till then, been regarded as the eye of the armoured squadrons, which were barely necessary. In fact, the aircraft-carrier was a means of attack which, on the open sea, was more deadly than the battleship; it was a defence in the struggle against submarines; and it was a mobile base for the support aircraft in landing operations. And so it became the queen of the fleets, dethroning the great gun bearing battleships.

In the post-War period, after the Korean episode, the aircraft-carrier's pre-eminent position in the United States Fleet was reinforced by the presence on board of jet-bombers, capable of dropping atom bombs within a radius of 1,500 miles. In the case of surprise attack, aircraft-carriers on the open sea were in a much better position to act as a base for reprisal action. When atomic submarines came into service, equipped with intercontinental missiles, this tactical function of the aircraft-carrier was still valid. Today it has completely taken the place of the battleship, with its ability to drop vastly superior explosives on the enemy at a much greater distance, by means of its aircraft, than ever the 16 inch gun could do, and it guarantees a mobile air force which is ready to intervene even at the other end of the world from its departure base.

The American aircraft-carriers in ser-

Foch – France 1963. The *Foch* and *Clemenceau* are the first aircraft-carriers designed and built entirely in France. They are examples of the light, attack type. Displacement: 22,000 tons. Length: 845 ft. overall. Speed: 32 knots. Max. fuel range: 7,500 miles (at 18 knots). Aircraft: 30. Armament: 8 × 3·9 in. guns; catapults: 2. Crew: 2,700.

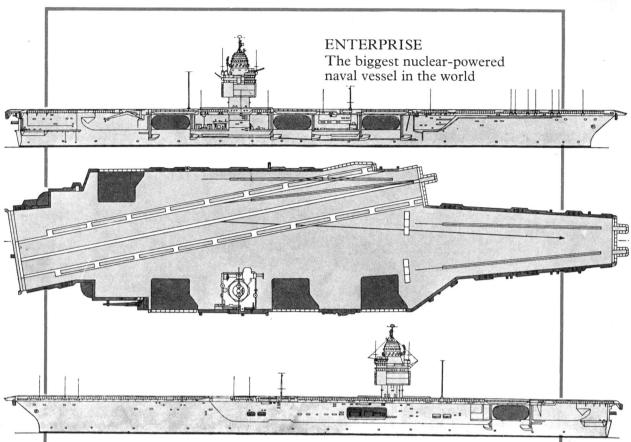

ENTERPRISE
The biggest nuclear-powered
naval vessel in the world

Enterprise – U.S.A. 1961. The biggest naval vessel in the world, seen from both sides and from above. Displacement: 75,700 tons. Length: 1,102 ft. Engines: geared turbines and 8 Westinghouse nuclear reactors. Speed 35 knots. Maximum endurance: 5 years at sea. Aircraft: 100. Armament: 4 Terrier guided missile launchers. Catapults: 4. Crew: 4,300. Builders: Newport News Shipyard. Estimated cost about £158 million.

vice today – almost all built after the War – are all either for attack or to give support, and one of them is nuclear-powered. The *Enterprise,* the biggest naval vessel in the world, is a veritable floating city, with a crew of 4,600 men and more than 100 aircraft. She can be at sea for five consecutive years without refuelling. Her generators supply enough electricity for a city of 200,000 people; her kitchens serve 12,000 meals every day; her laundries deal with 10,000 tons of washing every year.

The aircraft-carriers of the *Kitty Hawk* and *Forrestal* Class are not much smaller. American aircraft-carriers are all modern or have been brought up-to-date and are very efficient. Some of the old style carriers have been put on to other duties such as

executive command or as transport ships for assault troops. Only Britain and France can boast light attack aircraft-carriers that are of any importance and really efficient. The ships of the Argentine, Australia, Brazil, Canada and Holland are all former British carriers of the *Colossus* and *Majestic* Classes, built in the period from 1943-1950. Even though they have been modernised, they feel the weight of their years and cannot compare with the much larger and more powerful American aircraft-carriers.

In the naval forces of today, aircraft-carriers remain the strong point on which, in the case of hostilities breaking out, would rest the bulk of the actions over the widest possible area.

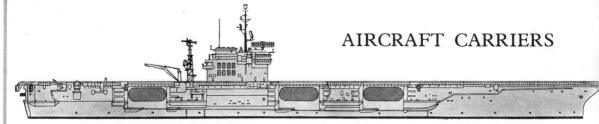

Kitty Hawk – U.S.A. 1961. Sister ship to the **Constellation.** The biggest traditionally propelled aircraft-carrier. Displacement: 60,000 tons. Length: 1,047 ft. overall. Speed: 36 knots. Aircraft: 90. Armament: 4 Terrier guided missile launchers, catapults: 4. Crew: 4,155. Builders: New York S.B. Corporation.

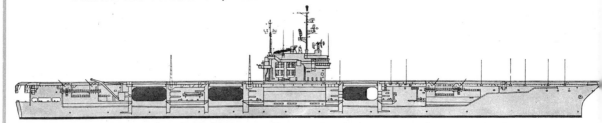

Forrestal – U.S.A. 1955. The same Class as the **Independence, Ranger** and **Saratoga.** Displacement: 59,650 tons. Length: 1,046 ft. overall. Speed: 35 knots. Aircraft: 90. Armament: 4 × 5 in. dual purpose guns, catapults: 4. Crew: 3,360. The **Forrestal** and her sister ships were the first aircraft-carriers to be put on the stocks in the U.S.A. after the War.

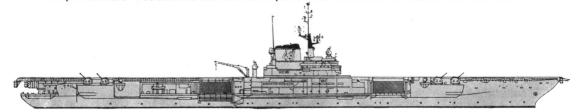

Coral Sea – U.S.A. 1947. She was laid down on 10th July, 1944, entered into service in 1947 and was employed in Korea. In 1957 she went back to the shipyards for radical modernisation. Displacement: 52,500 tons. Length: 968 ft. overall. Speed: 33 knots. Aircraft: 80. Armament: 3 × 5 in. guns. Catapults: 3. Crew: 3,960.

Franklin D. Roosevelt – U.S.A. 1945. Sister ship of the **Midway.** Went into service after the end of the War. From 1954-1960 they underwent modernisation that included the installation of an angled flight-deck. Displacement: 51,000 tons. 968 ft. overall. Speed: 33 knots. Reputed endurance: 15,000 miles. Aircraft: 80. Armament: 4 × 5 in. guns, catapults: 3. Crew: 3,550.

Essex – U.S.A. 1942. Over 20 aircraft-carriers of this Class were built during the War. Displacement: 30,800 tons. Length: 888 ft. overall. Speed: 33 knots. Reputed endurance: 18,000 miles. Aircraft: 46. Armament: 8 × 127 m.m. guns, catapults: 2. Crew: 3,230.

Boxer – U.S.A. 1945. **Essex** Class – was converted into an LPH (amphibious assault-helicopter-carrier). Displacement: 30,800 tons. Length: 888 ft. Speed: 33 knots. Reputed endurance: 18,000 miles. Helicopters: 30. Armament: 6 × 5 in. guns. Crew: 1000 plus helicopter crews and 1,500 landing team.

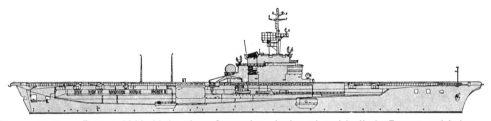

Clemenceau – France 1961. Light aircraft-carrier, designed and built in France, with her sister ship, the **Foch,** equipped with special radar systems to guide fighter-planes. Displacement: 22,000 tons. Length: 845 ft. overall. Speed: 32 knots. Endurance: 7,500 miles. Aircraft: 30. Armament: 8 × 3·9 in. guns, catapults: 2. Crew: 2,700.

Ark Royal – Gt. Britain 1955. The largest aircraft-carrier in the Royal Navy, designed for jet fighters and bombers. Displacement: 43,340 tons. Length: 810 ft. overall. Speed: 31·5 knots. Aircraft: 40 plus 8 helicopters. Armament: 4 × 5 in. and 14 anti-aircraft guns, catapults: 2. Crew: 2,300. Builders: Cammell Laird.

Victorious – Gt. Britain 1941/1958. She went into service in 1941 with the **Illustrious** and **Formidable.** Displacement: 30,530 tons. Length: 781 ft. overall. Speed: 31 knots. Aircraft: 25, plus 10 helicopters. Armament: 8 × 3 in. guns, catapults: 2. Crew: 2,400. She was built by Vickers-Armstrongs and rebuilt at Portsmouth.

Karel Doorman – Netherlands 1945/58. She was bought from Britain by the Low Countries in 1948 and completely modernised. Displacement: 15,892 tons. Length: 693 ft. Speed: 24 knots. Aircraft: 21. Armament: 10 × 40 mm. A.A. guns, catapults: 1. Crew: 1,460.

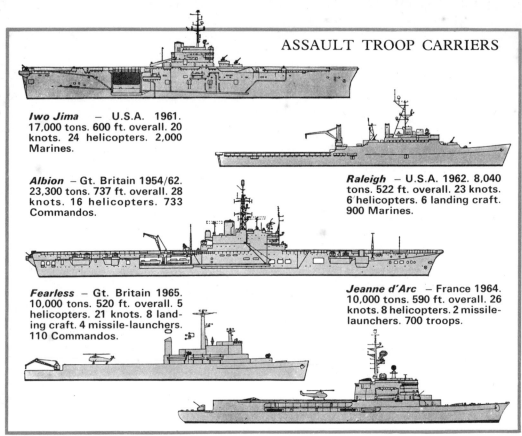

Iwo Jima – U.S.A. 1961. 17,000 tons. 600 ft. overall. 20 knots. 24 helicopters. 2,000 Marines.

Albion – Gt. Britain 1954/62. 23,300 tons. 737 ft. overall. 28 knots. 16 helicopters. 733 Commandos.

Raleigh – U.S.A. 1962. 8,040 tons. 522 ft. overall. 23 knots. 6 helicopters. 6 landing craft. 900 Marines.

Fearless – Gt. Britain 1965. 10,000 tons. 520 ft. overall. 5 helicopters. 21 knots. 8 landing craft. 4 missile-launchers. 110 Commandos.

Jeanne d'Arc – France 1964. 10,000 tons. 590 ft. overall. 26 knots. 8 helicopters. 2 missile-launchers. 700 troops.

ASSAULT TROOP CARRIERS

TWO new types of ship have emerged in recent years, first in the United States naval forces and then in the British and French. These are the "amphibious assault troop helicopter-carrier" and the "amphibious dock assault troop-carrier".

The first is either a modified aircraft-carrier or ship which has been specially designed to carry out a new duty – that of transporting large numbers of Marines or assault troops to wherever they may be needed, likewise their armament, equipment and heavy guns; all being off-loaded from ship to land by means of a big transport helicopter. These new ships are equipped to offer to the parachute troops, and others to be transported by air, much greater comfort than the old vessels and, above all, are capable of effecting the landing of both men and materials in the minimum of time, even when denied normal port facilities.

The amphibious dock transport ship has the same features as the helicopter carrier landing the troops in the traditional way of the Second World War, but with the landing craft stowed in the ship's internal dock, protected from possible enemy fire and from bad weather at sea. The United States' ships of the *Raleigh* class and those of the British *Fearless* class are of this second type. The former are equipped with six heavy helicopters and six landing-craft for 900, including the crew.

In this chapter we have linked up the helicopter-carriers (of which the U.S.A. already have six in service, the British two and the French one) with the amphibious dock transport ships because they have both been produced for the same ends – the transportation and well-timed landing of a force to intervene promptly wherever necessity demands it. The centres of localised war that smoulder in different corners of the world have taught the advisability of adopting these new types of ships, which were, perhaps, suggested by the bitter experiences of the Korean War.

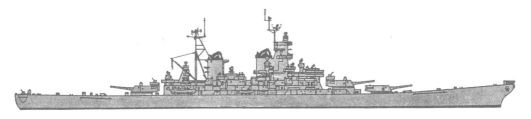

Iowa – U.S.A. 1943. The *Missouri, Wisconsin* and *New Jersey* were of the same Class. The last big American battleships (they took part in the final episodes of the Second World War) are in reserve. Displacement: 45,000 tons. Length: 887 ft. Speed: 33 knots. Armament: 9 × 16 in., 20 × 5 in., 130 A.A. guns. Crew: 2,700. Built by the New York Navy Yard.

BATTLESHIPS

THE last four battleships in the world – the giant *Iowa, Missouri, Wisconsin* and *New Jersey* – once the pride of the U.S. Navy – are waiting in a Pacific port to be condemned by the authorities for breaking up. And so the last examples of this type of ship will disappear – those "ships of the line" which were direct descendants of the *Dreadnought* of 1906 which, up to the Second World War, were considered the mainstay of every fleet, a determining element in sea warfare.

Their end has been brought about by the progress of aviation, linked with that of ship-building which has brought about the development of aircraft-carriers. The battleship with its 16 inch guns was once the only vessel which could fire 9 tons of explosive a distance of 25 miles. But today an aircraft-carrier's bombers can drop 100 tons of conventional explosive, apart from atomic bombs, up to a distance of 1,000 miles. There is no comparison!

Although the first mortal blow was inflicted to the battleship – very expensive and heavy, but a sadly easy target – by the aircraft-carrier in the Second World War, it was the new missile techniques that gave her the *coup de grâce*. Today a small missile-firing cruiser of only 6,000 tons has a deterrent power which is probably greater than the biggest battleship in the world with its 18 in. guns and perhaps a 100 smaller guns. Forty bombs and 18 aerial torpedoes were loaded aboard American aircraft-carriers to sink the great *Yamato*, which was regarded as invulnerable. With her, the concept of the big-gunship disappeared among the waves.

The battleship was responsible for many pages of glorious history – it was the symbol of sea-power. Its last shots were fired by the *Iowa* and her sister ship at Wonsan during the Korean War. Now it has gone, overtaken by the new techniques of the men who created it but not conquered by the sea over which the battleship reigned as queen for 50 years.

Missouri – U.S.A. 1944. The most perfect realisation of the concept of a battleship, with her 9 × 16 in. guns with a range of 23 miles and 130 A.A. guns. It was on board this ship that the Japanese surrender was signed; she marks the end of an epoch and of a type of warfare.

CRUISERS

THE old sailing ships were in the habit of using frigates to carry out reconnaissance duties to ascertain the size, route and speed of the enemy's fleets. After steam arrived, the same duties were entrusted to smaller and faster ships than the great "iron clads" – the cruisers. Already at the end of the last century, they were carrying out raids, pursuing merchant ships, and engaging in reconnaissance operations often far from base.

The armament and tonnage of the cruiser gradually increased until it became the most powerful and fastest ship in the squadron, after the battleship. The first to use cruisers in combat as ships of the line were the Japanese in their wars with China and Russia.

At the outbreak of the Second World War this type of ship had come a long way from its original form, so much so that it could under certain conditions stand up to a battleship. The pocket battleship *Admiral Graf Spee* was damaged by three British cruisers and her crew had no alternative than to scuttle her. In 1940/45, cruisers carried armament comparable to that of a regiment of artillery and their covering fire for landing parties was very valuable, if not the decisive factor.

Now that battleships have faded out, cruisers are the biggest attack ships in surface fleets, after the aircraft-carrier. The progress of missiles has produced the result that, although only of modest tonnage (from 6,000 to 17,000 tons), it has a deterrent power greater than that of the old-time ship of the line.

Today the cruiser is fully evolved and two principal categories can actually be defined among ships of this type: missile-launching and those with conventional armament. The missile-launching cruisers, in their turn, are divided between those that have already come off the stocks like the ones mentioned and those which have been converted from conventional cruisers. Up to now, there are only 2 of the first kind – the *Long Beach*, nuclear powered, of the U.S. Navy, and the *Andrea Doria* of the Italian Marina Militare.

The *Long Beach* was the first cruiser to be put on the stocks in America's shipyards after the end of the Second World War, besides being the first U.S. surface vessel with a range of 100,000 miles without re-fuelling. A powerful offensive ship, it is reckoned that she is also able to repel any attack that may come from the sky or from the depths of the sea, due to the variety of surface-surface, surface-air and surface-depth missiles with which she is armed. It is enough to say that her Terrier anti-aircraft missiles – more than 30 ft. long – are fitted with radar and with a special electronic apparatus which is capable of guiding them to a flying target up to 20 miles away and to an altitude of 12 miles. This

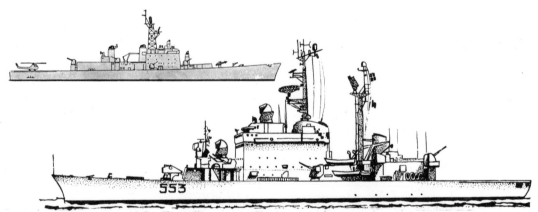

Andrea Doria – Italy 1964. First missile-launching escort cruiser to have been designed specifically as such, the *Andrea Doria* was built in Europe. She entered service in 1964 alongside her sister ship – *Caio Duilio*. Displacement: 6,000 tons. Length: 483 ft. overall. Speed 31 knots. Armament: 2 launchers for Terrier missiles; 8 × 3 in. A.A. guns. 6 torpedo tubes. 6 rocket-launchers. 4 helicopters. Crew: 450. Built by the Tirreno Shipyards.

Albany – U.S.A. 1946/59. A typical example of a heavy cruiser produced with traditional armament and converted into a missile-launcher. Unlike other ships – the *Canberra* and *Boston,* for example, in which the modification has been only partial – in the *Albany* her turrets with triple 8 in. guns have all disappeared, their places having been taken by launching apparatus for Talos and Tartar missiles. The anti-submarine equipment has also been brought up to date.

ship, which cost $339 million has, as her sole traditional weapons, two 5 inch guns! The *Andrea Doria,* a much smaller ship, is an example of a missile-launching escort cruiser, and three other ships will be lined up with her, two of which will be of greater tonnage. Their armament comprises: Terrier; anti-submarine torpedo-tube; rocket-launcher and 8 × 3 in. guns in single turrets.

All the other missile-launching cruisers in service in the United States, Italian, Dutch and Russian Fleets are converted ships. The United States have 11 missile-launchers apart from the *Long Beach,* most of which carry conventional armament as well as missiles. As for the Soviet Union, a few of their *Sverdlov* Class cruisers were experimentally converted into missile-launchers. There is no doubt that Russia, too, is currently in the process of modernis-

ing her traditional ships and building up a missile launching fleet.

Already the non-missile-launching cruisers can be regarded as out-of-date. All the same, the United States has some 13 heavy, and three light cruisers of this type, all of which were launched after 1945; Great Britain has one (not used as such) and France has two anti-aircraft cruisers. The ships of the Argentinian, Brazilian, Chilian, Greek, Indian, New Zealand, Pakistani, Peruvian and Spanish Fleets are all surplus from the Second World War – completely out-of-date by now.

The cruiser-type ship of tomorrow's fleets will chiefly, if not exclusively, be missile-launchers. When the transformation is complete, it will be possible to regard this category of ship as a worthy heir to the duties which, for the most part, were once entrusted to the doughty battleship.

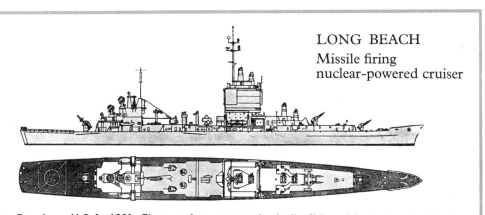

LONG BEACH
Missile firing
nuclear-powered cruiser

Long Beach – U.S.A. 1961. First nuclear-powered missile-firing ship in the world. Displacement: 14,200 tons. Length: 721 ft. Machinery: 4 Westinghouse nuclear reactors driving steam turbines. Speed: 30 knots. Armament: 6 missile-launchers, 1 rocket-launcher, 6 torpedo tubes. Crew: 960. Builders: Bethlehem Yard, Quincy.

MISSILE-LAUNCHING CRUISERS

De Zeven Provincien—Netherlands 1953. 9,529 tons. 609 ft. overall. 32 knots. 8 × 6 in. 16 A.A. guns. 2 Terrier missile-launchers. Crew: 848.

Giuseppe Garibaldi — Italy 1937/62. 9,800 tons. 613 ft. overall. 31 knots. 4 × 5·3 in., 8 × 3 in. A.A. guns. 2 Terrier and Polaris missile-launchers.

Albany — U.S.A. 1946/62. **Oregon** Class. 13,700 tons. 746 ft. overall. 34 knots. 2 × 5 in. guns. 6 missile-launchers. 1 rocket-launcher. 2 helicopters.

Little Rock — U.S.A. 1945/60. 10,670 tons. 610 ft. overall. 33 knots. 3 × 6 in., 2 × 5 in. guns, 2 missile-launchers. Built by Cramp Shipyard.

Canberra — U.S.A. 1943/56. 13,300 tons. 673 ft. overall. 34 knots. 6 × 8 in., 10 × 5 in., 12 × 3 in. A.A. guns. 4 Terrier missile-launchers.

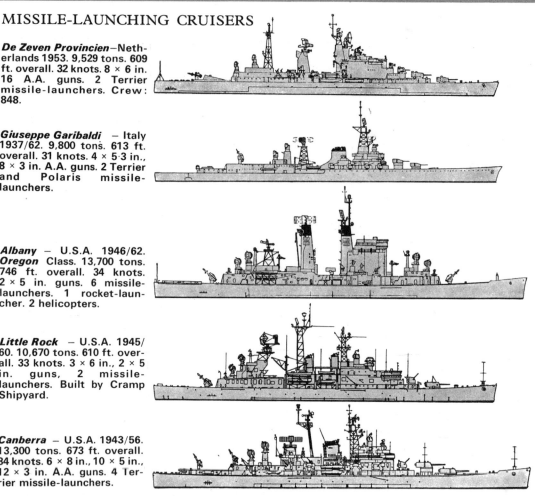

CRUISERS WITH TRADITIONAL ARMAMENT

Sverdlov — U.S.S.R. 1951/60. 15,450 tons. 689 ft. overall. 34 knots. 12 × 6 in., 12 × 3·9 in., 32 A.A. guns. 10 torpedo tubes. 250 mines.

Colbert — France 1959. 8,720 tons. 597 ft. overall. 32 knots. 16 × 5 in. and 20 smaller A.A. guns. 1 helicopter. Used as fleet command vessel.

Newport News — U.S.A. 1949. Heavy cruiser. 17,000 tons. 717 ft. overall. 33 knots. Armament: 9 × 8 in., 12 × 5 in., 16 × 3 in. guns. 1 helicopter. Crew: 1,668.

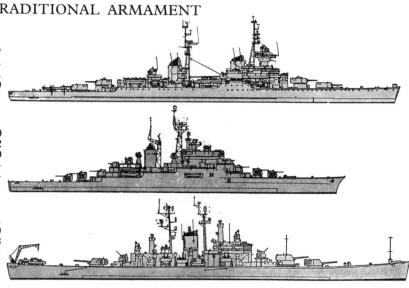

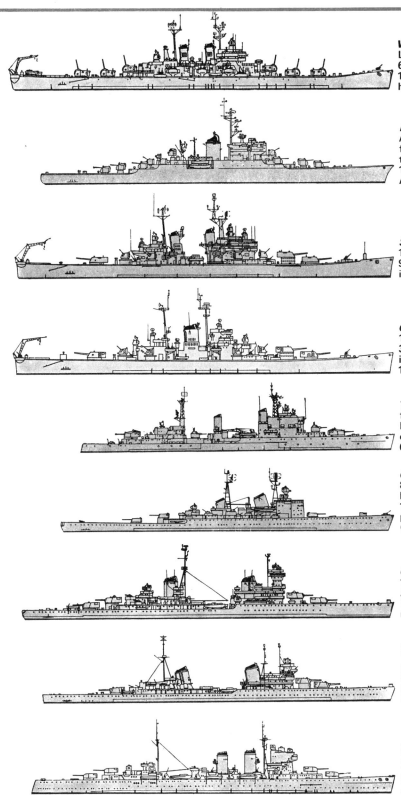

Worcester – U.S.A. 1948. Light cruiser. 14,700 tons. 679 ft. overall. 32 knots. 12 × 6 in., 24 × 3 in. guns. 1 helicopter. Crew: 1,700.

De Grasse – France 1955. Anti-aircraft type, used as a fleet command vessel. 9,380 tons. 617 ft. 33·5 knots. 16 × 5 in. and 12 smaller A.A. guns.

St. Paul – U.S.A. 1945. 13,600 tons. 673 ft. 34 knots. 9 × 8 in., 12 × 5 in., 14 × 3 in. guns. 1 helicopter.

Oregon City – U.S.A. 1946. 13,700 tons. 673 ft. overall. 33 knots. Armament: 9 × 8 in., 12 × 5 in. 20 × 3 in. guns. 1 helicopter. Crew: 1,750.

Tiger – Gt. Britain 1959. The final cruisers built for Royal Navy. 9,550 tons. 555 ft. overall. 31 knots. 4 × 6 in., 6 × 3 in. guns. Crew: 716.

Gota Lejon – Sweden 1947. 8,200 tons. 597 ft. overall. 33 knots. Armament: 7 × 6 in., 15 smaller A.A. guns. 6 torpedo tubes. 120 mines. Crew: 610.

Chapaev – U.S.S.R. 1950. 11,500 tons. 656 ft. 35 knots. Armament: 12 × 6 in., 8 × 4 in., 28 smaller A.A. guns. 200 mines.

Maxim Gorki – U.S.S.R. 1940. 8,800 tons. 626 ft. overall. 34 knots. 9 × 7·1 in., 8 × 4 in. A.A. 6 smaller A.A. guns. 6 torpedo tubes. 90 mines.

Canarias – Spain 1936. Modernised in 1953. 10,670 tons. 636 ft. 33 knots. 8 × 8 in., 8 × 4·7 in., 15 smaller A.A. guns. Crew: 948

DESTROYERS

AT the end of the 19th century, a new type of ship was created in Britain to oppose the torpedo-boat, the torpedo-boat destroyer. With the advent of the submarine and the aeroplane, and the decline of the torpedo-boat, its functions changed and it became known simply as a "destroyer". It would have been more appropriate simply to have officially defined it as a pursuit craft.

Since the First World War, destroyers were expected to operate against submarines and, in the Second World War, they had to carry out the most varied missions, making themselves quite indispensable in escortng Naval squadrons and convoys.

In the current situation, too, it is the destroyer that is mainly relied on for escort duties. The adoption of surface-air missiles and of anti-submarine torpedoes with automatic warheads has enormously increased the destroyer's usefulness which, ideally, must have a wide, full range, be capable of holding her own in any sea, be fitted with versatile armament and be able to stand up to all the different types of attack that are now possible. Today, destroyers are ideally suited as flotilla leaders, missile-launchers, radar duty vessels, anti-aircraft and anti-submarine-ships. Their tonnage ranges from a maximum of 7,600 to a minimum of 2,000 tons or just under, but the most suitable tonnage is held by some to be around 5,000 tons for flotilla leaders and 3,000 tons for the other purposes.

To be fully functional, modern destroyers should be missile-launchers and the fleets of the United States, Britain, Italy, France and Russia are already equipped with these. They are all ships

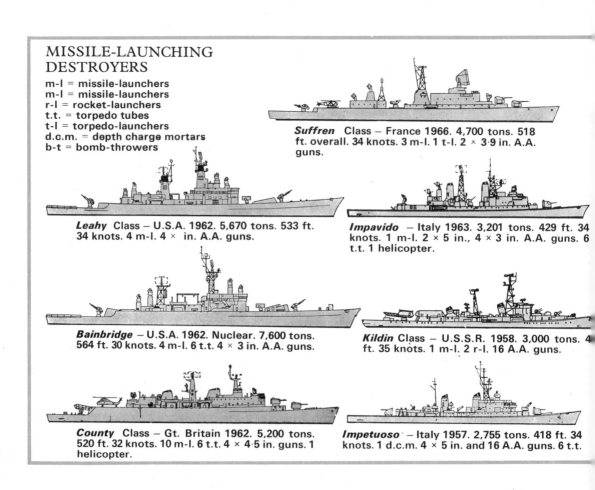

MISSILE-LAUNCHING DESTROYERS

m-l = missile-launchers
m-l = missile-launchers
r-l = rocket-launchers
t.t. = torpedo tubes
t-l = torpedo-launchers
d.c.m. = depth charge mortars
b-t = bomb-throwers

Suffren Class – France 1966. 4,700 tons. 518 ft. overall. 34 knots. 3 m-l. 1 t-l. 2 × 3·9 in. A.A. guns.

Leahy Class – U.S.A. 1962. 5,670 tons. 533 ft. 34 knots. 4 m-l. 4 × in. A.A. guns.

Impavido – Italy 1963. 3,201 tons. 429 ft. 34 knots. 1 m-l. 2 × 5 in., 4 × 3 in. A.A. guns. 6 t.t. 1 helicopter.

Bainbridge – U.S.A. 1962. Nuclear. 7,600 tons. 564 ft. 30 knots. 4 m-l. 6 t.t. 4 × 3 in. A.A. guns.

Kildin Class – U.S.S.R. 1958. 3,000 tons. 4 ft. 35 knots. 1 m-l. 2 r-l. 16 A.A. guns.

County Class – Gt. Britain 1962. 5,200 tons. 520 ft. 32 knots. 10 m-l. 6 t.t. 4 × 4·5 in. guns. 1 helicopter.

Impetuoso – Italy 1957. 2,755 tons. 418 ft. 34 knots. 1 d.c.m. 4 × 5 in. and 16 A.A. guns. 6 t.t.

Krupnyi – U.S.S.R. 1961. One of 12 in Class. 3,650 tons. Length: 453 ft. Speed: 34 knots. Armament: 2 missile-launchers, 16 A.A. guns. 6 torpedo-launchers.

which have been launched in the last few years and one of them, the *Bainbridge* is nuclear powered and belongs to the U.S. Navy. In practice, the destroyer of today may well take the place of the cruiser in the future. It seems that the British Navy may already be tending this way as they have several ships of this type on the stocks in the shipyards and no missile-launching cruisers.

The U.S.S.R. have fitted their *Krupnyi* Class destroyers with surface-to-surface missiles because they can be a means of attack not only against submarines and aircraft but also for big surface vessels. Nevertheless the majority of destroyers today in service in the world's fleets are still ships that took part in the Second World War, when they unequivocally revealed their amazing operative adaptability.

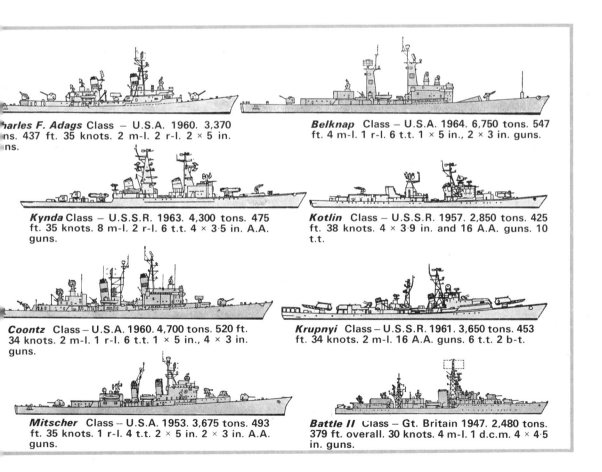

harles F. Adags Class – U.S.A. 1960. 3,370 ns. 437 ft. 35 knots. 2 m-l. 2 r-l. 2 × 5 in. ns.

Belknap Class – U.S.A. 1964. 6,750 tons. 547 ft. 4 m-l. 1 r-l. 6 t.t. 1 × 5 in., 2 × 3 in. guns.

Kynda Class – U.S.S.R. 1963. 4,300 tons. 475 ft. 35 knots. 8 m-l. 2 r-l. 6 t.t. 4 × 3·5 in. A.A. guns.

Kotlin Class – U.S.S.R. 1957. 2,850 tons. 425 ft. 38 knots. 4 × 3·9 in. and 16 A.A. guns. 10 t.t.

Coontz Class – U.S.A. 1960. 4,700 tons. 520 ft. 34 knots. 2 m-l. 1 r-l. 6 t.t. 1 × 5 in., 4 × 3 in. guns.

Krupnyi Class – U.S.S.R. 1961. 3,650 tons. 453 ft. 34 knots. 2 m-l. 16 A.A. guns. 6 t.t. 2 b-t.

Mitscher Class – U.S.A. 1953. 3,675 tons. 493 ft. 35 knots. 1 r-l. 4 t.t. 2 × 5 in. 2 × 3 in. A.A. guns.

Battle II Class – Gt. Britain 1947. 2,480 tons. 379 ft. overall. 30 knots. 4 m-l. 1 d.c.m. 4 × 4·5 in. guns.

DESTROYERS

St. Laurent Class – Canada 1957. 2,263 tons. 363 ft. 28 knots.

Mackenzie Class – Canada 1962. 2,366 tons. 366 ft. 28 knots. 4 × 3 in. guns.

Hamburg Class – W. Germany 1964. 3,340 tons. 439 ft. 35 knots. 7 torpedo tubes.

Ayanami Class – Japan 1958. 1,700 tons. 357 ft. 32 knots. 4 torpedo tubes.

Duperre Class – France 1957. 2,750 tons. 422 ft. 34 knots. 6 torpedo tubes.

Daring Class – Gt. Britain 1952. 2,800 tons. 390 ft. 30 knots. 5 torpedo tubes.

Friesland Class – Netherlands 1956. 2,497 tons. 380 ft. 36 knots.

Halland – Sweden 1955. 2,650 tons. 397 ft. 35 knots. 8 torpedo tubes.

Oquendo Class – Spain 1956. 3,496 tons. 391 ft. 38 knots. 6 torpedo tubes.

Forrest Sherman Class – U.S.A. 1956. 2,850 tons. 418 ft. 33 knots. 6 torpedo tubes.

Fletcher Class – U.S.A. 1942. 2,080 tons. 376 ft. 34 knots.

Gleaves Class – U.S.A. 1940. 1,700 tons. 348 ft. 34 knots. 5 torpedo tubes.

Allan W. Sumner Class – U.S.A. 1943. 58 ships. 2,200 tons. 376 ft. 33 knots. 8 torpedo tubes.

Gearing Class – U.S.A. 1944. 2,425 tons. 390 ft. 35 knots. 6 torpedo-launchers.

Kotling Class – U.S.S.R. 1957. 2,850 tons. 425 ft. 36 knots. 10 torpedo tubes.

Neustrashimyi – U.S.S.R. 1955. 3,200 tons. 433 ft. 38 knots. 10 torpedo tubes.

Skoryi Class – U.S.S.R. 1954. 2,600 tons. 420 ft. 36 knots. 10 torpedo tubes.

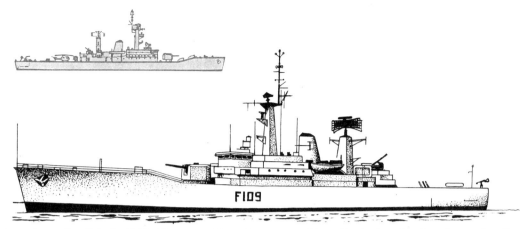

Leander – Gt. Britain 1963. Nineteen ships of the same Class. Typical anti-submarine and anti-aircraft frigate, built by Harland & Wolff, Belfast. Displacement: 2,250 tons. Length: 372 ft. overall. Speed: 30 knots. Armament: 1 quadruple Seacat A.A. missile-launcher; 1 three-barrelled depth charge thrower; 2 × 4·5 in. guns. Helicopters: 1 anti-submarine. Crew: 262.

FRIGATES AND CORVETTES

THE name "frigate" describes naval escort vessels, ships which are generally not unlike destroyers but which, nevertheless, do have a lower tonnage. Usually the biggest frigates do not exceed a displacement of 2,500 tons and do not go below 1,000 tons. Among ships of this type that have recently come into service are, for example, the British ones of the *Leander* Class, 2,300 tons, and the Italian ones of the *Bergamini* Class, 1,410 tons.

In practice, these ships are specifically designed for escorting convoys and so are mainly equipped with anti-submarine armament. Most of the more modern ones also carry one or two helicopters – valuable in sighting and pursuing under-water craft. Some frigates, on the other hand, are for general purposes, that is, both anti-submarine and anti-aircraft, besides radar look-out ships fitted with radar equipment to guide escort fighter planes.

This type of ship has developed a lot since the Second World War to meet the needs of merchant shipping for protection in case of war. In the event of a nuclear war, ships in convoy would have to travel at great distances apart to avoid becoming a single objective for an atomic attack – this would mean a great increase in the numbers of escort vessels needed on anti-submarine patrol.

Corvettes are similar in concept to destroyers but much smaller and suited to coastal escort work. Both in frigates and in corvettes, the torpedo-tubes are mainly for anti-submarine work, that is, they are suitable for launching homing torpedoes – really awe-inspiring offensive weapons against submarines.

Köln – West Germany 1958. Displacement: 2,100 tons. Length: 357 ft. overall. Speed: 32 knots. Armament: 2 × 3·9 in., 6 smaller A.A. guns, 2 anti-submarine torpedo tubes, 2 depth charge mortars. The *Köln* is an anti-submarine frigate and convoy escort vessel. Diesel and gas turbine machinery.

FRIGATES

t.t. = torpedo tubes
b-t = bomb-throwers
d.c.m. = depth charge mortars
t-l = torpedo-launchers
r-l = rocket-launchers

Commandant Riviere Class – France 1962. 1,750 tons. 334 ft. 25 knots. 3 × 3·9 in. guns. 6 t.t. 1 helicopter.

L'Alsacien – France 1956, 1,295 tons. 327 ft. 27 knots. 12 t.t. 2 b-t.

Centauro Class – Italy 1957. 1,680 tons. 339 ft. 26 knots. 2 t.t. 4 b-t. 4 × 3 in. guns.

Alpino – Italy 1965. 2,000 tons. 371 ft. 28 knots. 6 × 3 in. guns. 6 t.t. 1 d.c.m. 2 helicopters.

Isuzu Class – Japan 1961. 1,490 tons. 308 ft. 25 knots. 4 × 3 in. guns. 4 tt.. 2 t-l. 1 r-l.

Bergamini Class – Italy 1961. 1,410 tons. 308 ft. 24 knots. 3 × 3 in. guns. 6 t.t. 1 b-t. 1 helicopter.

Tribal Class – Gt. Britain 1961. 2,300 tons. 360 ft. 28 knots. 2 × 4·5 in. guns. 1 helicopter.

Rothesay Class – Gt. Britain 1960. 2,150 tons. 369 ft. 30 knots. 2 × 4·5 in. guns. 2 d.c.m. 12 t.t.

Leopard Class – Gt. Britain 1957. 2,300 tons. 339 ft. 25 knots 4 × 4·5 in. guns. 1 × 1½ in. d.c.m.

Salisbury Class – Gt. Britain 1958. 2,170 tons. 339 ft. 25 knots. 2 × 4·5 in, 2 A.A. guns.

Garcia Class – U.S.A. 1965 on. 2,624 tons. 414 ft. 27 knots. 2 × 5 in. guns. 6 t.t.

John C. Butler Class – U.S.A. 1944. 1,350 tons. 306 ft. 24 knots. 2 × 5 in., 2 × 1·5 in. A.A. guns. 1 or 2 d.c.m.

Buckley Class – U.S.A. 1943. 1,400 tons. 306 ft. 24 knots. 3 × 3 in., 8 × 1½ in. guns. 6 t.t.

Edsall Class – U.S.A. 1943. 1,200 tons. 306 ft. 21 knots. 3 × 3 in., 12 smaller guns. 8 b-t.

Bostwick Class – U.S.A. 1943. 1,240 tons. 306 ft. 20 knots. 3 × 3 in., 2 × 1½ in. guns. 3 t.t.

Kola – U.S.S.R. 1946. 1,500 tons. 305 ft. 31 knots. 4 × 3·9 in. guns. 3 t.t.

Riga Class – U.S.S.R. 1955. 1,200 tons. 295 ft. 28 knots. 3 × 3·9 in. guns. 3 t.t. 4 d.c.m.

MINELAYERS AND MINESWEEPERS

IT is calculated that more than 500,000 mines were laid by the various belligerent countries in the waters around the European coasts in the course of the Second World War and their effects were not long in making themselves felt. Mines sank more shipping than did submarines and aircraft put together.

In order to lay these devices, of which many types exist – contact, magnetic, acoustic, limpet, etc. – the countries involved in the War made use of every means, from aircraft to destroyers, from fishing-boats to submarines, besides ships which were especially equipped for the purpose like the British *Manxman* and the American *Terror*.

An equally important problem for every Fleet was the cleaning up of the seas on which their ships had to pass. During the War, the British used no less than 1,300 minesweepers and the Germans 3,000. These ships (sometimes called the "little sea-brushes") have had to be employed after the end of the War, to try and rid the seas of these constant hazards to shipping. Today all naval forces are equipped with squadrons of minesweepers – ships which are more or less modern but which are still ready to go into action because, in the event of a conventional war, the mine will still be a deadly weapon.

Manxman – Gt. Britain 1940. Minelayer of Second World War. Displacement: 3,000 tons. Length: 418 ft. Speed: originally 40 knots. Armament: now 6 × 1½ in. guns and 50 mines. Crew: 240.

Terror – U.S.A. 1942. Now Fleet minelayer. Displacement: 5,875 tons. Length: 454 ft. Speed: 20 knots. Armament: 4 × 5 in., 24 × 1½ in. guns. 800 mines. Crew: 400.

MINESWEEPERS

Falster – Denmark 1963. 1,800 tons. 252 ft. 16·5 knots. 4 × 3 in. guns. 400 mines.

Algerine Class – Gt. Britain 1942. 1,040 tons. 225 ft. 16·5 knots. 1 × 4 in. gun.

Bredsker – Sweden 1940. 450 tons. 187 ft. 17 knots. 1 × 4·1 in., 1 × 1½ in. guns.

Agile Class – U.S.A. 1955. 665 tons. 171 ft. 15·5 knots. 1 × 1½ in. gun.

Admirable Class – U.S.A. 1943. 650 tons. 184 ft. 15 knots. 1 × 3 in. gun.

Ability Class – U.S.A. 1957. 801 tons. 189 ft. 15 knots. 1 × 1½ in. gun.

T 58 Class U.S.S.R. 1959. 600 tons. 220 ft. 18 knots. 4 × 1·8 in. guns.

T 43 Class – U.S.S.R. 1959. 500 tons. 200 ft. 18 knots. 4 × 1·45 in. guns.

Fugas Class – U.S.S.R. 1938. 441 tons. 203 ft. 18 knots. 1 × 3·9 in. gun.

Nautilus – U.S.A. 1955. First nuclear-propelled submarine in the world. On 3rd August, 1958 it reached the North Pole under water, having navigated under a 100 ft. thick ice-cap. From Alaska she reached Greenland, opening up a new way between the Pacific and the Atlantic.

SUBMARINES

IN 1955 the first real "sub-marine" made its appearance with the nuclear propelled *Nautilus* – a ship specifically built to operate while submerged and even able to stay down for very long periods. Prior to the Second World War it was necessary to surface to recharge the diesel batteries of the electric motors for underwater work, and it was only possible to remain submerged for a relatively short time.

The submarine's evolution has been completed with the *Nautilus* – only 60 years from the advent of this type of craft. In two world wars, the submarine showed itself to be a formidable means of attack and almost invulnerable to the new atomic weapons in the experimental test at Bikini on 1st July, 1946. In fact, a submarine which was immersed on that occasion at 500 yards from the target sustained only very minor damage, whilst the surface craft – cruisers and destroyers – all sank. Research on this type of ship, particularly that carried out in the United States, has led to the adoption of nuclear propelled engines and today the sub-

ATOMICALLY PROPELLED SUBMARINES

Where speeds are indicated in knots, the first figure represents surface speed and the second figure speed when submerged.

Lafayette Class – U.S.A. 1963/66. Better known as *Polaris* 7,250 tons. 425 ft. 1 nuclear reactor. 20/35 knots. 16 Polaris launching ramps, 4 torpedo tubes. Crew: 140.

Halibut – U.S.A. 1960. 3,650 tons. 350 ft. 1 nuclear reactor. 18-25 knots. 4 torpedo tubes. Crew: 97. The U.S. Navy's first guided missile, nuclear-propelled submarine.

Triton – U.S.A. 1959. One of the largest in the world, and equipped as a radar station. 5,900 tons. 447 ft. 2 nuclear reactors. 27/30 knots. 6 torpedo tubes. Crew: 170.

Seawolf – U.S.A. 1957. Second nuclear submarine, experimental type. 3,260 tons, 338 ft. 1 nuclear reactor. 19/20 knots. 6 torpedo tubes. Crew: 105.

Nautilus – U.S.A. 1955. The first experimental nuclear-powered submarine. 3,180 tons. 319 ft. 1 nuclear reactor. 20 / 23 knots. 6 torpedo tubes. Crew: 104.

Dreadnought – Gt. Britain 1963. First British nuclear-propelled submarine which bears a famous name. It is of the anti-submarine type and has a characteristic shape in the form of a whale. The **Dreadnought** is equipped with an American nuclear reactor but later vessels have British ones.

marine is almost invisible as it can remain submerged for weeks. It is as fast as a surface craft, a deadly weapon of attack especially now that the new magnetic torpedoes have been brought into use (they explode as they pass under their objective), also the acoustic torpedoes (that automatically go towards the sound of the propellers), and the sinusoidal trajectory torpedoes (that go at a speed of 50 knots in the waters around the convoy until they reach a target). The new systems of look-out and of locating the enemy, such as the ultrasonic "sonar-asdic" and radar in submersion, have greatly broadened the offensive possibilities of this ship.

When the trial launching of a Polaris missile was carried out in submersion on 20th June, 1960, capable of carrying a nuclear charge of the power of 0·1 to 0·8 megatons to a distance of 1,500 miles, the submarine justifiably became a part of the strategic picture of total atomic warfare. A mobile base for launching nuclear devices, difficult to locate, it has greater opportunities than land bases of avoiding surprise atomic attack and so be able to carry out a reprisal.

Ethan Allen Class U.S.A. 1961. Five ships equipped with Polaris launching ramps. 6,900 tons. 410 ft. 1 nuclear reactor. 20/35 knots. 16 Polaris missile-launchers. 4 torpedo tubes. Crew: 112.

George Washington Class – U.S.A. 1959. Five ships. Currently all in service. 5,600 tons. 382 ft. 1 nuclear reactor. 20/35 knots. 16 Polaris missile-launchers. 6 torpedo tubes. Crew: 112.

Tullibee – U.S.A. 1960. 2,175 tons. 261 ft. 1 nuclear reactor. 13/15 knots. 4 torpedo tubes. Crew: 56.

Skate Class – U.S.A. 1958. 2,360 tons. 267 ft. 1 nuclear reactor. 15/25 knots. 6 torpedo tubes.

Skipjack Class – U.S.A. 1960. 2,830 tons. 252 ft. 1 nuclear reactor. 16/35 knots. 6 torpedo tubes (24 torpedoes on board). Crew: 90.

Thresher Class – U.S.A. 1962/65. 3,750 tons. 278 ft. 1 nuclear reactor. 20/35 knots. 4 torpedo tubes. Crew: 99.

Dreadnought Gt. Britain 1963. 3,000 tons. 265 ft. 1 nuclear reactor. 30 knots. 6 anti-submarine torpedo tubes. Crew: 88.

Leninski Komsomol – U.S.S.R. 1960. 3,200 tons. 328 ft. 1 nuclear reactor. 25/30 knots. 6 torpedo tubes. Crew: 88.

The United States, quite convinced of this new rôle for submarines, now has around 50 of the Polaris carrying type which the Soviet Union has an unspecified number fitted with inter-continental missiles. This new purpose has not diminished the submarine's usefulness as a traditional weapon. In the naval services now there are many different types of these craft which are kept supplied at sea by depot-ships. Amongst them are atomic missile-launchers; ocean-going submarines for attack purposes, both atomic and traditional; anti-submarine; radar look-out; Commando transport; coastal; pocket; target; mine-laying. Of course, even the traditionally propelled submarines, can now stay submerged a long time, thanks to the perfection of the "Schnorkel" system, which allows air to be renewed in the interior of the submarine by means of a hinged surface tube without the craft having to emerge.

The fact that the United States and, above all, the Soviet Union, have enormous submarine Fleets, with hundreds of units, shows clearly to what extent they are now regarded as the backbone of naval strength for modern warfare.

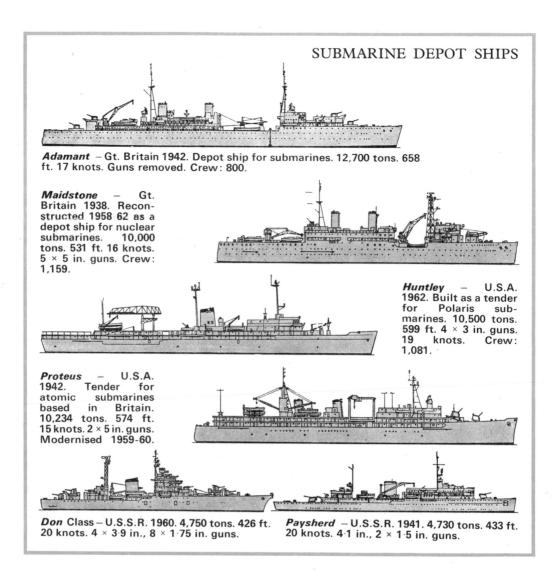

SUBMARINE DEPOT SHIPS

Adamant – Gt. Britain 1942. Depot ship for submarines. 12,700 tons. 658 ft. 17 knots. Guns removed. Crew: 800.

Maidstone – Gt. Britain 1938. Reconstructed 1958-62 as a depot ship for nuclear submarines. 10,000 tons. 531 ft. 16 knots. 5 × 5 in. guns. Crew: 1,159.

Huntley – U.S.A. 1962. Built as a tender for Polaris submarines. 10,500 tons. 599 ft. 4 × 3 in. guns. 19 knots. Crew: 1,081.

Proteus – U.S.A. 1942. Tender for atomic submarines based in Britain. 10,234 tons. 574 ft. 15 knots. 2 × 5 in. guns. Modernised 1959-60.

Don Class – U.S.S.R. 1960. 4,750 tons. 426 ft. 20 knots. 4 × 3·9 in., 8 × 1·75 in. guns.

Paysherd – U.S.S.R. 1941. 4,730 tons. 433 ft. 20 knots. 4·1 in., 2 × 1·5 in. guns.

TRADITIONALLY POWERED SUBMARINES

Delfinen Class – Denmark 1958. Four ships. 550 tons. 177 ft. 13/12 knots. 4 torpedo tubes. Crew: 30.

Daphne Class – France 1960/67. 850 tons. 190 ft. 16 knots. 12 torpedo tubes.

Narval Class – France 1957. 1,200 tons. 256 ft. 16/18 knots. 8 torpedo tubes. Crew: 58.

Arethuse Class – France 1958. Four ships. 400 tons. 164 ft. 16/18 knots. 4 torpedo tubes. Crew: 39.

U Class – W. Germany 1962/67. 450 tons. 144 ft. 11/17 knots. 8 torpedo tubes.

Hayashio Class – Japan 1962. 750 tons. 193 ft. 12/15 knots. 3 torpedo tubes. Crew: 40.

Oyashio – Japan 1960. 1,130 tons. 258 ft. 13/19 knots. 4 torpedo tubes. Crew: 65.

Oberon Class – Gt. Britain 1961. 1,610 tons. 295 ft. 20/15 knots. 8 torpedo tubes. Crew: 68.

T Class – Gt. Britain 1944. 60. 1,090 tons. 273 ft. 15 knots. 6 torpedo tubes. Crew: 65.

A Class – Gt. Britain 1948. 14 ships. 1,120 tons. 283 ft. 19/8 knots. 6 torpedo tubes.

Pietro Calvi – Italy 1944/59. Rebuilt 1961. 800 tons. 216 ft. 4 torpedo tubes.

Dolfijn – Netherlands 1960. 1,140 tons. 260 ft. 14·5/17 knots. 8 torpedo tubes. Crew: 64.

Hajen Class – Sweden 1956. Six ships. 720 tons. 216 ft. 4 torpedo tubes. Crew 44.

Najad Class – Sweden 1943. 550 tons. 200 ft. 16/10 knots. 20 mines. 4 torpedo tubes. Crew: 32.

Abborren Class – Sweden 1944. 388 tons. 164 ft. 14/9 knots. 4 torpedo tubes. Crew: 23

Sailfish Class – U.S.A. 1956. 2,425 tons. 350 ft. 20/15 knots. 6 torpedo tubes. Crew: 96.

Grayback Class – U.S.A. 1958. 2,980 tons. 332 ft. 20/18 knots. Crew: 67.

Barbel Class – U.S.A. 1959. 1,750 tons. 219 ft. 15/25 knots. 6 torpedo tubes. Crew: 77.

Tang Class – U.S.A. 1951. 1,615 tons. 278 ft. 20/18 knots. 8 torpedo tubes. Crew: 83.

Requin – U.S.A. 1945. One of the **Tench** Class, 1,570 tons. 312 ft. 20/10 knots. 6 torpedo tubes. Crew: 80.

Balao Class – U.S.A. 1943. 1,526 tons. 311 ft. 20/17 knots. 10 torpedo tubes. Crew: 80.

G Class – U.S.S.R. 1960. 2,350 tons, 320 ft. 17 knots. 3 vertical missile tubes. 10 torpedo tubes.

F Class – U.S.S.R. 1960. 2,000 tons. 300 ft. Speed: 20/15 knots. 8 torpedo tubes. Crew: 70.

Z Class – U.S.S.R. 1958. 2,100 tons. 295 ft. 20/15 knots. 2 missile-launchers. 8 torpedo tubes.

R. Class – U.S.S.R. 1959. 1,100 tons. 246 ft. 18·5/15 knots. 6 torpedo tubes. Crew: 65.

W Class – U.S.S.R. 1950-57. 1,030 tons 240 ft. 17/15 knots. 8 torpedo tubes. Crew: 60.

MV Class – U.S.S.R. 1946. 350 tons. 167 ft. 13/10 knots. 2 torpedo tubes. Crew: 24.

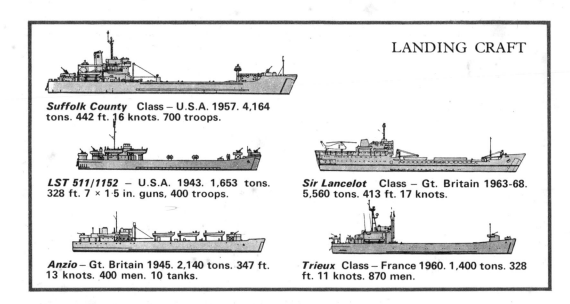

LANDING CRAFT

Suffolk County Class – U.S.A. 1957. 4,164 tons. 442 ft. 16 knots. 700 troops.

LST 511/1152 – U.S.A. 1943. 1,653 tons. 328 ft. 7 × 1·5 in. guns, 400 troops.

Anzio – Gt. Britain 1945. 2,140 tons. 347 ft. 13 knots. 400 men. 10 tanks.

Sir Lancelot Class – Gt. Britain 1963-68. 5,560 tons. 413 ft. 17 knots.

Trieux Class – France 1960. 1,400 tons. 328 ft. 11 knots. 870 men.

OTHER NAVAL SHIPS

A MODERN Navy includes many other types of ships besides those mentioned in the foregoing pages. These consist of operational ships – such as landing-craft and command vessels – and of auxiliary ships which constitute so to speak, the supply lines for the front line and are allocated according to the nature of the duties the naval squadrons are expected to undertake. Even just a list of all the types of auxiliaries that exist, how many there are of them and what functions they are respectively called upon to carry out, would require more space than has been dedicated to aircraft-carriers in this book. Suffice it to say that, this category ranges from ice-breakers to support craft for aircraft-carriers, destroyers and submarines; from tugs to transport ships for men, munitions and materials; from tankers to netlayers; from hydrographic and oceanographic research ships to communication link-up ships.

The United States have the largest

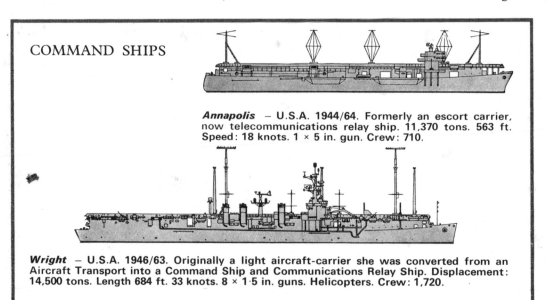

COMMAND SHIPS

Annapolis – U.S.A. 1944/64. Formerly an escort carrier, now telecommunications relay ship. 11,370 tons. 563 ft. Speed: 18 knots. 1 × 5 in. gun. Crew: 710.

Wright – U.S.A. 1946/63. Originally a light aircraft-carrier she was converted from an Aircraft Transport into a Command Ship and Communications Relay Ship. Displacement: 14,500 tons. Length 684 ft. 33 knots. 8 × 1·5 in. guns. Helicopters. Crew: 1,720.

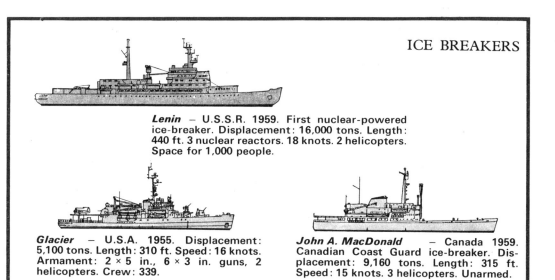

ICE BREAKERS

Lenin – U.S.S.R. 1959. First nuclear-powered ice-breaker. Displacement: 16,000 tons. Length: 440 ft. 3 nuclear reactors. 18 knots. 2 helicopters. Space for 1,000 people.

Glacier – U.S.A. 1955. Displacement: 5,100 tons. Length: 310 ft. Speed: 16 knots. Armament: 2 × 5 in., 6 × 3 in. guns, 2 helicopters. Crew: 339.

John A. MacDonald – Canada 1959. Canadian Coast Guard ice-breaker. Displacement: 9,160 tons. Length: 315 ft. Speed: 15 knots. 3 helicopters. Unarmed.

number and greatest variety of auxiliary ships. The higher the number of operational ships, the more necessary is the support of ships that can carry out the supplying and the maintenance of vessels which are thousands of miles from base, meeting every possible need. A conventionally propelled aircraft-carrier would be of little use if it could not be guaranteed fuel for its engines and munitions and bombs for its aircraft, and the necessities of life for its crew, in any sea.

For example, the first nuclear powered ship to have been launched from a Soviet shipyard was in fact, an auxiliary ship – the ice-breaker *Lenin,* of very great value to her Merchant shipping and her Navy should it be called on to operate in seas closed by ice. This is proof of how auxiliary ships are certainly no less important than those which are actually on operational service and with which they create a complete, indivisable whole, perfectly co-ordinated.

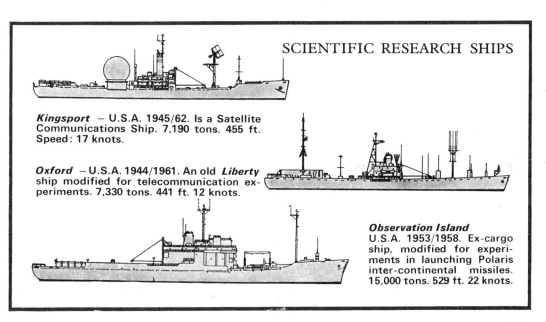

SCIENTIFIC RESEARCH SHIPS

Kingsport – U.S.A. 1945/62. Is a Satellite Communications Ship. 7,190 tons. 455 ft. Speed: 17 knots.

Oxford – U.S.A. 1944/1961. An old *Liberty* ship modified for telecommunication experiments. 7,330 tons. 441 ft. 12 knots.

Observation Island
U.S.A. 1953/1958. Ex-cargo ship, modified for experiments in launching Polaris inter-continental missiles. 15,000 tons. 529 ft. 22 knots.

TRAINING SHIPS

THE efficiency of naval forces today rests on two fundamental elements: the up-to-dateness of the ships and the standard to which crews are trained. And the more a naval force is equipped with ships of advanced design, the more highly qualified must be the personnel who man them, from the captain to the humble sailor.

Technical improvements, which have radically transformed armament and equipment of warships, have created the need for new specialists. Alongside the helmsmen, radio-telegraphists, gunners, and torpedo specialists who are all expected to carry out much more difficult duties than in the past, are today grouped the radar-operators, asdic and sonar operators, electrical mechanics and electronic technicians.

Gone is the time when a young recruit, after a short period at the depot, was put aboard an operational ship where he would gradually learn to carry out his duties correctly – mainly by practice. Now, a recruit must continue his studies at school desks almost uninterruptedly in order to specialise before going on to ships which must, at all times, be ready to operate to the limit of their capacity.

The preparation of the men costs no less than the fitting out of new ships – Naval Academies, and other training establish-

Amerigo Vespucci – Italy 1931. Three-masted with steel hull.

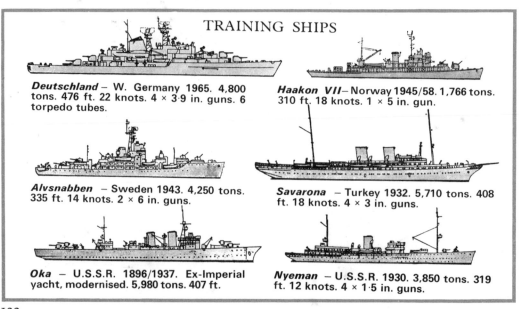

TRAINING SHIPS

Deutschland – W. Germany 1965. 4,800 tons. 476 ft. 22 knots. 4 × 3·9 in. guns. 6 torpedo tubes.

Haakon VII – Norway 1945/58. 1,766 tons. 310 ft. 18 knots. 1 × 5 in. gun.

Alvsnabben – Sweden 1943. 4,250 tons. 335 ft. 14 knots. 2 × 6 in. guns.

Savarona – Turkey 1932. 5,710 tons. 408 ft. 18 knots. 4 × 3 in. guns.

Oka – U.S.S.R. 1896/1937. Ex-Imperial yacht, modernised. 5,980 tons. 407 ft.

Nyeman – U.S.S.R. 1930. 3,850 tons. 319 ft. 12 knots. 4 × 1·5 in. guns.

ments – all must be equipped with more efficient and modern teaching equipment in order to fulfil their task properly. And, alongside the halls of theoretical studies are the training ships – sailing ships, cruisers that have been converted into testing-grounds for gunners and naval engineers, modern ships which have been carefully planned as being the synthesis of all the instruments and equipment that the youngster must have practice in using. The last great sails that are seen at sea to-day are mostly those of the schooners, and square-riggers, belonging to the largest Naval Academies – in which are to be found the Naval officers of the future. It is not possible to be a good captain of modern steel ships if one has not sailed as they used to sail in days gone by – if one has not become familiar with the winds, with handling a ship, and with the problems of sail.

There are not more than about 15 sailing ships used for training currently in service and all are fitted with emergency auxiliary engines. Some are feeling their age, others have only recently been launched. In these ships of yesterday – which may even appear to be anachronistic in this era of nuclear propulsion – are prepared the officers of tomorrow's navies, not only in technical matters but also in spirit. Although times have changed and ships may not be the same as they once were, the qualities needed for a good sailor are still the same – courage, loyalty, and a spirit of self-sacrifice.

Libertad – Argentine 1956. 3,025 tons. 301 ft. 2 diesels. 13 knots. 1 × 3 in. gun.

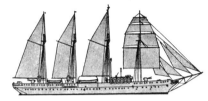

Almirante Saldanha – Brazil 1934. 3,325 tons. 307 ft. 1 engine. 11 knots. 4 × 4 in., 1 × 3 in. guns.

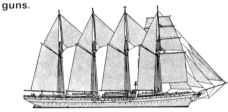

Esmeralda – Chile 1952. Four-masted schooner. 3,040 tons. 308 ft. 1 engine. 11 knots.

Gorch Fock – W. Germany 1958. 21,150 sq. ft. of sail. 1,760 tons. 257 ft. 1 engine. 11 knots.

Amerigo Vespucci – Italy. 2,500 sq. yd. of sail. 3,550 tons. 270 ft. Speed: 10 knots.

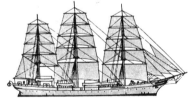

Dar Pomorza – Poland 1909. Built at Hamburg. 1,561 tons. 240 ft. 1 engine.

Sagres – Portugal 1937. Built for Germany. 1,415 tons. 229 ft. 2 diesels. 10 knots.

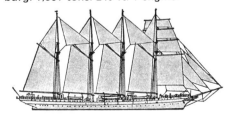

Juan Sebastian de Alcano – Spain 1927. 3,420 tons. 309 ft. 1 engine. 9.5 knots.

MERCHANT NAVIES

The above figures are taken from the latest available Statistical Tables issued by "Lloyd's Register of Shipping" in October 1967.

MORE than 44,000 merchant ships of all types are on the world's seas today, to a total of about 182 million tons gross – more than double the amount in service at the outbreak of the Second World War. It is a great achievement, but one that will, according to the experts, be exceeded in the years to come.

The situation is the direct consequence of the growth in maritime transport requirements which have developed since the end of the last war. However, the composition of today's merchant fleets is substantially different from that of 1939. Many factors have contributed to this: the competition from jet air lines; revised distribution of raw materials in the world, with the exhaustion of some sources and the discovery of new ones; the emergence of new independent countries in varying stages of development, with the consequent opening up of new markets; a greater degree of general well-being, which in itself creates a demand; these and a hundred other elements have had a direct influence not only on the number, but also on the types of merchant ships launched during the post-war period.

The transportation of ever larger quantities of oil, both crude and refined, has caused a colossal increase in the number of tankers which make up one-third of all merchant shipping now in service. The need for transporting minerals in large quantities has resulted in the development of a new type, the bulk carrier which, as regards size, is often the rival of the giant tanker.

In terms of gross tonnage, the largest merchant fleet in the world is that registered in Liberia. The United Kingdom comes a very close second as regards tonnage, but in fact has three times as many ships. Then comes the United States including a reserve fleet of over 7 million tons – as third, with Norway fourth, Japan fifth, Russia sixth and Greece seventh, followed by Italy, West Germany, France and the Netherlands. This shows how the after-effects of the War have now been erased and are no longer more than a bad memory.

At the end of the Second World War the total world tonnage of power driven mer-

Queen Elizabeth – Gt. Britain 1940. The world's largest liner. Launched 1940. During the Second World War she transported some 811,325 soldiers. She entered the Cunard Line's passenger service between Southampton and New York in 1946. Was withdrawn from this service in the autumn of 1968 following her sale to America for use as a floating hotel. Gross tonnage: 82,998. Length: 1,031 ft. Service speed: 28·5 knots. Passengers: 2,260.

cantile shipping (69,317,000) was, in fact, slightly greater than at the beginning (68,509,000).

Nevertheless, this was solely due to the colossal effort of the Allies who alone could boast great merchant fleets. It is, in fact, true that the Allied losses amounted to 21 million tons out of the total shipping lost of 28 million tons, but it is also true that the United States, Britain and Canada launched 94 million tons from 1939-1945, thus replacing the ships sunk and with a good margin in excess. However, France, Italy, Germany, Norway, the Netherlands and Japan, who had seen their mercantile fleets reduced to nothing, were not able to do likewise. Evidence that these countries, too, have now regained positions of importance in the division of world tonnage confirms that merchant fleets in general have fully recovered. A large percentage of the cargo shipping now in service consists of modern ships, better adapted to specialised needs and so more economical to operate, and these have gone ahead, taking the place of the older

ones of many of the "Liberty" ships which, at the end of the War, met the needs of the world's trade routes.

Today the merchant fleets of Great Britain and the U.S.A. are still numerically the largest in the world; and these two nations are well in the forefront of the revolutionary switch-over to very large, ultra-fast cargo liners specially designed to carry containers. Since 1962 the Japanese merchant fleet has almost doubled in size, while Russia's fleet has now passed the 10 million ton mark. Liberia has now far surpassed Panama as a flag of convenience, one which, on a large scale, was first chosen by American owners, as a means of avoiding Government restrictions, manning standards and taxes. About 1,500 ships are now registered in Liberia and most are tankers or bulk carriers of large size, which accounts for the high tonnage total. Norway continues her role as the world's great carrier for other nations. For the world's cargo fleets as a whole the present is a period of continued expansion and ever faster technological development.

France – France 1961. The longest liner in the world, her length of 1,035 ft. exceeds that of the ***Queen Elizabeth*** by 4 ft. Her eight boilers develop 160,000 h.p. During the season she sails between Le Havre and New York, a crossing which takes less than five days, and also goes cruising. 66,348 tons gross. Quadruple screw steam turbines. Speed: 30 knots. Passengers: 2,000.

United States – U.S.A. 1952. Flagship of the United States Lines. She has retained the "Blue Riband" since July, 1952, when she completed the crossing from New York to Le Havre in 3 days, 10 hours, 40 minutes, at an average speed of 35·59 knots. Maximum speed is 42 knots. She cost 72 million dollars, and was designed for rapid conversion into a troopship. 53,329 tons. Length: 990 ft. Steam turbines. Crew: 1,000. Passengers: 1,926.

PASSENGER SHIPS

ANY study of passenger ships means, above all, prior attention to the big trans-Atlantic liners. Traditionally the most important ocean passenger route is that between Europe and North America and it is almost the only one for which the ships used have been built almost exclusively for the carriage of passengers. On the other services, dual-purpose ships are used which are able to carry considerable numbers of passengers besides varying quantities of cargo. Having said that, it is interesting to note that, in the immediate post-war period, in spite of the competition from air transport which has overtaken them, the trans-Atlantic routes have known moments of greatness. Atlantic passenger traffic really reached its height before the outbreak of the First World War, especially in 1913, with 2,576,000 passengers. On the whole, these were emigrants, for whom primarily the trans-Atlantic routes had developed so amazingly in just one century.

Between 1920 and 1930, when the migratory flood was interrupted, the trans-Atlantic services concentrated on carrying an average of about 65,000 passengers every year, mostly made up of business men and tourists. It was for the particular needs of these that the large luxury liners were evolved, floating cities like the *Ile de France, Rex, Normandie,* and *Queen Mary,* all rigorously employed in a competitive struggle in which the possession of the "Blue Riband" was something of fundamental importance because of its prestige value. During the Second World War these big ships were converted into troop-carriers and by 1945 very few of them had survived. The *Normandie,* for example, ended up in flames in New York harbour while the great giants of the Italian seas had all been sunk. To provide for the needs of trans-Atlantic traffic in the early post-war period, the *Queen Mary* and the *Queen Elizabeth* were used, having been re-adapted for carrying civilian passengers, as well as smaller ships belonging to Britain, America, France, Holland and Italy.

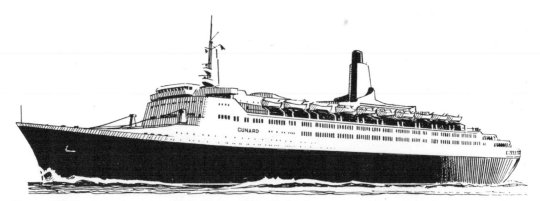

Queen Elizabeth 2 – Great Britain 1968. Built at Clydebank for the Cunard Line, launched on 20th September, 1967, and made first commercial voyage in April 1969. Intended mainly for cruising. Length: 963 ft., breadth 105 ft. 13 decks. Twin screw, geared turbines, 110,000 h.p. Service speed 28½ knots. Gross tonnage 65,863. Passengers: 2,025.

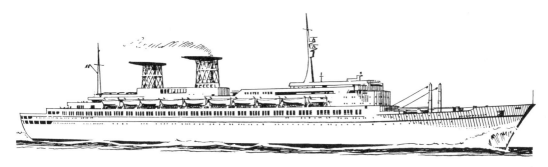

Michelangelo – Italy 1965. Flagship of the Italia Line, and with sister ship ***Raffaello*** is employed on the Italy-New York service. Built by Ansaldo, Genoa. 45,911 tons gross. Length 905 ft., breadth 102 ft. Twin screw, geared turbines, 26½ knots. Passengers: 1,775.

Regular trans-Atlantic air services were started up immediately after the end of the War and were based on air force experience gained from 1939 to 1945. But at first this new means of transport did not seem to worry the shipping companies. In 1948, for example, against 501,000 passengers carried by sea, only 252,000 had gone by air. Nevertheless, the situation was to change rapidly. The increase in sea traffic was proportionally less than the increase in air traffic – in 1953, 892,000 passengers went by sea and 507,000 by air; in 1955, 964,000 and 652,000 respectively; in 1957, 1,036,000 and 968,000. The point of reversal came in 1958, the year in which shipping started to register a decrease in the number of people carried, whilst the air lines went ahead with their development – 957,000 sea passengers against 1,193,000 air passengers. Today the battle for the trans-Atlantic passenger trade has been overwhelmingly won by the jet plane. It is only necessary to realise that, in 1963, out of 3,210,000 people who crossed the Ocean both ways, some 2,422,000 did so in aircraft and just about 788,000 in ships, to be fully convinced.

Some years back the directors of the shipping companies were faced with very serious problems. They were compelled to ask themselves whether air traffic would reach the point where it would totally eliminate sea transport. Also, would the number of passengers wishing to travel by sea be enough to justify and support the expense of keeping the trans-Atlantic ships up-to-date? Again, would new ships have to be very large, of medium size or small, in order to be economical in running? These were only some of the many questions that the companies had to ask – but the replies they received were generally positive and reassuring. Air traffic would never completely supersede sea traffic – and the continually increasing number of people wishing to cross the Atlantic every year would always guarantee sufficient passengers to keep the maritime services alive. To compete with aircraft, it was thought sufficient to offer attractive prices, good conditions of com-

Leonardo da Vinci – Italy 1960. One of the most elegant passenger ships in the world, she was the flagship of the Italia Line until the ***Michelangelo*** came into service. She has eleven decks, nine of them for passengers, and is fitted with stabilisers. 33,340 tons. Length: 767 ft. Engines: steam turbines. Speed 23 knots. Crew: 570. Passengers: 1,326. Built by Ansaldo.

Canberra – Gt. Britain 1961. The biggest passenger ship to be constructed in Britain since the *Queen Elizabeth*. She was built by Harland & Wolff, Belfast for the P & O Line, for service on the Australian trade run and for cruising. She can carry 2,200 passengers, first and tourist. A great deal of use has been made of aluminium in the superstructure. 45,733 tons. Length: 818 ft. Engines: twin screw, turbo-electric. Speed: 27·5 knots.

fort and regularity of services which, combined with the undoubted fascination of a sea voyage (a fascination which is still very much alive today), would justify the enormous outlay involved.

So all the companies which involved North American services before the War built new ships, each one finer than the last, like the *France, United States, Cristoforo Colombo, Leonardo da Vinci, Michelangelo* and the *Raffaello*.

The Italian concern which was particularly involved in the revival of this type of shipping was the Italia line, which had found itself almost completely crippled at the end of the War, to the extent of 88% of its tonnage. Of the 37 ships under its flag in 1939, only 6 remained by 1945. In spite of this, the *Saturnia* set sail for New York from Genoa on 20th January, 1947, and so the services on the "sunshine route" were once again brought into operation.

By 1955 the Italian merchant navy had succeeded in regaining the second position in North Atlantic traffic which she had held before the War. Further evidence that the Italian Company still believed in the vitality of sea traffic was given by the delivery of the new *Michelangelo* and *Raffaello* – ships which may be regarded as typical of the type of vessel which will meet the needs of those passengers who choose the ship rather than the aeroplane, who prefer to spend five days making the crossing, rather than a mere matter of hours, and enjoy a voyage which is both a diversion and a rest.

Inevitably passenger ships are becoming used more and more for tourist cruises which have been on the increase now for quite a few years, and became even more popular as longer and more varied itineraries have been thought up.

The liners built immediately after the War were of various tonnages ranging from 20,000 – 30,000 tons, with a speed

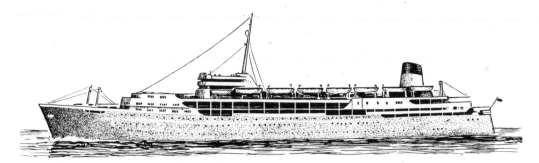

Southern Cross – Gt. Britain 1955. The first engines-aft passenger ship to have been built in Britain. Besides leaving the best space available for her passengers, this arrangement gives the ship a unique appearance. She operates on the Shaw Savill Line's round the world service. 19,313 tons. Length: 604 ft. Twin screw turbines. Speed: 20 knots. Passengers: 1,164.

Rotterdam – Netherlands 1959. Flagship of the Holland-America Line; like the ***Southern Cross*** her turbines are placed aft of amidships. She was the first European passenger liner to have twin exhausts instead of the usual funnel. Her layout is unusual for her first and tourist class rooms are placed on alternate decks. 38,621 tons. Length: 749 ft. Twin screw turbines. Speed: 21·5 knots. Crew: 776. Passengers: 1,360.

potential of about 21 knots. On the other hand, those which have been built more recently are much bigger, around 40,000 tons, and capable of exceeding 25 knots. In the new ships, light alloys and plastic materials have been increasingly used, reducing weight and so allowing for increased speed. Greatly improved safety measures have also been incorporated so as to reduce the danger of fire on board and to guarantee all passengers being rescued in the unfortunate event of a serious accident. These precautions are the result of recent international regulations, the aim of which has been to eliminate the spectre of tragedies at sea for all time. Another characteristic of newly built passenger ships is the reduction in the number of passenger classes. It seems likely that soon there will only be First and Tourist classes on all liners, the goal being to be able to guarantee maximum comfort to all passengers. Many interesting experiments have been

carried out by owners and builders and one of the ideas which has latterly been applied to passenger ships has been the placing of the machinery aft, as in tankers, so leaving the more important midship portions of the ship clear for the better arrangement of the public rooms and cabins.

Alas, on the North Atlantic a new stage will be reached during the winter of 1968-69, for then – during a three month period – none of the leading liners will be operating between the USA and Europe, all being diverted for more profitable off-season cruising. So the trans-Atlantic air lines will have their first period of virtual monopoly. It now seems unlikely that any more large passenger liners will be launched and the *Hamburg* and the *Queen Elizabeth 2* may well be the last of their type. Cruising, however continues to prosper, but competition is fierce.

Kentavros – Greece 1941-64. This vessel, of 2,805 tons gross, was bought from the U.S. Navy and completely rebuilt for Mediterranean cruises. Owned by Kavounides Lines, Piraeus, she is 311 ft. long and has a top speed of 17 knots. 220 passengers, but no cargo.

PASSENGER SHIPS CURRENTLY IN SERVICE

Oriana – Gt. Britain 1960. P & O Line on U.K. – Australia and trans-Pacific services. 41,915 tons gross. 804 ft. Twin screw, turbines. Speed: 27·5 knots. Passengers: 2,000.

Windsor Castle – Gt. Britain 1960. Flagship of the Union-Castle Line. 37,647 tons. 783 ft. Twin screw, turbines. Speed: 23·5 knots. Passengers: 830.

Hanseatic – W. Germany 1964. Hamburg-Atlantic Line's cruise ship. Built in France. 25,320 tons gross. Length o.a. 628 ft. Twin screw, turbines, 20 knots.

Guglielmo Marconi – Italy 1963. On the Italy-Australia run. 27,905 tons. 701 ft. Twin screw, turbines. 24 knots. Passengers: 1,700.

Giulio Cesare – Italy 1951. The first large motor passenger ship to be built in Italy after the Second World War. 27,078 tons. 680 ft. Speed: 21 knots. Passengers: 1,186.

Empress of England – Gt. Britain 1957. On the Liverpool-Montreal run. 25,585 tons. 640 ft. Twin screw, turbines. Speed: 20 knots. Passengers: 972.

Infante Dom Henrique – Portugal 1961. On the East African route. Built in Belgium. 23,306 tons. 642 ft. Twin screw turbines. 21 knots.

Independence – U.S.A. 1950. Owned by American Export Isbrandtsen Lines. 23,754 tons gross. Length 683 ft. Twin screw, turbines, $22\frac{1}{2}$ knots. Passengers: 1,100.

Carmania – Gt. Britain 1954. Built as *Saxonia* for Cunard Line; used since 1963 as cruise ship. Sistership *Franconia*. Twin screw, turbines, 20 knots.

Federico C. – Italy 1958. On the Genoa-South American service. 20,416 tons. 605 ft. Twin screw, turbines. Speed: 21 knots. Passengers: 1,259.

Nevasa – Gt. Britain 1956. British India Line educational cruise ship. 20,746 tons. Length 609 ft. Twin screw turbines, 17 knots. Passengers: 1,100 (pupils).

Principe Perfeito – Portugal 1961. Built in Britain. On the Lisbon-Lorenzo Marques run. 19,393 tons. 625 ft. Twin screw turbines. 20 knots. Passengers: 1,200.

Ancerville – France 1962. Operates on the Marseilles-Las Palmas-Dakar route. 14,224 tons. 551 ft. Twin screw, diesel engines. Speed: 22½ knots. Passengers: 733.

Rossini – Italy 1951. One of three employed on services to Central America. 13,325 tons. 528 ft. Twin screw, diesels. 18 knots. 552 passengers.

Verdi – Italy 1951. Previously called the *Oceania* was modernised when transferred from the Lloyd Triestino to the Italia Line.

Stockholm – Sweden 1948. Survived collision with the *Andrea Doria*. Now the East German *Volkerfreundschaft*. 12,165 tons. 524 ft. Diesels. 19 knots.

Ausonia – Italy 1957. On the East Mediterranean services. 11,879 tons. Length: 522 ft. Twin screw, turbines. Speed: 21 knots. Passengers: 529.

Victoria – Italy 1953. Operates on the Lloyd Triestino's Far Eastern service. 11,695 tons. 522 ft. Twin screw diesels. 19 knots. 431 passengers.

Montserrat – Spain 1945. Employed on U.K. – Central American service. 9,008 tons. 455 ft. Single screw, turbine. 17 knots. Passengers: 840.

Amerikanis – Greece 1952-68. Originally the 17,042-ton *Kenya Castle*. Used mainly as cruise ship. Length o.a. 576 ft. Twin screw, turbines, 18 knots.

President Cleveland – U.S.A. 1947. A passenger and cargo ship employed on the San Francisco – Far East service of the American President Lines. She and the *President Wilson* are sister ships, the flagship of the fleet being the more up to date *President Roosevelt*. Gross tonnage: 15,456 tons. Length: 609 ft. Turbo-electric drive. Speed: 19 knots. Passengers: 684.

PASSENGER AND CARGO SHIPS

IN order of importance, the passenger sea routes which come immediately after those of the North Atlantic are the ones that link Great Britain with Australia; the United States with the Far East; and Italy (and, of course, the Mediterranean) with South America, Africa and Australia. Ships on these services are of two main types – they are either passenger ships with special facilities for carrying some cargo, such as the *President Cleveland,* or they are the classical cargo-liners. The former are ships designed to carry several hundred (perhaps over a thousand) passengers as well as mail and general cargo. On the other hand, the cargo-liners – as their name suggests – are real cargo carriers, used on a regular route, which also have cabins for a maximum of 12 passengers, usually 1st class. Their spacious holds can carry every type of general cargo, their deep tanks liquids, such as latex and vegetable oils, while the many

with refrigerated space carry perishables, such as fruit, dairy produce and meat.

The cargo-liners of today, of which the *Port Auckland* and the *Viminale* are splendid examples, base their economy on cargo, passengers being of secondary importance. Whilst air travel for passengers from Australia to Europe, for example, is a strong competitor of sea travel, it has not yet made any impact as far as goods are concerned, this because of the high cost of air freight.

The most recently built cargo-liners are of up to 15,000 tons gross and have speeds of about 18-22 knots. The accommodation for the few passengers that they carry is particularly comfortable and spacious. It is hardly surprising that many persons prefer to travel by such ships rather than by large liners, for not only is the service more personal, but there is generally the added attraction of more time being spent in the various ports of call.

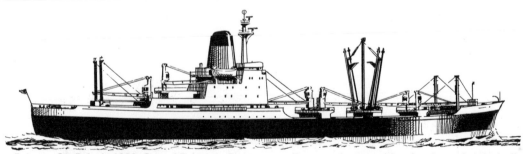

Priam – Gt. Britain 1966. One of Britain's finest cargo liners and name-ship of a class of eight built in Britain and Japan. Four are owned by Blue Funnel Line and four by its subsidiary, the Glen Line. Length 564 ft. 12,094 tons gross, 11,150 tons deadweight. Single screw, diesel. Service speed: 21½ knots plus.

Tunadal – Sweden 1967. This specialist ship, designed to carry pulp, is owned by the Swedish Cellulose Co. Shown with two hatches open, and arms of travelling Munck gantry extended in unloading position. 9,355 tons gross. Length 504 ft. Twin Pielstick diesels are geared to a single shaft.

DRY CARGO SHIPS

CARGO ships are primarily divided into two main categories – dry cargo and liquid cargo. This second group – tankers – has assumed such importance from the immediately post-war period up to the present day as to merit a separate section. The first group, in turn, is divided into cargo-liners – about which we have already written – tramps and bulk carriers.

The old, well-known cargo ships are undoubtedly the "tramps". They are real wanderers of the seas, not employed regularly on any pre-determined route, but constantly plying for loads in the ports of the five continents. The cargo-liners and ships for carrying mineral ores and cereals represent severe and growing competition nowadays to these tramps.

For some years after the end of the Second World War, the "Liberty" ship represented the classical "tramp". It is worth remembering that, during the War, the United States started mass-producing these cargo steamers of 10,000 tons cargo capacity which were capable of a modest 1⸰.5 knots, and were indeed aptly named "Liberty" ships.

A "Liberty" ship, said to be made up of 9,300 pieces, was built in a maximum of 50 days and one was actually produced in the record time of 4 days 15 hours 24 minutes! The U.S.A. launched 542 vessels of this type in 1942, and 1,253 in 1943, until they reached a production figure of three every day! The 2,650 "Liberty" ships built totalled 27 million tons gross – little less than half the tonnage of all merchant shipping by the end of the War. Many of them were handed over to shipowners of other countries and coped with the needs of international trade during the immediate post-war period. By now the majority

Enrico C – Italy 1943. One of some 2,650 pre-fabricated "Liberty" ships built in the U.S. during the latter part of the Second World War. She bore the name *Frank H. Evers* until 1946 when she was sold to Giacomo Costa of Genoa. She traded as the *Enrico C* until 1963, when she became the Liberian registered *Nicolas A*. 7,160 tons gross. Length: 422 ft. Speed: 10½ knots.

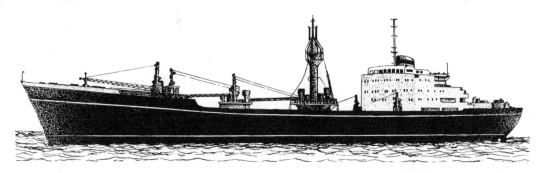

Beloretsk – U.S.S.R. 1962. Sister ship – *Belovodsk.* One of the more modern Soviet merchant ships. She was built, with three others, in Denmark. She is a classical cargo vessel with a dead-weight (cargo) capacity of 14,485 tons. The Soviet Union has an extremely large number of cargo ships, tankers and trawlers on order, nearly all of them from other countries. Gross measurement: 10,651 tons gross. Length: 526 ft. Engines: Diesel. Speed: 18.5 knots. Crew: 38.

of them have been discarded, having been replaced – like the "tramps" – by more suitable and economical ships. The current trend of shipowners shows a preference for vessels of about 8,000 tons gross for trans-oceanic traffic and of about 5,000 tons for coastal traffic.

Bulk carriers have evolved as the result of the increased necessity for transporting mineral ores, cereals and coal. Somewhat similar in appearance to oil tankers, their design would seem to have been evolved from those of the cargo carriers on the American and Canadian Great Lakes. Both types can carry large amounts of cargo in bulk in their holds, which can be loaded and unloaded by machinery available in the docks; therefore relatively few of these ships carry the necessary equipment themselves. They are the giants of the dry cargo ships – their gross tonnage

has continued to increase in the last few years and now often exceeds 80,000 tons. A further increase in size is unlikely until the ports are better equipped to deal with them. To realise just how important these great bulk carriers are to trade, suffice it to say that in 1963, 103 million tons of iron ore, 51 million tons of coal, 73 million tons of cereal, 31 million tons of chemical fertilisers, 20 million tons of sugar and 18 million tons of bauxite were carried by sea.

In 1963, dry cargo ships constituted 47.5% of the world's merchant shipping, bulk carriers alone accounting for 11.6% – a noticeable increase on the situation in the preceding years. It is foreseeable that this percentage will tend to rise even more in the future, as a direct consequence of the growing need for transportation by sea of raw materials.

Canadoc – Canada 1961. When new was the biggest ship to have been built in Canada. Her machinery is placed aft and almost all her length of 605 ft. is occupied by holds for cereals and mineral ores – which can take up to 15,465 tons. More than 700 ships of this type are employed on the Great Lakes. 10,061 tons gross. Single screw, diesel. Speed: 15 knots.

CARGO SHIPS

Polar Equador – W. Germany 1967. One of six "Polar" class refrigerated cargo ships of the Hamburg-South American Line. 5,617 tons gross, 7,500 tons d.w. Length 485 ft. Engines: two 16-cylinder Pielstick diesels, 22½ knots.

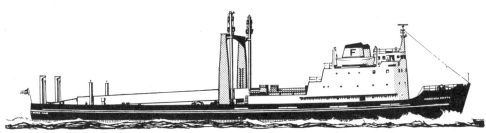

Aberthaw Fisher – Gt. Britain 1966. Sister ship *Kingsnorth Fisher*. Heavy load carriers, specially adapted for transporting transformers, etc, and owned by James Fisher & Sons. 2,355 tons gross, diesel-electric machinery, 11 knots.

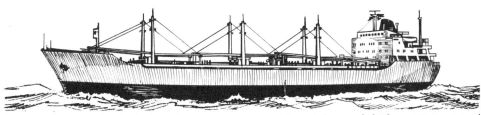

Ferder – Norway 1962. Designed to carry cars – on hinged, internal decks – one way, and bulk cargoes the other. Employed on long-term charter to Volkswagen. Can carry 1,220 cars at a time. 17,870 tons deadweight. Length: 500 ft. Speed: 15 knots.

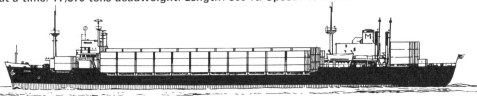

Hawaiian – U.S.A. 1946. Rebuilt to carry containers. Owners: Matson Navigation Co., San Francisco. 14,113 tons gross, 20,644 tons d.w. Length 633 ft. (originally 523 ft.). Geared turbines, 15½ knots.

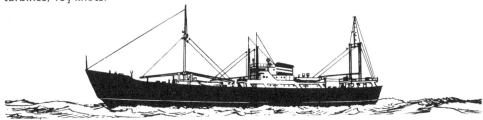

Polaris – Finland 1956. Built in Holland for the Finland Steamship Co., Helsinki, this small cargo ship is designed for regular North Sea and Baltic services. 1,519 tons gross. 2,257 tons deadweight. Length: 307 ft. Single screw, diesel. Speed: 14 knots.

Manhattan – U.S.A. 1962. When new was the largest merchant ship to have been built in the United States and one of the biggest oil tankers in the world. She was constructed by the Bethlehem Steel Company – the Company which launched the first missile-launching nuclear cruiser, *Long Beach* – and has a deadweight tonnage of some 108,588. 65,740 tons gross. Length: 1,050 ft. 4 turbines. Speed: 17·7 knots.

OIL TANKERS

AT the outbreak of the First World War in 1914, the total tanker tonnage did not exceed 1½ million tons. Twenty-five years later, at the start of the Second World War, it was approaching 11,500,000 tons – equal to about 17% of the entire gross tonnage of merchant shipping. The extraordinary growth – both in numbers and in size – of oil tankers became obvious after 1950 when crude oil had to be carried in larger and larger quantities by sea from the oil fields to the refineries and from there to the points of consumption, this being due to the steadily increasing demand for oil products.

In 1952, the world's tanker tonnage had already reached 20 million tons, equal to 23% of the world's merchant shipping. In 1963, 11 years later, it amounted to 46,900,000 tons, 33% – equal to 69,340,233 tons deadweight capacity.

The exceptional development of tankers is one of the most interesting phenomena to have occurred in recent years in merchant shipping. In building these new ships, the oil companies have obviously played a rôle of extreme importance but it is worth noting that 65% of the entire tonnage of tankers is owned by independent shipowners, some of whom were in at the beginning and realised the importance of this type of ship and have made huge profits.

Great Britain no longer has the world's largest tanker fleet, this position now being held by Liberia. The latest world tonnage figures, those issued by Lloyd's Register of Shipping late in 1967, show that Liberian registered tankers numbered 582 and had a gross tonnage of 12,945,197. The Norwegian fleet held second position with 510 ships of 9,899,619 tons, Great Britain and Northern Ireland coming third, with 596 tankers of 7,845,283 tons. The Japanese fleet, numerically large, comprised 1,222 vessels of 5,849,549 tons. The United

Nissho Maru – Japan 1962. She, too, for a while, was the world's largest tanker. Her main dimensions are length: 955 ft., breadth: 141 ft., depth: 73 ft. She has a gross tonnage of 74,868, her deadweight being 130,250 tons. She was built in Japan for the Idemitsu Tanker Co., who are one of the most important crude oil importers in Japan. Single screw, turbines. Speed: 16½ knots.

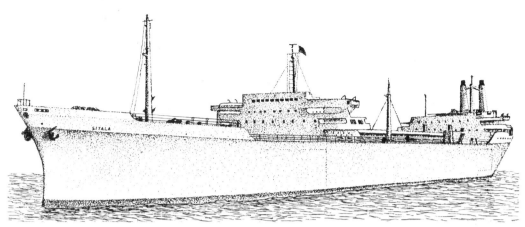

Sitala – France 1961. When built at St Nazaire – Penhoet for the Societe Maritime Shell, she became the flagship of that Company's tanker fleet. She was among the first tankers to break from the traditional single funnel and have twin stacks; the provision of a helicopter deck was also unusual. Dead-weight tonnage 73,148. Gross measurement: 49,410. Length: 849 ft. Single screw, turbines, Speed: 16½ knots.

States were in the next – fifth – position with 386 of 4,544,158 tons. The U.S.S.R., France, Panama and Italy all had over 2 million but under 3 million tons, while Greece, Holland, Sweden, West Germany and Denmark followed in that order, with over 1 million but under 2 million tons of tankers apiece.

In only a few years, the tanker itself has undergone a great transformation and has become progressively larger. In 1959, for example, the average tonnage of tankers was about 20,000 tons; a year later it had already passed the 50,000 ton mark, and there are already many that exceed 100,000 tons gross. Its speed has gradually increased, too, having risen from 11 knots in 1958 to about 16 knots today.

Tankers are now the largest of merchant ships. In 1962 the *Nissho Maru* became the world's greatest oil carrier, her dimensions being 954 ft. × 141 ft. She had a gross tonnage of 74,868 and a deadweight (carrying capacity) of 130,250 tons, but in 1966 she was eclipsed by the *Idemetsu Maru*. The latter had a length of 1,122 ft. and a breadth of 163 ft. Her gross and dead-weight tonnages were 107,957 and 206,006 respectively. Like so many of the giant tankers these two were for the Persian Gulf – Japan trade. However, yet larger tankers have been built – to bring crude oil from Kuwait to the Gulf Oil Company's terminal at Bantry Bay. The first of these, one of a class of six, the *Universe Ireland* was completed in the summer of 1968 and raised the size record to a new level – 312,000 tons deadweight. In addition to the classic types of tankers, designed to carry either crude or refined products, lubricating oil or, in some cases, "parcels" of several different grades simultaneously, other tankers have been specially designed to carry gases in liquified form. For these too, there is a growing demand.

St. Nikolai – W. Germany 1965. Motor tanker built at Hamburg for the Hamburg-South American Line. When completed she had the largest-bore diesel engine ever put in a ship. Machinery remote controlled. 39,520 tons gross, 63,260 tons d.w. Length 773 ft., breadth 110 ft. M.A.N. type diesel, 22,500 b.h.p., 17.2 knots.

OIL TANKERS

Esso Austria – Panama 1962. Built in France, for the Esso Group who transferred her to a Panamanian subsidiary. 45,445 tons gross. 78,786 tons deadweight. 851 ft. Turbine. 17 knots.

Jaricha – Norway 1962. Built in Germany. This tanker has a gross tonnage of 32,878 tons. Deadweight tonnage: 52,203. 740 ft. 2 turbines. Speed: 15·75 knots.

Agip Trieste – Italy 1964. One of three motor tankers built in Italy for **Soc. Nazionale Metandotti,** Milan. 30,109 tons gross, 49,000 tons deadweight. Length: 750 ft. Speed: 17 knots.

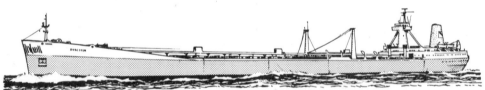

Borgsten – Norway 1964. Motor tanker built at Sunderland. 49,054 tons gross, 86,800 tons' d.w. Length 869 ft., breadth 122 ft. One 10-cylinder B & W diesel, $15\frac{1}{2}$ knots.

Anadara – Gt. Britain 1959. One of a series of 50 handy sized, general purpose tankers. All are turbine driven. 18,500 tons deadweight. Length 559 ft. Speed: $14\frac{1}{2}$ knots.

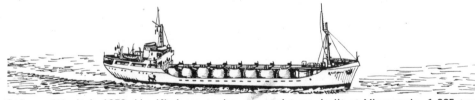

Agipgas III – Italy 1959. Liquified gas tanker, coastal type, built at Viarreggio. 1,385 tons gross, 925 tons deadweight. Length: 261 ft. Renamed **Petrobras Leste,** 1960.

Appia – Italy 1961. The development of the passenger and car ferry has been one of the most notable advances of recent years. Owned by the Adriatica Line, this one operates between Brindisi and Patras, in conjunction with the Greek-owned *Egnatia*. She loads private cars and commercial vehicles through the stern door. 8,016 tons gross. Length: 403 ft. Twin screw diesels. Speed: 17 knots. 835 passengers by day, 719 at night.

SPECIAL PURPOSE SHIPS

THE merchant navies of today comprise many other types of ships than liners, passenger ships, tramps, cargo liners, bulk carriers and tankers. It is hard to imagine just how many specially designed types there are, to meet particular needs – from ferries to refrigerated ships, from banana carriers to whalers, from cable-layers to those built for the study of ocean phenomena, from lightships to oil prospecting ships, from floating cranes to tugs. Of all these, ferries and tugs are certainly the most numerous. Of the former there are many different types of various sizes and shapes, all suited to the particular type of work they are expected to do. For instance, the ferries which can take two trains, many cars and large numbers of passengers on the shuttle service between Calabria and Sicily are substantially different from those which have plied for some years between Italy and Greece, ferries which have to cross a stretch of sea considerably longer than the Straits of Messina.

The Greek trans-Adriatic ferries are the real giants, but quite dissimilar from those which link the islands of the North in Finland, Norway and Denmark. In nearly every case, however, they have one characteristic in common – a stern or side doors to facilitate the speedy and easy loading and unloading of vehicles. They are equipped with dining saloons and, if employed on the longer routes, a certain number of cabins and rest rooms, too. Indeed, the most recent ferries can vie, in elegance and speed, with the traditional passenger ships.

Various types of deep-sea tug also form part of the great family of ships. They vary in size and shape, some having displacements of over 1,000 tons and speeds of around 16 knots. They are built so as to be able to stand up to even the most severe ocean storms and are equipped with

Fort Fleur d'Epee – France 1961. This refrigerated banana carrier has accommodation for 12 passengers and is one of a fleet of over a dozen trading to the Caribbean area. Some fruit ships are built for charter work and operate on a variety of routes. High speed is an essential feature. 5,014 tons gross. Length: 373 ft. Single screw, diesel, 19½ knots.

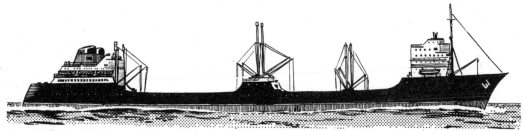

Will em Barendsz — Netherlands 1955. This whale factory ship was one of the last to be built outside Russia and Japan. Owing to the shortage of whales she was sold to South Africa and is now used as a fish factory, working with a flotilla of trawlers. The main features are the large oil tank space, vast factory area above and, on top, the flensing deck, to which the whales were hauled via the stern ramp. 23,155 tons gross. Length: 677 ft. Crew (as whaler) 506.

powerful engines that enable them to tow ships very many times larger than they are themselves. The tugs used in port are very much smaller than the sea-going ones and are indispensable in bringing large ships into dock. In this connection, it is interesting to note that the tugs of New York Harbour are quite different from all others, in that they generally carry out the manoeuvre by pushing rather than by pulling. They are equipped with a special type of fender at the bows for this purpose, which incidentally gives them a very distinctive appearance. Tugs are, however, very valuable craft and it is often due to them that accidents on the high seas do not become tragedies. Their readiness to intervene, regardless of the size of the sea which may be running, often enables ships, apparently doomed to sink, to arrive safely in port.

Le Havre — France. Lightship. Such craft seldom exceed 400 tons and are about 100-150 ft. long. They are equipped with powerful lighting plant and are moored at positions off the coast which are particularly dangerous.

Less numerous, but no less important – particularly in the merchant navies of Nordic countries – have been the whalers which, at one and the same time, served both as floating factories for processing whale meat and oils as well as workshops for the flotilla of small catchers which hunted and killed these marine animals. Equipped with stern ramps and great derricks with which to lift the enormous creatures on deck, they used to cruise for months, returning to their ports of origin with holds full of oil and other products from the processed whales. Now however such ships are almost all Japanese or Russian owned.

Refrigerated ships are more common, ships in which special compartments are maintained at the correct temperature for the safe transportation of such things as fruit, fish and frozen meat, all of which would quickly perish on board traditional ships.

Romantic, even if not very common, are the lightships. These are special vessels equipped with a powerful light which are generally anchored a long way from the coast, to give warning of sand-banks or rocky reefs. They usually have no engines and are towed into position by tugs, or special tenders, where they remain to carry out their valuable work.

Cable-layers are other ships which are infrequently seen. As their name suggests, they are ships designed specially for the laying and maintenance of under-water telecommunication cables. They are a great deal smaller than the gigantic *Great Eastern* which laid the first trans-Atlantic cable, but they are equipped instead with a mass of equipment which makes it possible to carry out the difficult and delicate repairs in the minimum of time. Many small islands are still waiting to be linked

Trieste – U.S.A. 1953. Bathyscaphe for scientific research, designed by A. Piccard, built in Italy and owned by the U.S. Navy. It has reached a depth of 3,500 ft.

Denise – France 1959. "Plunging saucer", a submerging disc designed by Jacques-Yves Cousteau. It is equipped with a tele-camera, hydrophones and mechanical arms.

telephonically to each other and with their nearest mainlands and, of course, cables which have already been laid need constant and careful attention. It seems likely, therefore, that the decline of the cable-ship (which generally belongs to a tele-communications company) is not yet in sight – and is probably very far away.

For some years now, research workers and technical experts have been giving a lot of attention to the sea bed. There is great determination to discover the

mystery of the under-water abysses in which there are believed to be incredible treasures – not the coffers filled with gold of the galleons returning from the Indies but rather deposits of oil, mineral ores, etc. In addition, it must not be forgotten that plants grow on the sea-bed which are adaptable for use as food and therefore capable of solving the problem of food for all, in the future, for a world whose population is so rapidly increasing. Even now, the sea bottom gives a good harvest of oil

Salernum – Italy 1956. Cable ship. For the laying and repair of the world's underwater cables this is a fleet of specially designed and equipped ships. These ships range in size from about 1,000 tons gross to 11,000 tons. The *Salernum* was the first of this type to be built in Italy and has a gross tonnage of 2,834. Her length is 340 ft. and twin screw diesel-electric machinery gives her a speed of 15 knots.

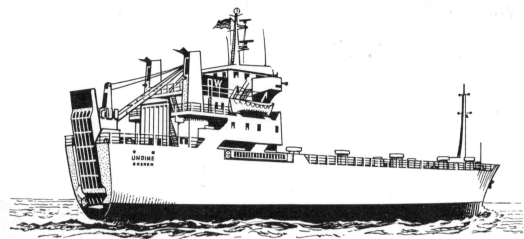

Undine – W. Germany 1966. Stern-loading vehicle carrier, owned by O. Wallenius Bremen G.m.b.H. 1,961 tons gross. Length 271 ft. One Borsig diesel, also a bow-thruster propeller, for easy manoeuvring. 13 knots. Her owners are specialists in the mass-transportation of newly assembled cars.

and special types of ships are used to prospect and to drill for it, amongst which are some enormous crane pontoons and great workshop units.

Underwater equipment has been very much on the increase during the last few years for exploring the sea-bed, like Professor Piccard's bathyscaphe, the *Trieste;* Cousteau's under-water disc, the *Denise;* and the bathyscaphe, *Archimede.* In fact, one is not really dealing with ships now, but with oceanographic research units which, nevertheless, deserve the greatest possible attention. Thanks to the bathyscaphe, *Trieste,* which was built in Italy by the Navalmeccanica company and is cur-

rently American owned, it has become possible to explore the famous depression of the Mariana Islands and for a survey of data to be made which is of extreme scientific interest. The *Trieste* also made possible the discovery of the wreck of the *Thresher,* the American nuclear submarine which sank in mysterious circumstances in April, 1963.

It may well be that it will be due to these means of exploration that the navies of the future will find new routes, new ways to exist and to expand, new possibilities of facilitating contact between peoples, their business interests and improvement in their general well-being.

Zwarte Zee – Holland (Netherlands) 1963. When built at Kinderdijk for L. Smit & Co., Rotterdam, was the world's largest, most powerful dieseldriven salvage tug. 1,539 tons gross. Length 254 ft. Two M.A.N. type diesels of 9,000 b.h.p. drive a single shaft. 20 knots. Crew 31, plus 20 salvage men.

SHIPS
TOMORROW

The future of nuclear-powered ships,
hydrofoils and hovercraft

L OOKING at the profound changes which the ship has undergone during the period covered by the last 150 years, from the
arrival of steam to the first nuclear propulsion experiments, it must
be concluded that it is impossible to foresee what the ship of tomorrow will be like – "tomorrow" being taken as more than ten
years hence. Considering the speed with which technical advances
follow one another, it is not unlikely that, in the near future, something will radically transform the very concept of a naval or a
merchant ship. It is wiser, therefore, and more realistic, to concentrate on what is already being worked on and may well be seen in
practical form in the years to come.

The atomic submarine and attack aircraft-carrier must still
continue to share pride of place in the naval forces, whilst still greater
improvement and development will be seen in the lighter escort
craft of the frigate and corvette types.

For war-ships, the use of nuclear propulsion is not governed by
motives of economy, as with merchant ships, and it obviously has
advantages which far outweigh its disadvantages. It is therefore
reasonable to foresee its greater application to underwater craft and
large surface vessels such as aircraft-carriers and cruisers.

It is in the sphere of merchant shipping that it seems the greatest
changes must take place – research is, in fact, going on into the
economic use of nuclear energy for large cargo ships, into the possibility of building submarines for commercial use and of using large
sea-going hydrofoils and hovercraft. If all these experiments were
to give positive results, the merchant ships of tomorrow would be able
to go around the world several times without refuelling; passengers
in hydrofoils would be able to cross the Atlantic in only 30 hours; and
the fantastic world of the unfathomed depths would be open to
anyone. How correct these forecasts may be, only the future itself
will show.

Savannah – U.S.A. 1962. This, the first nuclear propelled merchant ship, was a joint project of the U.S. Atomic Energy Commission and the U.S. Department of Commerce. Her reactor weighs 2,500 tons, but the amount of enriched uranium oxide used is so small that she can be at sea for $3\frac{1}{2}$ years. 15,585 tons gross. Length: 595 ft. Speed: $20\frac{1}{4}$ knots.

THE FUTURE OF NUCLEAR PROPULSION

THE first merchant ship equipped with nuclear powered engines was launched at Camden, N.J. on 21st July, 1959. The launching of the N.S. *Savannah*, (that is, the "Nuclear Ship Savannah"), was a historic event of no less importance than the first voyage across the Atlantic carried out in 1819 with the somewhat infrequent aid of steam by the American ship of the same name.

The *Savannah*, of 15,585 tons gross and 595 ft. in length, was built to carry cargo and 60 passengers. She is fitted with a water pressurised nuclear reactor and has been described as a "floating laboratory at the service of the whole of humanity". The many and complex problems involved in adapting nuclear powered engines for ships destined for civil use have been faced for the first time, in constructing this ship. These problems are substantially different from those involved in adapting nuclear power to naval craft, which have already been resolved. Above all, the American technical experts have had to find the right answer to the question of anti-radiation screens which had to combine complete efficiency with reasonable weight and bulk. They had to resolve the problem of waste elimination from the reactor. They had to take all appropriate precautions to avoid absolutely the danger of atomic radiation, even in the event of collision or sinking. The *Savannah*, which is currently operating between the USA and Mediterranean ports, is tangible proof of the possibility of the nuclear powered engine being applied to a merchant ship. It is the point from which further experiments and tests can be based, not only for American experts but also for those of all the other countries interested in the de-

Nuclear powered underwater tanker – U.S.A. The U.S. Navy has plans for an underwater tanker with a carrying capacity of 20,000 tons and equipped with a nuclear energy engine. If it comes into use for military purposes, it could be the prototype for a series of mercantile oil carrying submarines which would gradually replace the huge tankers of today.

Japan's nuclear-propelled ship which is being built at Tokyo is due for delivery in March, 1972. Besides a crew of 59 she will carry 20 scientists. Her indirect-cycle, water-moderated and water-cooled reactor will have a thermal output of 36 Mw. Provisional figures show a length of 426 ft. and a gross tonnage of 8,350.

velopment of their shipping. In the future, however, the widespread use of nuclear propulsion in ships for commercial purposes will be determined almost exclusively by economic factors.

Although it is, in fact, true that a nuclear ship can offer greater loading capacity, that it does away with the necessity of calling at ports solely for refuelling and that it gives increased cruising speed, it is also true that a nuclear reactor today costs infinitely more than a conventional engine. The radio-active fuel, too, costs more in comparing equal performances, although occupies less space than diesel oil or coal. It will just be a matter of seeing how soon the costs of nuclear reactors – once they have come out of their restrictive testing period – can be regarded as competitive with those of traditional engines. This could happen much sooner than might be expected, as a result of research being carried out in this connection by experts throughout the world, who are examining the different types of reactors in detail; also the functional characteristics of the ships in which they would be used.

The first European nuclear propelled ship was launched in Germany in 1964, the *Otto Hahn*, of 17,000 tons – a typical cargo vessel. In Italy, technical experts of the Fiat and Ansaldo Companies, in conjunction with Euratom and the National Committee of Nuclear Energy, are preparing plans for an oil tanker. Research has been carried out in Britain for a bulk carrier, but appears to have been shelved. In Japan however, there is a nuclear propelled ship under construction and she is due for delivery in 1972. According to widespread opinion, nuclear powered engines will be particularly suitable for very large cargo ships, either tankers or bulk carriers, since the space needed for nuclear fuel would be fractional compared to that necessary for a large conventionally powered ship making a long voyage. This space would become available for cargo. There are those who maintain that the nuclear powered engine will be in competition with the conventional one by 1970. If this is so, it should soon be possible to count commercial atomic ships by the score.

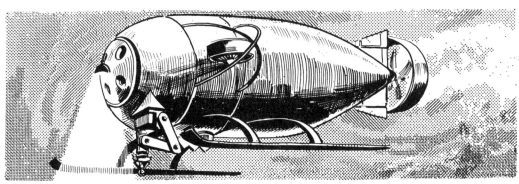

Underwater craft for scientific research – U.S.A. 1964. Ordered by the U.S. Navy for scientific explorations at depth, she can submerge to 6,000 ft. She is equipped with a tele-camera and mechanical prehensile arms. The results of the United States' oceanographic research programme may well influence future trends in merchant shipping.

Ocean-going hydrofoil – U.S.A. 1964. Following the example of the Italians who were the first to build hydrofoils, the Americans have produced this 72·5 ton ocean-going hydrofoil which is 104 ft. long. She is capable of carrying over 30 tons, divided between fuel and cargo. She is equipped with two turbines and has a speed of over 50 knots. She rests on her four fins, which emerge with the craft itself from the water, at just over half-speed.

From an aesthetic point of view, the principal characteristic of the nuclear ship is the absence of any traditional funnel which is no longer necessary since the combustion of uranium unlike coal, fuel or diesel oil, does not generate exhaust gas. It is, of course, probable that still more important structural modifications to the hulls will be carried out, as research progresses on nuclear propulsion. Some experts are already considering housing the

Hovercraft SR. N3 – Gt. Britain 1964. This vehicle travels just above the surface of the water, supported by a cushion of air which is created by her four powerful Bristol Siddeley engines. Length: 77 ft. Width: 30 ft. Weight: 37·5 tons. She can carry 150 passengers.

reactor in a special "gondola" under the hull, submerged in water, which would rest on fins like the present day hydrofoil, to give greater speed.

With nuclear propulsion, it would be possible to build merchant submarines, particularly for carrying oil products. As already mentioned, unlike traditional engines atomic powered engines do not need air in order to function and are therefore especially suitable for this purpose. The underwater tanker could be equipped with smaller, less costly nuclear-powered engines than those in surface craft of the same load capacity. Without going into technical details, it is enough to say that, to obtain a speed of 40 knots with a surface craft, it would be necessary to have a horsepower of, for example, 1,100,000, whilst for an underwater craft of equal capacity 300,000 h.p. would be enough. Besides the lower cost of the reactor, another point in favour of this idea is that a constant speed could be guaranteed, quite independent of weather conditions, and the possibility of following new routes – even Arctic ones – thus considerably shortening the distances to be covered, would become a reality. It seems that the American Navy has a project under way for just such a craft – an underwater tanker with a gross tonnage of 20,000 tons, whose importance experimentally would undoubtedly be enormous.

From all that has been said so far, it can be deduced that, as with naval forces, the future of merchant shipping lies in nuclear propulsion. Years of research and experimenting will certainly be necessary – perhaps even some failures – but it would be completely illogical for such a revolutionary discovery as nuclear fission to remain undeveloped in this field. It could be a serious mistake to underestimate the value of nuclear energy – no less serious than the scepticism with which the first steps in thermic energy were greeted at the beginning of the 19th century.

In the meantime, other sections of technical experts are actively engaged on planning and improving devices to relieve the hull from the resistance of water, making greater speeds possible. Ships that can make use of the results of their work are divided into two categories – the hydrofoil and the hovercraft (craft which ride on a cushion of air).

In the case of the hydrofoil, 4 fins – 2 large ones forward and 2 smaller ones aft – project from the hull, which has a traditional shape. In motion, the whole craft rises above the surface, only resting on the fins which offer a very reduced surface to the resistance of the water. It is capable of reaching considerable speeds. The first hydrofoils were built some years ago in Italy and many are currently in use in the Channel Islands, Scandinavia, the Mediterranean, Japan and Russia – several of which are capable of carrying up to 100 passengers at a speed of 40 knots. Recently,

an American Naval coastal look-out vessel, built in the Grumman aircraft factory, has confronted waves of more than 10 ft. high without harm, reaching a speed of more than 59 knots. This would seem to prove that the experts have succeeded in overcoming the greatest difficulty which stood in the way of using hydrofoils on the high seas – the force of the sea itself.

Currently, ocean-going hydrofoils of 200 tons, with a potential speed in the region of 70 knots, are said to be under construction in the United States. At the same time, a trans-ocean hydrofoil is being planned of 1,000 tons. It should be able to carry hundreds of passengers at the incredible speed of 97 knots. If this type of ship successfully passes its tests, transAtlantic traffic would be radically changed, for such a hydrofoil would be able to cover the route from New York to Le Havre in less than 30 hours – or one-third of the time now taken by the fastest liner currently in service.

The development of hovercraft is much further advanced and in Britain a number of these are already in commercial operation. In hovercraft, jets of compressed air, produced by large turbines, keep the vehicle just above the surface of the sea or

Princess Margaret – Gt. Britain 1968. "Mountbatten" class (SR.N4) hovercraft built at East Cowes. Operated from August 1968 on Dover-Boulogne service. Length 130 ft., breadth 78 ft. Four Rolls Royce "Marine Proteus" gas turbines. Service speed: 40-50 knots. Can take 30 cars and 254 passengers.

land and airscrews, powered by conventional engines, provide the drive which enables it to attain considerable speed. To be strictly accurate these craft are not ships (lifesaving equipment conforms to aircraft requirements) in the true sense of the word since they can also operate over dry land, swamp and ice but since the surfaces they travel over must be reasonably smooth they seem more suited to maritime use.

It was in the English Channel and the Isle of Wight areas that the first commercial hovercraft services were introduced. History was made in the spring of 1966 when Hoverlloyd, a subsidiary of the Swedish Lloyd, started the world's first international hovercraft service. This was between Ramsgate and Calais, the two craft used being 36-seater SR.N6s. A few weeks later the Isle of Wight (Cowes) – Southampton hovercraft service was introduced by British Rail, this likewise with a 56-knot SR.N6. Later a second service from Ryde to Portsmouth was introduced. Hoverlloyd's plans to put a giant SR.N4

craft into service were so long delayed through official obstruction – eventually overcome – into the building of a new terminal that it was British Rail which, in July 1968, inaugurated the first "Mountbatten" class SR.N4 service – between Dover and Boulogne. This 165-ton craft which is 77 ft. wide and 42 ft. high, has a 7 ft. high skirt of plastic covered nylon weave. It has a top speed of 77 knots and is designed to carry up to 800 passengers or 254 passengers and 30 cars.

This brief survey of new projects and developments in the realm of shipping projects shows how difficult it is to make accurate forecasts for the future and how, at the same time, interesting innovations can certainly be expected. What is quite certain is that mankind is still not satisfied with his achievements on the sea and that the development of the ship – which was started in prehistoric times – still cannot be said to have reached completion. Even today, when we navigate in space and regard Mars as no longer an unattainable goal, the sea retains its importance.

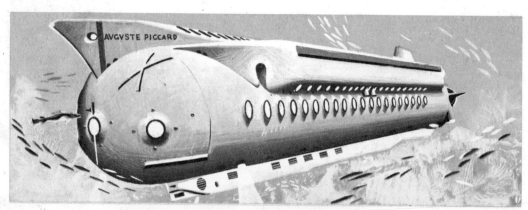

Perhaps, in not too many years' time, it will be a common thing to travel in a submarine from Genoa to Naples, looking out at the mysterious marine depths from large port-holes. That this forecast may be anything but guesswork and sheer fancy is shown by this observation submarine, named the *Auguste Piccard,* which goes down about 500 ft. into the waters of Lake Lemano with passengers on board. Designed and built by the great Jacques Piccard, it offers a view of the underwater flora and fauna in complete comfort and safety. Progress advances at such a rate that the surprises of "tomorrow" may arrive much sooner than we imagine.